Critical Acclaim for the Revised Edition of
The Making of a Quagmire

In the voluminous literature on America's Vietnam war, Halberstam's is one of the very few first-hand records to emerge as a classic. This shortened, revised edition is likely to ensure its keeping that reputation. The vividness of this enterprising and courageous correspondent's account will still grip the attention of any reader. Halberstam's devastating critique of the U.S. role in Vietnam is all the more telling because when he wrote this he was still something of a hawk—a firm believer in the objectives pursued there by the United States. This revised edition of his book should make it easier for today's college generation to understand what in hindsight appears to so many of them to be bizarre and incomprehensible.

Making clear that the United States *created* its own quagmire in Vietnam, Halberstam's knowledgeable assessment of the U.S. record is so devastating that the reader will soon appreciate why he so discomfited the Kennedy Administration, and why that President took the controversial step of trying to get *The New York Times* to pull him out of Vietnam. . . .

In being condensed by a third, this new college edition has lost nothing of significance bearing on Vietnam and is now of a length more suitable for college courses than the original. And it is all the more so because of Daniel Singal's sound and substantial introduction, one which alerts the reader to both the book's virtues and its few weaknesses—mainly important background information which was difficult to come by when it was written.

Anyone whose teaching covers the Vietnam war should find this book helpful in kindling students' interest and valuable in increasing their understanding of that Washington-made quagmire.

—GEORGE MCT. KAHIN, *Cornell University*

As was the case in 1965, the book still deserves the widest possible audience. It is as fresh and stimulating as when it first appeared. Halberstam's capacity to cut through the illusions and self-deception that characterized American and Vietnamese behavior in the early 1960s still makes a fascinating story. If anything, the book now has an even greater impact on the reader, who has the advantage of hindsight and can see how astute Halberstam's observations were at the time.

. . . This new edition of the book will be very well received by college instructors and will get wide use in courses on American foreign policy generally and on Vietnam in particular. The book may also find its way into courses on post-1945 United States history and on international relations given in political science departments. It will have a considerable appeal to instructors not only as an analysis of what went wrong in Vietnam but also as a contemporary document in which a brilliant journalist struggled with painful questions about American foreign policy in what then looked like a vital area of the world for American interests. As it did in 1965, Halberstam's book will provoke vigorous discussion. Students will marvel at how the United States allowed itself to be so misled in South Vietnam and will use the book to make connections to more recent events in Central America and the Middle East.

—ROBERT DALLEK, *University of California at Los Angeles*

The book was invaluable to me when I went to Vietnam in 1966; and it remains invaluable today as a unique first-hand account of the period 1962–1963 in South Vietnam. Looking back, that period was the crucial one politically: the government in Saigon then had its chance to become the government of South Vietnam and failed. It was defeated politically by the Vietcong. That failure was decisive: it was never reversed in spite of the introduction of a half a million American troops and fifteen more years of war. . . . In *The Making of a Quagmire* Halberstam gives us both an analysis of events and the texture of the time in Saigon. The new introduction is excellent and should help to give the book the audience it deserves.

—FRANCES FITZGERALD, Pulitzer Prize-winning author of *Fire in the Lake: The Vietnamese and the Americans in Vietnam*

An important work of analytical journalism in 1965, *The Making of a Quagmire* is today part of the documentary history of the Vietnam war. It presents a contemporary point of view that must be studied if the course of the war is to be understood.

—MARTIN SHERWIN, *Tufts University*

Few journalists did more to educate Americans about the harsh realities of the Vietnam War than David Halberstam. . . .

Halberstam went to Vietnam during the Kennedy buildup of 1962. His account of his tour there covers in often vivid and compelling detail the guerrilla war in the Mekong Delta, America's stormy and eventually fateful relationship with the Ngo family, the Buddhist revolt of 1963, and the subsequent overthrow and murder of Ngo Dinh Diem. It offers numerous insights into the conflict between the American press and the U.S. government that began in these years and ultimately played a major role in the war. . . .

The Making of a Quagmire is a valuable introduction to Vietnam in the era of John F. Kennedy and Ngo Dinh Diem. This new edition should be most useful for courses on American involvement in Vietnam.

—GEORGE C. HERRING, *University of Kentucky*

THE MAKING OF A QUAGMIRE

BOOKS BY DAVID HALBERSTAM

The Noblest Roman

The Making of a Quagmire

One Very Hot Day

The Unfinished Odyssey of Robert Kennedy

Ho

The Powers That Be

The Breaks of the Game

The Amateurs

The Reckoning

The Best and the Brightest

The Making of a Quagmire

America and Vietnam During the Kennedy Era

REVISED EDITION

David Halberstam

Edited with an Introduction by Daniel J. Singal

Boston, Massachusetts   Burr Ridge, Illinois
Dubuque, Iowa   Madison, Wisconsin   New York, New York
San Francisco, California   St. Louis, Missouri

Grateful acknowledgment is made to the following for the permission granted to use copyrighted material in this volume:

Articles by Robert Trumbull, David Halberstam, and Peter Grose. Copyright © 1947, 1963, 1964 by The New York Times Company. Reprinted by permission.

Excerpts from the *Time* cover story "The New Frontier." Copyright © 1950 by Time, Inc.

Excerpt from "Last Act in Indochina" by Graham Greene. Reprinted from *The New Republic*, May 16, 1955.

Article by Marguerite Higgins. Copyright © 1963 by New York Herald Tribune Inc.

Cover photo: Bill Strode/Black Star

McGraw-Hill

A Division of The McGraw-Hill Companies

This is a Borzoi Book published by Alfred A. Knopf, Inc.

Revised Edition

7 8 9 BKM BKM 9 0 9 8 7 6 5 4 3 2 1

Copyright © 1964, 1965, 1988 by David Halberstam

Library of Congress Cataloging-in-Publication Data

Halberstam, David.
  The making of a quagmire.

  1. Vietnam—Politics and government—1945–1975.
2. United States—Foreign relations—Vietnam.
3. Vietnam—Foreign relations—United States.
I. Singal, Daniel Joseph, 1944– . II. Title.
DS556.9.H344   1987   959.704   87-2723
ISBN 0-394-36860-6

Manufactured in the United States of America

For my mother, Mrs. Blanche Halberstam,
and in memory of my father, the late Dr. Charles Halberstam

Just remember one thing: there are no dumb Asians.

—Advice to the author from Robert Trumbull, Old Asia Hand and *New York Times* correspondent in Southeast Asia—September 3, 1962

Author's Note

This book is a reporter's story, and as such it belongs as much to those others who were there: Mert Perry, Neil Sheehan, Nguyen Ngoc Rao, Mal Browne, Ray Herndon, Horst Faas, Peter Arnett, Pham Xuan An, John Sharkey, Nick Turner, Francois Sully, Vo Huynh, Ha Thuc Can and Charley Mohr.

Contents

Introduction

by Daniel J. Singal

When *The Making of a Quagmire* first appeared in April 1965, its prospects could not have seemed brighter. During the previous two months, the administration of President Lyndon B. Johnson had sharply escalated American involvement in the long-simmering conflict between Communist and anti-Communist forces in Vietnam, introducing U.S. combat troops and initiating a massive bombing campaign against North Vietnam. As a result, the American public was finally beginning to pay serious attention to events in Southeast Asia; Vietnam was at last becoming headline news. It was thus hard to imagine better circumstances for a firsthand account of the war by an author such as David Halberstam, a 1955 graduate of Harvard College who had reported on the civil rights movement for newspapers in the South before making his mark during the early 1960s as a *New York Times* correspondent in the Congo and Vietnam, earning a Pulitzer Prize for his skillful coverage of Vietnam from mid-1962 to late 1963.

But unfortunately the accelerating pace of events would soon overtake the book, thanks primarily to Johnson's fateful decision in the summer of 1965 to "Americanize" the war. The subsequent escalation proceeded swiftly: at the time *The Making of a Quagmire* arrived in print, only 56,000 American soldiers were in Vietnam; a year later the number was up to 216,400; and by the end of 1966, it had reached 383,500. The buildup elicited a predictable response from the North Vietnamese, who started committing their own main-force army units to battle. Given these developments, Halberstam's narrative, which concerned a period when Americans saw action only as "advisers" to the South Vietnamese army (or ARVN), suddenly seemed dated. The same held true for his chronicle of South Vietnamese politics during the regime of President Ngo Dinh Diem, the monklike autocrat whom the United States had helped to overthrow in November 1963. With Diem gone, replaced by military leaders considered far more amenable to American influence, it appeared that the game in Vietnam had drastically changed—that a new era had commenced in which Halberstam's observations and analysis, excellent though they might be, were no longer relevant.

Finally, there was the problem of political perspective. By early 1966, as the scope of the American commitment to South Vietnam became unmistakable, public opinion within the United States rapidly polarized, with people taking strong stands on the war as either "hawks" or "doves." *The Making of a Quagmire,* however, did not fit readily into either of these ornithological categories. On the one hand, Halberstam's conspicuous patriotism and admiration for American military advisers in the field made his narrative suspect among the doves. Some in the antiwar camp also complained about what they called his "quagmire thesis," which held, as they understood it, that the United States had stumbled into Vietnam accidentally, rather than as the consequence of a deliberate and misguided policy (in fact, Halberstam takes the latter position; as its very title suggests, the book contends that the United States *made* its Vietnam quagmire). Hawks, on the other hand, could not help noticing that, whatever Halberstam's intentions, the evidence he presented added up to a damning indictment of the American performance in Indochina. Though ostensibly an argument for increasing our efforts to achieve victory, his book at the same time conveyed the impression that the war was inherently unwinnable. In short, neither side in the fierce national debate could take much comfort from *The Making of a Quagmire,* which, one suspects, along with its supposed obsolescence, was why it did not find its deserved place among the classic works on Vietnam but instead slowly faded into obscurity, going out of print in 1977 with only sixteen thousand copies sold.

Ironically, however, what is most striking about the book in retrospect is how durable its portrait of the American experience in Vietnam has turned out to be. Put simply, *The Making of a Quagmire* penetrates to the heart of that experience, capturing not only the sorry details of the Diem period but also the fundamental errors and misconceptions that continued to shape American policy until the final collapse of South Vietnam in 1975. The reason for this may lie, again ironically, in the advantage that Halberstam enjoyed of being on the scene before the great American buildup, when it was still possible to focus on the *real* war in South Vietnam—the contest between the Communist insurgents in the countryside and the feckless government in Saigon for the political loyalty of the peasantry who made up the overwhelming majority of the population. For it was there, at the level of the individual village, that the long-term battle would be won or lost, as Halberstam clearly perceived, and as American decision makers so frequently forgot. Massive search-and-destroy missions, B-52 raids, defoliation, and all the other accoutrements of the Americanized war would divert attention from this basic struggle between Saigon and the Vietcong, but in the end it was the American combat effort itself that would prove to be the side show; for when the GIs returned home following the 1973 armistice, the situation quickly reverted to the one Halberstam had depicted, with the Saigon government helplessly succumbing to the military and political superiority of its adversary.

Indeed, one might argue that the relatively brief period that Halberstam witnessed and reported on so well was the most decisive in the entire war: in his phrase, "a crucial moment of truth" during which the ultimate outcome was determined. For this was when the National Liberation Front (or NLF, as the guerrillas' political arm was called) gained effective political control of the Mekong Delta, that fertile region ideally suited for rice cultivation that stretches for two hundred miles south of Saigon, providing a livelihood for most of the country's rural population. Losing the Delta, as Halberstam repeatedly insists, meant losing the bulk of the peasantry of South Vietnam, and losing the peasantry was the sure harbinger of military defeat. The NLF's impressive advances in this area were duly recognized by General Maxwell D. Taylor, President John F. Kennedy's chief adviser on Vietnam, in an October 1961 report that led to an ambitious attempt to upgrade the ARVN in early 1962. Following Taylor's recommendations, the United States both increased the number of American advisers assigned to ARVN units and provided helicopters and amphibious personnel carriers to enable the ARVN to pursue its elusive enemy across difficult terrain like the swampy Delta. But, as Halberstam reports, though this "booster shot" helped for a short time, it, like all prior and subsequent infusions of American aid, soon proved a dismal failure. The summer of 1963 found the NLF "winning by default in the Delta," with the situation virtually "beyond recall." In explaining how that failure came about, he pinpoints why the United States, despite its immense resources and firepower, would finally lose in Vietnam.

The main problem, Halberstam tells us, was that so few Americans, along with their ARVN counterparts, adequately comprehended the political nature of the war. Just the opposite was true on the other side: for the NLF, he writes, "the war was entirely political; its military aspects were simply a means to permit them to practice their political techniques." Everything the NLF did was designed to gain the allegiance of the people; winning new territory, inflicting heavy casualties on the ARVN, and disrupting the operations of the South Vietnamese government were deemed important *only* if they contributed to that overriding political objective. This was why NLF cadres attempted, when possible, to live among the people, often working in the fields alongside them, providing education and medical aid, taking up their grievances, and promising them land and social services following a Communist victory. Well-disciplined and politically aware, NLF troops, moreover, made every effort to avoid harming civilians during military operations. Their terror tactics were almost always carried out with scalpel-like precision, aimed typically at corrupt local officials who symbolized the heavy-handed Diem regime. Putting the head of a decapitated tax collector on public display was thus calculated to please as much as to intimidate village residents. In this way, Halberstam writes, the NLF succeeded in making guerrilla war "virtually an art form."

By contrast, the ARVN seemed entirely incapable of waging this sort of conflict. Halberstam's detailed accounts of the combat missions he went on make clear how poorly trained and motivated the ARVN was, and how little attention its leaders paid to cultivating popular support. Recounting his first operation in the Delta, for example, he describes two incidents in which civilians were wantonly killed: the first when an inexperienced helicopter gunner opened fire on a farmer standing innocently in a field and the second when an ARVN platoon moving through a village mistook an impoverished peasant for a Vietcong agent and shot him. Such errors, which occurred all too often and in which the ARVN command took virtually no interest, quite obviously did not endear the Saigon government to its would-be constituents, which was the central strategic task. Neither did the extraordinary destruction unleashed by the modern weapons that the United States supplied to South Vietnam. Rather, as Halberstam notes, from the standpoint of the peasants, the availability of jet aircraft, helicopter gunships, and powerful munitions "meant more bombings, more deaths, and more suffering." Colonel John Paul Vann, the American expert on counterinsurgency warfare from whom Halberstam learned so much, was keenly aware of the folly here. "The best weapon" for this sort of war, Vann is quoted as saying, ". . . would be a knife, but I'm afraid we can't do it that way. The worst is an airplane. The next worst is artillery. Barring a knife, the best is a rifle—you know who you're killing." But that was a lesson that neither the ARVN nor the American high command ever managed to learn, while the NLF mastered it thoroughly.

Indeed, it is apparent from Halberstam that, with few exceptions, South Vietnamese forces felt minimal compunction about injuring or harassing civilians. ARVN soldiers, in the course of inspection sweeps through villages, routinely stole whatever they could find. Women were subjected to harsh methods of interrogation; young men, if present, might be conscripted into the army for long service at scandalously low pay. For most peasant families, contact with the government centered on the payment of taxes, while the money allocated to provide them with schools, medical care, and other services typically found its way into the pockets of Diem's appointed officials. To be sure, part of the reason for this was the NLF policy of assassinating those few capable local leaders who refused it cooperation. But then again, Saigon made almost no effort to afford its loyalists even rudimentary protection. ARVN units moved through the countryside by day but retreated to their bases at night, leaving the villages open to the NLF, which could quickly retaliate against any civilian who had demonstrated support for the government. Again and again Halberstam registers his amazement at how those in high positions in Saigon, both South Vietnamese and American, remained oblivious to these problems in the face of the enemy's continuing success.

NLF political advances, in turn, had direct military significance. In guerrilla warfare, nothing is more vital than obtaining accurate intelligence—knowing where the other side's units are located, how large they are, and where they are headed. In Vietnam the chief source of such information was the peasantry. "Unless the population was willing to tell the troops where the Vietcong had hidden," observes Halberstam, "the Government had a nearly impossible task—and at that time the population wasn't telling." A clear instance of this was the battle of Go Cong, when over five hundred NLF soldiers "had been able to gather near a major center in a heavily populated area, without one single peasant warning the government." This network of support was invaluable to the NLF for more than just intelligence; it could also be relied on for setting up secure hiding places, procuring necessary provisions, and providing dedicated recruits. Try as they might, government forces met little or no success breaking into this network, as we see repeatedly in *The Making of a Quagmire.* On one occasion, an ARVN captain, who seems an unusually skillful interrogator, informs Halberstam during the sweep of a village that the woman who has refused to help them is probably an NLF sympathizer, but that arresting her would only ensure her children's dedication to the guerrillas. "Do they teach about this at Fort Bragg?" he asks in frustration.

In this fashion, Halberstam depicts in full detail the military and political cycle through which the ARVN's position became hopeless. The more the NLF cornered the loyalty of the people, the better the intelligence it was able to gather and the more likely it became that the NLF would score highly visible military victories. Since the peasants naturally gravitated toward the winning side, those victories served to strengthen their attachment to the NLF, which led in due course to still better NLF intelligence and still more successful attacks against the government. Also feeding the cycle was the growing number of sophisticated weapons that the guerrillas captured as a by-product of those attacks; the larger their arsenal, the more troops they were able to field and the more damage they could inflict on government installations. At the same time, ARVN soldiers—relegated to long, frustrating marches in pursuit of an enemy they almost never saw (but who seemed able to find them at will)—quickly lost their sense of morale. That, in turn, further eroded their military discipline, increased their tendency to mistreat villagers, and in general rendered them even less likely to inspire the confidence of the people. By the late summer of 1963, according to Halberstam, this downward spiral had proceeded to the point where the ARVN had lost its initial overwhelming advantage of numbers, with NLF battalions growing so large that the ARVN was terrified of engaging them. "In a war which was so largely psychological," he writes, ". . . this was disastrous."

Did the ARVN ever have a chance to win? At the time, Halberstam seemed to think so, but the facts he supplies suggest otherwise. The problem, one can now see, stemmed from the very nature of the social order in South Vietnam, which continued to reflect both long-standing tradition and the legacy of French colonialism. Again and again he shows how South Vietnamese military officers and government officials were caught up in a deep-seated system of class prerogative and corruption that undermined their ability to rally the people or to offer a viable political alternative to the NLF. Perhaps nothing illustrates this better than Colonel Vann's abortive campaign to set an example for his Vietnamese counterparts by walking through combat missions in the rice paddies. What even the best Americans like Vann couldn't fathom, Halberstam astutely points out, "was the power of the mandarin legacy: the whole point of being a major or colonel was that you *didn't* have to go into the field. . . ." In one of the most insightful paragraphs in the book, he expounds on this basic internal contradiction that was to debilitate the U.S. effort:

> What the Americans were attempting to do, by setting examples like this, epitomized our entire problem in Vietnam. They were trying to persuade an inflexible military ally, who had very little social or political sense about its own people, to do what the Americans knew must be done, but this would force the Vietnamese officers to give up the very things that really mattered to them and that motivated them in the first place. How could anyone make the Vietnamese officers see, almost overnight, that the purpose of promotion was not primarily to separate them from the misery whence they came, but to get them to inspire and lead others?

Vann's chief weakness, Halberstam adds, was his belief that capable advisers like himself could uproot this powerful cultural tradition and "buck the system"; rather, "the system was stronger than the men bucking it."

Compounding this dilemma was the vivid memory of French rule. Few colonial regimes were more bitterly resented by a subject people than that of France in Indochina. Thus it did not help that so many officials of the Diem administration and officers of the ARVN came from families that had collaborated in some fashion with the French, prospering through appointments in the French army or civil service, while Ho Chi Minh and his Vietminh guerrillas had been responsible for expelling the colonial oppressors in 1954. The great majority of the Saigon elite were not only educated in French schools but spoke French instead of Vietnamese as their primary language; in many cases, the families had also converted to Catholicism in order to curry favor with their French patrons. Accordingly, as *New York Times* columnist James Reston reported from Vietnam in 1965, the people in the countryside viewed their rulers in Saigon as "the successors of the French colonial regime, with upper-class urban Vietnamese replacing the French"—a fact that made it difficult, if not impossible, for Saigon to compete with Hanoi or the NLF on the grounds of Vietnamese nationalism at a time when the fires of nationalism were raging throughout the society. Worse still, the South Vietnamese elite's growing dependence on American aid made it appear that it had merely exchanged one foreign master for another. Thus again the fatal trap: the more Saigon turned to the United States for help, the less political loyalty it could command at home. Yet it was obvious that without increased American support, the government would quickly collapse. Given all of these entrenched political realities, it is hard to see how any policy that the United States might have adopted would have allowed its South Vietnamese ally to triumph.

As the evidence that Halberstam presents also demonstrates, it was these unyielding realities that were primarily responsible for the dramatic downfall of Ngo Dinh Diem. The Eisenhower administration had installed Diem in power in 1954 because of his strong credentials as both a nationalist and an anti-Communist, but the Americans had failed to understand how thoroughly he was steeped in mandarin culture. Though successful at first in cleaning up the gangster sects that had plagued Saigon, he also believed, in Halberstam's words, "that he represented God to his people," and that "he could do no wrong and had discharged his obligations if he remained morally and spiritually correct." Trusting no one except his blood relatives, Diem had, by the early 1960s, fallen under the sway of his paranoid and ruthless brother and sister-in-law, Ngo Dinh Nhu and the notorious Madame Nhu, which gave rise to what Halberstam calls "a suspicious, unresponsive and archaic family dictatorship." Along with its endemic repression, inefficiency, and corruption, the regime was beset by an extraordinary dreamworld mentality, perfectly exemplified by the parade Diem staged to commemorate the anniversary of his ascent to power —a parade that wound its way through the empty streets of downtown Saigon because no spectators were allowed to watch it. Yet, precisely because it saw no alternative, the United States committed itself to a policy of, as one wit put it, "sink or swim with Ngo Dinh Diem." No matter what Diem and Nhu did, it seemed, the Americans would cheerfully and blindly back them.

The second half of *The Making of a Quagmire* recounts the process by which this American policy disintegrated under the pressure of internal events within South Vietnam. It explains how the Buddhists, who represented the overwhelming majority of the country's population, took increasing umbrage at the way a small minority of Saigon Catholics monopolized top positions in government and the military, often receiving appointments in preference to non-Catholics of greater ability (the Buddhist movement, by contrast, "was clearly one of the few in the country where men of true talent, instead of second-raters, had risen to the top"). In addition, the Buddhists saw Catholicism as "the religion of the West and of colonialism," connoting a betrayal of Vietnamese nationalism as well as unfair social privilege. This deep-rooted resentment, inflamed by a series of foolish acts by the Diem regime, led the Buddhists in the spring of 1963 to hold massive street demonstrations, initiated on some occasions by monks who actually doused themselves with gasoline and set themselves on fire. More than anything else, it was Diem's failure to respond sensibly to this widespread unrest, capped by Nhu's savage attack on the Buddhist pagodas in August, that eroded the brothers' support in Washington and set the stage for the coup that would remove them from power.

The relief brought by Diem's downfall would, of course, prove only

temporary, for the United States was to persevere in its policy of supporting autocratic rulers of urban, Roman Catholic background while Vietnam
itself remained predominantly rural and Buddhist. The tendency of
American officials to focus almost exclusively on the military situation and
to ignore festering political problems in Saigon would also continue una-
bated into the Johnson and Nixon administrations. As a consequence,
Halberstam's analysis of the weaknesses of the Diem regime applies all too
well to those of Diem's successors, especially that of Nguyen Van Thieu,
the military strongman who served as president of South Vietnam from
1967 to 1975 and who, in hindsight, appears in essence as a shrewder
version of Diem. In short, one is again struck by how remarkably prescient
The Making of a Quagmire was in setting forth the basic causes of the
American debacle in Vietnam.

Equally striking is the skill with which Halberstam tells his tale, especially his facility in enabling the reader to experience vicariously what he
is describing. We join him on combat missions jumping from his helicopter
into a rice paddy, landing shoulder-deep in the murky water and splashing
alongside the ARVN troops toward the village tree line where enemy
snipers may be waiting. He shares with us the discomfort of his soggy
shoes, the terror of being exposed to possible automatic weapons fire with
no way to run or hide, and the trials of being a large-sized American
reporter crossing a Delta canal on thin poles of rounded bamboo while an
entire ARVN platoon watches and laughs. The book is filled with such
firsthand recollections that epitomize what life in the war zone was actually like—memories enhanced by Halberstam's razor-sharp powers of ob-
servation and characterization. Take, for example, his portrait of Madame
Nhu during a public appearance as "the only one of the family who walked
the way a dictator should walk—with flair and obvious enjoyment, trailed
by a line of attendants—turning slowly first to the right, then to the left
in acknowledging the crowd." Or his profile of General Ton That Dinh,
one of the key plotters in the coup against Diem, who wept on hearing
the news that the President had been killed, but "was not so grief-stricken
that it prevented him from dancing at a party that night." It is incisive
detail of this sort, culled from personal experience, that so often gives the
book the immediacy and rich texture one associates with a competent
work of literature (Halberstam a few years later would, in fact, publish a
novel set in Vietnam).

The Making of a Quagmire is also noteworthy for the density and
reliability of its facts, a virtue stemming from the collaborative approach
which Halberstam and his colleagues in the Saigon press corps used in
going about their work. Far more than is usual in modern journalism, this
talented group of reporters—most of them young and two of them Vietnamese—decided to pool information and sources. In part, this joint effort
reflected the close friendships that existed among them (Halberstam and
Neil Sheehan, as it happened, had been editors on the same college newspaper a decade earlier) and in part a desire to band together for mutual

protection in a hostile environment where their work came under frequent attack. One also senses that the nature of the story itself, with its complex layers of intrigue and deception, led them to work together closely. Especially dangerous in this regard was the elaborate network of confidential informants that they created—an intelligence operation, as Halberstam proudly observes, that consistently outperformed that of the CIA but which, with its reliance on anonymous sources (many with personal axes to grind), could in such a volatile situation easily have misled a reporter working on his own. Precisely because Halberstam and his friends kept verifying information with each other, however, they made remarkably few mistakes. Indeed, their achievement stands as a case example of how investigative journalism should be done.*

To be sure, there are a few places where Halberstam's narrative of the Diem coup errs. Most notably, Halberstam seems to have been unaware of how heavily involved the United States was with the ARVN officers plotting against the President. Thanks to the availability of previously classified documents, we now know that a special CIA agent met regularly with the generals, transferred messages between them and the American government, and was present in their headquarters the night of the coup. Halberstam also gives Ambassador Henry Cabot Lodge more credit for breaking the American commitment to the Ngo family than the evidence will support. He leaves the impression that upon arriving in Saigon in August 1963, Lodge instantly sized up the political situation and then cleverly convinced other members of the administration to accept his views. Although Lodge was certainly a major player in the drama, it is apparent that the Kennedy administration had been giving serious consideration to removing Nhu and possibly Diem too well before Lodge arrived in Vietnam—indeed, effecting that shift in policy was Kennedy's main reason for sending Lodge. But these and other factual flaws seem relatively minor; what is striking from the vantage point of a quarter-century is how well Halberstam's rendition of this highly complicated event still holds up.

More serious, perhaps, is the Cold War bias that periodically clouds his judgment. That bias should be no surprise: having come of age in the early 1950s, when such attitudes went virtually unquestioned in the United States, Halberstam naturally arrived in Vietnam with the assumption that any Communist-led movement was inherently evil and deserved to be eradicated. We see this, for instance, in the double standard that he adopts toward the ARVN and NLF: over and over he insists that the ARVN troops must learn to be better fighters and to pursue and kill the enemy relent-

---

*Their profession, it should be noted, did not fail to recognize this achievement. In addition to the 1964 Pulitzer Prize, awarded jointly to Halberstam and Malcolm Browne, Halberstam, Browne, and Neil Sheehan shared the first Louis M. Lyons Award, given by the Nieman Foundation at Harvard University, for reporting "the truth as they saw it in the Vietnam conflict . . . without yielding to unrelenting pressure." For his work in Vietnam, Halberstam also received the 1964 George Polk Memorial Award for foreign reporting.

lessly; yet when NLF units demonstrate military aggressiveness, he writes as if they were bloodthirsty and immoral. And although he knows that the NLF is dramatically outnumbered and underarmed, he can't forgive it for resorting to ambushes and sudden nighttime raids. His criticism of American policy, accordingly, comes from a "hawk" perspective; he wants somehow to win the war against the NLF, not to curtail American involvement.

Yet when Halberstam attempts, in his concluding chapter, to puzzle out what the United States should do next, his anti-Communist instincts give way to a tough-minded realism based on all he has seen and learned in Vietnam. Though he has little enthusiasm for American withdrawal and believes a compromise settlement would lead swiftly to a Communist takeover, he also understands that introducing American combat troops would almost certainly produce disaster. His comments, published just as the Johnson administration was embarking on its massive escalation of the conflict, turned out to be all too prophetic:

> If only 5 percent of the population in the South is committed to the Vietcong, the arrival of U.S. combat units would probably make enemies out of fence-sitters; certainly the guerrillas' cause would become a broader and more popular one. Whatever military gains were brought by U.S. troops might soon be countered by the political loss; the war would begin to parallel the French experience. It would be a war without fronts, fought against an elusive enemy, and extremely difficult for the American people to understand. The misconceptions, misinformation and lack of candor displayed by American officialdom in the past in Indochina does not give anyone confidence that our government would explain the conflict.

At the book's end, Halberstam, for all his hawkish enthusiasm, is left with the realization that the contest in Vietnam is all but over and that the best the United States can now do is to identify and study its mistakes so as to avoid repeating them elsewhere. The book's final sentence encapsulates those lessons well: "Before we ever plant the flag again, we must make sure that grounds for mutual self-interest exist, that the situation has not deteriorated beyond control and, above all, that we are wanted."

This verdict on the American effort in Vietnam was put forth even more forcefully in an article that Halberstam wrote for *Harper's* after a visit to Vietnam at the height of the American buildup in late 1967. "Return to Vietnam," which appears as the epilogue to the present volume, represents an extended exercise in déjà vu; it shows, in his words, "how little had really changed" since the Diem era, even though the United States had almost entirely taken over the war. All the same errors and illusions are present, giving rise to the same predictable and tragic results.

The heart of the matter, he reports, is that "We are not building a nation" in South Vietnam—or, as one U.S. official tells him, there is nothing "local" that is "viable." It is possible, the official explains, to make progress for a time by sending American units into a given area, but "pull the American boots out . . . and it would go Red in a week." The reason for the lack of progress in this essential task of "nation building," Halberstam now states outright, lies in the class structure of the society, with its chasm between the privileged and the poor and its pervasive corruption. The movement led by Ho Chi Minh had succeeded in tapping the wealth of human resources within the peasantry by offering a vision of an independent Vietnam, without artificial social barriers, where people could rise as high as their talents would permit. But in the American client state of South Vietnam, a person's life prospects continued to depend on family status and a willingness to adopt Western ways. This fact was visible throughout the South Vietnamese government and especially in the ARVN, whose officers in 1967 still represented "a microcosm of existing privilege in Vietnam." "The enemy," Halberstam sums up, "has had a revolution, and we, failing to have one, have tried to compensate for it piecemeal. But we have never really changed the order of society. Rather, our presence . . . has tended to confirm and strengthen the existing order."

If anything, the massive American presence had exacerbated the problems of this "rotting society." Material corruption seemed everywhere in 1967, from the docks, where American goods flowed in; to the bars, which were frequented by GIs for drugs and prostitutes; to the construction taking place in all the major cities under the stimulus of American involvement. Up and down the governmental ladder, from village officials to President Thieu's palace advisers, it seemed that nothing could be accomplished without a bribe or kickback. While certainly not what planners in Washington had intended, this corruption was nonetheless an unavoidable by-product of the Americanized war and could only get worse as the influx of dollars and American resources kept growing. In Halberstam's words, "the more resources we feed into this country, the more we weaken the fiber and the more we corrode our own Vietnamese."

In short, the epilogue serves to corroborate Halberstam's earlier conclusion in *The Making of a Quagmire* that the United States had, in effect, exhausted all its viable options in Vietnam during the Kennedy era. With the ARVN hopelessly "defeated" by 1965, American combat divisions had been sent in to block an NLF and North Vietnamese victory. That narrow purpose had been accomplished—the U.S. soldiers "had staved off defeat" —but because no progress had or could be made in winning over the majority of the people, "the real power of the Vietcong [had] not been affected." In fact, exactly as Halberstam had anticipated, the more American military power was applied, the more the people of South Vietnam were alienated from the Saigon government and the easier the Communists' political task became. The end result was thus stalemate, "neither victory nor defeat," with the United States trapped in the unenviable position of attempting to forestall the inevitable at a tremendous cost in blood and treasure.

The story that *The Making of a Quagmire* tells, then, assuredly does not make happy reading. But it is one which desperately needs retelling as the nation continues to learn how to exercise the responsibilities of a superpower in a world that seems to get smaller every year. And few writers to date have presented that story more lucidly, vividly, or wisely than David Halberstam does in this book.

A Note on the Text

This edition of *The Making of a Quagmire* differs in a number of ways from the original one. Approximately one-third of the text has been cut in an effort to eliminate material that seemed clearly redundant or that did not relate directly to the Vietnam war. Thus several passages—and in certain cases, whole chapters—pertaining to David Halberstam's earlier stint as a reporter in the Congo, or dealing with his philosophical reflections on world politics in the mid-1960s, were removed. Moreover, content footnotes were added by the editor to help identify important persons and events from the Vietnam period that may no longer be familiar. Part and chapter titles have also been added by the editor. These changes should serve to make the book more accessible and useful for the great majority of contemporary readers; however, scholars working on Vietnam or on Halberstam himself may also wish to consult the 1965 edition.

Part I

EDGING TOWARD CALAMITY: VIETNAM IN THE EARLY 1960s

Chapter 1

Coming into a Troubled Land

I arrived in Saigon at a time of singularly bad feeling toward foreign correspondents. Francois Sully, the *Newsweek* correspondent in Saigon and for seventeen years a resident of Indochina, had just been ordered out by the Vietnamese government—or rather by Madame Nhu.* Several official protests about the expulsion had failed, and though at first the American authorities had referred to the banishment as a misunderstanding which would soon be cleared up, it became clear that there was no misunderstanding at all. According to the unofficial explanation, Sully was being expelled because he had offended Madame Nhu in a *Newsweek* article: a quotation from Madame Nhu about the Vietcong ("The enemy has more drive") had been used under a photo of her Paramilitary Girls' organization—a cadre which she usually referred to as "my little darlings," and whose members drew better pay than the Government soldiers in the field. Cables from *Newsweek*'s highest executives, pointing out that Francois had nothing to do with writing captions, were of no avail.

The campaign against Sully had gone according to the prevailing style. At first there was criticism in the local, controlled press—some of it personal, some of it political. "The colonialist journalist Sully was seen on the Rue Catinat eating Vietnamese rice," went one particularly good story—implying that Sully was not only telling stale lies about the country, but was virtually taking food from the mouths of starving Vietnamese. Then the Women's Solidarity Movement, controlled by Madame Nhu, called for Sully's expulsion. Sure enough, an official announcement of the expulsion was made.

Francois thus became something of a hero to many Vietnamese. In a store he was stopped by two young girls and asked for his autograph; later in the day when he went by to pay his taxes, amounting to several hundred

*The wife of Ngo Dinh Nhu, and thus the sister-in-law of President Diem, Madame Nhu was regarded—along with her husband—as the real power behind the throne in the South Vietnamese government. Known for her sharp tongue, she once told an interviewer that "Halberstam should be barbecued, and I would be glad to supply the fluid and match."

dollars, the local official smiled, shook his hand, called him a true friend of Vietnam and said there would be no tax collection.

The night I arrived in Saigon there was a farewell party for Francois in the *Newsweek* room at the Caravelle Hotel. The most striking quality about that gathering was an atmosphere which reminded me strongly of my working days as a reporter in Mississippi: we all seemed to be outsiders. There was no one there from the mainstream of the American embassy or the American military mission—just as in Mississippi comparable gatherings of reporters never included the leaders of the Chamber of Commerce, the mayor or a local legislator.

What was disturbing to me on my arrival was that none of the American officials was talking about the substance of Sully's stories. Yet his fellow newsmen considered his sources very good, particularly his military information. He often heard of Government defeats before other reporters; indeed, he was told of events which his sources were afraid to tell the President, Ngo Dinh Diem. This did not increase Sully's popularity at the Palace, and since he angered Diem and thus made the embassy's life more difficult, it seemed to me that the embassy protests on his behalf were largely perfunctory.

It had become clear to me very soon after my arrival in Saigon that the relationship between the American mission and the American press in Vietnam was quite different from any other in the rest of the world. In Vietnam there was a sharp and unfortunate polarization of the press reporting on the one hand, and the official position on the other. This was no overnight development; nor was it, as was claimed later, a product of the Buddhist crisis, for that was still eight months away. (Curiously, it was the Buddhist crisis that finally cost the Diem government the support of most of the remaining members of the American community and impelled them to take the viewpoint of the reporters.)

The existing dichotomy had been a long time in developing. It began at the time of the Indochina war in the late forties, when French officials, and then American officials, spoke optimistically about the war against the Vietminh, and the reporters reserved their judgment. Indeed, one of the first shots was fired by Robert Trumbull, the *New York Times* correspondent in Indochina at the time, who wrote an exceedingly pessimistic and stunningly prophetic story from Saigon in early *1947*, just a few weeks after the war had begun—an account which immediately aroused the ire of French officials, who felt Trumbull was trying to sabotage them. (Ironically, sixteen years later Trumbull, then chief of our correspondents in Southeast Asia, was still around to see other officials predict similar victories and criticize other reporters.)

His story began:

SAIGON, January 27—It is difficult to see how France can achieve a military victory in Indochina in a reasonable length of time, even with the promised reinforcements and with superior arms.

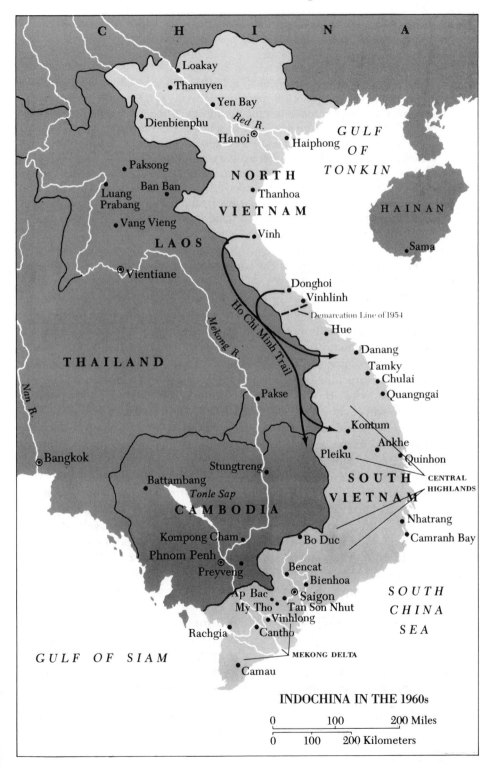

C H I N A

Loakay

Thanuyen

Yen Bay

Dienbienphu

Red R.

Hanoi ◎

Haiphong

GULF

OF

TONKIN

Paksong

NORTH

Ban Ban

Luang
Prabang

Thanhoa

VIETNAM

HAINAN

Vang Vieng

L A O S

Vinh

Sama

◎ Vientiane

Donghoi

Vinhlinh

Demarcation Line of 1954

Ho Chi Minh Trail

Mekong R.

Hue

Danang

T H A I L A N D

Tamky
Chulai

Nan R.

Quangngai

Pakse

Kontum

Ankhe

Pleiku
Quinhon

◎ Bangkok

Stungtreng

S O U T H

CENTRAL
HIGHLANDS

Battambang

Tonle Sap

C A M B O D I A

VIETNAM

Nhatrang

Camranh Bay

Kompong Cham

Bo Duc

Phnom Penh ◎

Preyveng

Bencat

Bienhoa

SOUTH

Ap Bac

◎ Saigon

CHINA

My Tho

Tan Son Nhut

Vinhlong

SEA

Rachgia

Cantho

GULF   OF   SIAM

MEKONG DELTA

Camau

INDOCHINA IN THE 1960s

0   100   200 Miles

0   100   200 Kilometers

France faces a clever foe. It is a foe that employs elusive guerrilla tactics over a vast area and fights to the last man when occasionally pinned down. There will probably always be more armed hostile Annamese in Indochina than there are Frenchmen. . . .

The Vietnamese are clever saboteurs. They cut vital highways with tremendous hand-dug pits, carefully carrying away the dirt from the hole so that the French forces must forage for filler material. When the Vietnamese sever a railroad line, as they have done in scores of places, they take away not only the tracks and ties, but also the gravel roadbed . . .

In any stand-up fight in which artillery could be employed, the French, with what armament they have, would undoubtedly be victorious every time. But the Vietnamese do not fight that way. Against superior odds they retreat, leaving nothing behind but ashes and ruins. By night they return in small bands again and again, making life uncomfortable for the foe. . . .

The split between the American press and the American officials in Vietnam continued throughout the bitter years of the Indochina war and it continued to exist during the war of the Vietnamese government against the Vietcong. Faced with this historical blindness to the efficacy of guerrilla warfare, newsmen had become increasingly dubious, until by the time I arrived the feeling was strong, bitter and personal. Although the embassy occasionally chided the Ngo government for its attacks on the press, such high officials as Ambassador Frederick Nolting, Jr., General Paul Donal Harkins and the CIA station chief John H. Richardson were basically more sympathetic to the Vietnamese Government viewpoint. They felt we were inaccurate and biased; they thought the war was being won, and they longed for control over us. "The American commitment," said an embassy white paper prepared in January 1963 for General Earle Wheeler, Chief of Staff of the Army, "has been badly hampered by irresponsible, astigmatic and sensationalized reporting."

The polarization had become more pronounced as the United States stepped up its commitment to a new high in monetary and military aid and prestige, and as our activities became more and more involved with that of a suspicious, unresponsive and archaic family dictatorship. American officialdom in Vietnam became enthusiastic boosters of the Government; in fact, they were part of the Ngo team.* As virtual participants in the struggle, they were in sharp contrast to American missions throughout the rest of the underdeveloped world.

In general, a relationship of mutual respect exists between ambassadors and reporters in most underdeveloped countries; if anything, reporters—and *New York Times* reporters in particular—may be treated too well. A reporter must always be aware that an ambassador in a small country which has no immediate crisis may view the press as the best way

---

*"Ngo" refers to the family of President Ngo Dinh Diem, which included his brother, Ngo Dinh Nhu, and sister-in-law, Madame Nhu. In Vietnamese culture, a person's first name is the family name.

to break through State Department channels and get his country and its problems to the White House at breakfast.

But in Vietnam these relationships simply did not exist. The split between the reporters and the mission was basic; it had foundered on the policy itself. It was not, as some were later to claim, the result of a bad press policy, or poor handling of the press, or inept news management. News management cannot turn a bad government into a good one; from time to time it can hide the story of, say, one military defeat, but in the end it cannot conceal the fact that an enemy with superior drive and motivation is gaining ground.

The split between the American press and the American mission was very much the product of our country's traditional freedoms and attitudes. There was a conflict between these and the pressures of the Cold War, which often push the United States into complicated, difficult and essentially alien situations. We reporters were the heirs of a traditional American freedom: the right of a journalist to write what he sees, whether the news is good or bad for his own country. We did not have to worry about the alternatives of policy making. The ambassadors and generals, on the other hand, were the heirs of a new dilemma: the discord between this country's traditional instincts, and its duties and responsibilities in the Cold War.

Our commitment to the Diem regime changed drastically in late 1961, after President Kennedy had sent General Maxwell D. Taylor* to Vietnam on a special mission to see what could be done to keep the country from falling to the Communists. From the position of a relatively cool backstage backer with only about six hundred advisers in the country—a relationship not too different from many others throughout the underdeveloped world —the United States had gone operative. It committed itself fully to Vietnam, and placed its prestige in Southeast Asia at stake—and in the hands of the Ngo family. This position, moreover, put the Kennedy Administration in jeopardy; a "Kennedy War," and a losing war at that, could have an influence in the next election. In October of 1961 we decided to increase American troops in advisory and supporting roles to over sixteen thousand, and to boost our economic aid to one and a half million dollars a day. Yet in so doing we were tied to the Ngo family; the United States could be no more politically sophisticated, no more aggressive, no more sensitive or responsive than the Ngo family.

Not only were we getting deeply involved in a situation where we could be no more effective than the established government, we were making a major commitment during a crisis in whose making we had played only a minor part. Moreover, we were making it at a time when

---

*As a trusted consultant on military matters and later chairman of the Joint Chiefs of Staff, General Taylor played a key role in shaping American policy toward Vietnam in the Kennedy Administration.

the war had already been under way for a long time and when there were really few new ideas or panaceas left for a very tortured country.

True, Vietnam had become vital to our national interest at the time of the 1961 commitment, but during many of the formative years that culminated in the crisis it had had very little priority at all; it had seemed far away. In the years immediately after World War II, when the struggle for Indochina began, U.S. attention was not focused on Vietnam: America was primarily concerned with trying to promote economic recovery in Western Europe and to establish a stable Japan. The question of change in the vast colonial empires of our Allies was very remote. President Roosevelt had been somewhat interested in Indochina; he believed that if the French resumed colonial control after the war, the results could only be disastrous. But Roosevelt died in early 1945, and Truman was less interested in Southeast Asia, simply because other issues were more pressing. In this vacuum the French returned to business as usual in Indochina.

The Vietnamese are not a phlegmatic people, and for centuries they have revolted against their oppressors. Bright, sophisticated people, traditional warriors, they have never accepted the rule of outsiders. During the thirties there was an increasing subsurface desire for independence; the defeats the white man suffered at the hands of Asians at the beginning of World War II simply accelerated these hopes. With victory for the Allies in sight, the Vietnamese had hopes of some sort of independence, perhaps at first as part of a French union. The French quelled these hopes, but they could not dampen the desire for independence; it simply became a matter of who would exploit nationalism most effectively.

It was not the West. Instead it was Ho Chi Minh,* an old Bolshevik and the brilliant leader of the Vietnamese Communist Party. Ho ("Uncle Ho" to the peasants)—a thin, slight figure, with a wisp of a beard, who looks like any pedicab driver in Vietnam—performed his mission brilliantly. He dissolved his own Vietnamese Communist Party in order to secure a broader base for a Communist-nationalist movement. Communist goals and Communist figures became secondary; emphasis was placed on a popular front. The cause was a national and patriotic one, and it camouflaged the hard-core Communist apparatus. Many nationalists joined who were not Communists; others who opposed the Communists were liquidated, sometimes by the Vietminh (which means, literally, Viet nationalist), sometimes by the French. Slowly but steadily the anti-Communist nationalism of Vietnam was strangled and destroyed; by the end of the war with the French it was never to be a serious force again.

At first the French considered the Vietminh nothing but peasant-bandits, and they consistently underestimated their strength, dedication, leadership and ability. Ho went to Paris in 1946 to make a last desperate

---

*Leader of the Vietminh in its battle against French rule and then President of North Vietnam from 1954 until his death in 1969, Ho Chi Minh had campaigned continuously for his country's independence from 1919 onward and thus became the symbolic embodiment of Vietnamese nationalism.

appeal for some political concessions, but the French were unbending; they did not sense as quickly as the British the changes that were coming over the colonial world. As for the United States, the brand-new world of anticolonialism, postcolonialism and neocolonialism was something it would discover belatedly in the late fifties.

In 1946 the French Indochina war began. There were many instances of great gallantry, but the bravery of the individual French soldier in fighting the war exceeded the motives of the French government. Asians were on one side and white men on the other, and though many Vietnamese did fight and die for the French they were never offered any real incentive. One of the cruelest ironies in Vietnam today is an inscription like the following, which can be seen on countless Vietnamese tombstones: NGUYEN VAN DAN—MORT POUR LA FRANCE.*

The French were confident about the outcome of the war. They had elite troops and the finest of weapons; they had tanks and airplanes. For them, the enemy was *les jaunes,* "the yellow ones." But though they lacked the equipment, the Vietminh at least knew what kind of war was being fought. They had discipline, absolute political superiority and a knowledge of the land and of the people; above all else they had a cause. They also had developed techniques of guerrilla warfare similar to those which Mao Tse-tung was using so effectively against the Chinese Nationalists. Gradually, in small actions at first, they began to ambush French troops, to capture French weapons and turn these over to their own elite troops—who would thereby capture more. The French controlled the highways and the cities; the Vietminh controlled the people. The French moved during the day, and the face they presented was always a military one; the Vietminh moved at night, lecturing the people, distributing medicine, promising land reform, reducing rents, teaching some of the youngsters to read and write, promising a better society.

The Vietminh troops adhered to the strictest discipline, as the Vietcong do now, in dealing with the population. Severe punishment was meted out for such offenses as the rape of peasant women or for lesser infractions like the stealing of peasant pigs; often the troops worked by the side of the farmers in the field. Whereas the French had a limited military intelligence network, every farmer became an agent for the Vietminh. In the colonialists' eyes every Vietnamese was a potential spy.

The French would hold static points; if it took fifty soldiers to man an outpost, the Vietminh could not successfully mount an attack with fifty of their own troops. But knowing exactly where the French would be they could attack with two hundred or two hundred and fifty men, and in the end they would capture fifty more weapons. "Is the enemy strong? One avoids him," wrote Vo Nguyen Giap, the Vietminh military commander. "Is he weak? One attacks."

Slowly the insurgents gained strength. They used classic guerrilla tech-

---

*Nguyen Van Dan—Died for France.

niques, emphasizing political education, always trying to confuse the enemy about the extent of their forces in any area. Eventually the French came to rely more and more on air power and napalm. This terrified the Vietminh, but it failed to deter them, for the war had become a great national cause, a war to force the white man out of Vietnam. To a young Vietnamese with any drive there were only two choices: either he joined the French, was paid money and fought to keep the French in Vietnam —taking a chance that they might some day leave; or he joined the so-called People's Army to drive them out. For a generation of inspired young Vietnamese the choice was clear.

One of the real problems of South Vietnam today is that a vast percentage of the vital, able people of the country became deeply involved with the Vietminh before they realized the full extent of its Communist role; by the time they did, they were so far along that they remained committed to what was to become the Hanoi government, in North Vietnam.

But politically the French gave the Vietnamese little. The best they offered was the discredited playboy Bao Dai.* Writing of him in a cover story in May 1950, *Time* reflected the Western mood and attitude:

> It is Bao Dai's mission and the U.S.-French hope to rally his countrymen to the anti-Communist camp of the West. In this undertaking he needs time. "Nothing can be done overnight," he says. He needs time to organize an effective native government, train an army and militia that can restore order in the village, win over the doubtful fence-sitters among the intelligentsia. Besides a military shield he also needs a display of winning strength and patient understanding by Western allies. As a national leader Bao Dai has his weaknesses, and largely because of this he does not enjoy the kind of popularity achieved by India's Jawaharlal Nehru . . .

In the early fifties the French were still predicting imminent victory, backed now by the Americans, who were their silent partners and were giving military and economic aid. Our military echoed the optimism of the French, even while the Vietminh strengthened their rural control. By 1952, Giap had divisions of troops, and was growing stronger. In the field, the French line officers' respect for the enemy continued to grow.

In 1954 the end came, militarily and politically. The French, seeking a set-piece battle, found themselves encamped at Dienbienphu, a fort deep in the mountains near Laos, reachable only by air. There the French high command hoped the Vietminh would attack, there they would break the back of Giap's forces. The French conceded the high ground to the enemy, and were dug in down in a valley. They believed that the Vietminh could never bring artillery and anti-aircraft guns to the site—and even if they did, they could not use them properly.

On March 13, 1954, the battle began. The French clearly were out-

*Bao Dai, a puppet of the French colonial government, served as chief of state of Vietnam from 1949 to 1955. He was ousted from power in October 1955 by Ngo Dinh Diem.

gunned; the Vietminh had not only the high ground but the artillery, and they knew how to use it. The French artillery commander committed suicide the first night, and very soon the outcome of the battle became a foregone conclusion. The French fought bravely, but there was no way for them to be reinforced; planes bringing in air supplies ran into concentrated anti-aircraft fire from perfectly camouflaged positions, from guns which had been brought in piecemeal, on the backs of coolies. The French lost sixteen thousand two hundred men—captured or killed—and they lost a war.

The day after Dienbienphu fell the Geneva Conference began. It resulted in another Vietminh victory: the partitioning of the country, with the northern, industrial half going to the Vietminh.* The French Indochina war had been what might be called a popular war, and its political legacy to the West was appalling; the Vietminh, who garnered almost all the talented people of a generation, was identified in the public mind as the side which drove the French out. Today Ho Chi Minh remains the closest thing to a national hero in both the North and the South. When Vietnam was divided in 1954 the North had the sense of dynamism, the leadership, a form of government whereby men rose through their ability, and an ideology which made the system work. In the South there was only the residue of that eight-year war.

South Vietnam was disorganized; there was no governmental authority; all anti-Communist feeling was identified with the French; the Vietminh were viewed by the people as liberators; the people were tired of war; the whole administrative structure was riddled with the worst kind of corruption practiced by the French and imitated by the Vietnamese—a legacy which is still a major problem. Any leader hoping to set up a stable government in the South would have to be both anti-French and anti-Communist, and eight years of fratricidal war had depleted the country of almost any qualified potential leader. The ruler of South Vietnam, Emperor Bao Dai—the corrupt playboy and French puppet—summoned Ngo Dinh Diem from his monastery in the United States to take over the country. Diem had been Minister of the Interior under the French in the thirties and belonged to an artistocratic, highly influential Vietnamese

---

*It should be noted that most scholars today, relying on evidence that has become available since *The Making of a Quagmire* was written, would strongly disagree with the account of the events of 1954 presented here. There seems little doubt that the Geneva Conference of that year was anything but "another Vietminh victory"; rather, under heavy pressure from the People's Republic of China and the Soviet Union (both of whom were pursuing their own narrow national interests), Ho Chi Minh was cheated out of much of the territory his army had won on the battlefield and forced to settle for only half the country. It is true that the Geneva Accords stipulated that this partition was to be temporary and that elections were to be held in 1956 to reunify Vietnam, but, as events soon showed, that was a promise that could easily be broken. Clearly, given the military realities at the time, the outcome of the conference represented a major diplomatic defeat for the Vietminh. Also, it is not really true, as Halberstam states below, that "there was no governmental authority" in the south at this time. The Geneva Accords provided for France to govern the territory below the Seventeenth Parallel until the 1956 elections took place.

family. A reluctant United States also backed Diem; in the ashes of postwar Vietnam there was no one else capable, and no one else who wanted the job. The significance of Diem was not so much what he was, but where he came from—the fact that to find him, officials had to look outside the country. It was a time of human bankruptcy in South Vietnam and Diem was the one straw for a grasping America. The Saigon intellectuals were discredited for what had often been a dilettante attitude during the Indo-china war; many of the other educated Vietnamese in Saigon were what became known as "Saigon bourgeoisie"—more French than the French, corrupt and weak. No real anti-Communist military hero had emerged during the years that the Vietnamese had fought alongside the French against their fellow countrymen; the political alternatives were largely war lords, gangsters or discredited puppets. Diem it had to be.*

In those days the Americans were not unaware of the difficulties ahead. Many in the American mission at the time were against Diem; others recognized his numerous failings, but admitted that there was no other choice. In 1955 General Lawton Collins, President Eisenhower's special envoy to Vietnam, argued strongly against Diem, claiming that he was aloof, obstinate, suspicious and unwilling to accept American advice. His reports were countered by those of Colonel Edward Lansdale, the chief U.S. intelligence agent in Saigon at the time. Lansdale, who a few years before had played a vital role in the Philippines in defeating the Huk guerrillas and had helped bring Ramon Magsaysay to international promi-nence, sent his reports directly to Allen W. Dulles, then head of the CIA. Lansdale persuaded Dulles that he must support Diem; in turn, Dulles influenced his brother, then Secretary of State. (Ironically, nine years later several key associates of Lansdale who were still in Saigon played a vital role in Diem's downfall.) Thus, on what is known in the boxing world as a split decision, began the uneasy relationship between Diem and the Americans.

---

*Again, most historians would say that Diem was the sole available choice only from the standpoint of the American desire to preserve South Vietnam as an independent, anti-Communist nation in violation of the Geneva Accords. France, for example, preferred Buu Hoi, who was also anti-Communist and who enjoyed considerable support within the South Vietnamese Army. But Buu Hoi favored holding the reunification elections that had been agreed upon at Geneva on schedule in July 1956, and thus was unacceptable to the Eisen-hower administration.

Chapter 2

Latter-Day Mandarins: The Ngo Family

After I had been in Vietnam for a few months, Madame Nhu granted me an interview.

The Americans, she said, were very silly in their attitude toward President Diem. They always wanted him to go out and mingle with the people, and wave to them and shake their hands and do those things which the Americans themselves like to do. But the President, she said, was very shy, and he could never do this; he would feel foolish and he would never be able to hide this from the people. The Americans did not understand him, she said.

Ngo Dinh Diem had been a prominent nationalist in the thirties, a respected mandarin and public servant who had resigned his position as Minister of the Interior of Annam because the French had reneged on promises that he would be allowed to rule freely. He was a member of an aristocratic old family, a devout Roman Catholic and an early and articulate anti-Communist—something rare in an underdeveloped nation where the Communists were in the luxurious position of being the social critics and of being identified with nascent anticolonialism. Because of Diem's reputation as a nationalist, Ho Chi Minh asked him to join Ho's popular front in 1945. Diem refused; the Communists had murdered his eldest brother, Ngo Dinh Khoi, and this had only further increased his hatred for them.

It is true that as a young man Diem was well known as both a nationalist and an anti-Communist, but although his country was undergoing a decade of insurgence he kept himself strangely apart from revolutionary feeling. The excitement of independence, the techniques of mass crowd appeal remained alien to him; his nationalism stemmed more from a sense of responsibility than from anything else. In his youth he had taken vows of chastity, and as an adult he led virtually a monastic life, both in Vietnam and later in exile, where he spent the vital years of the Indochina war. During the last two of these years he stayed at Maryknoll Seminary in Ossining, New York, and in this country he often met such Americans as

13

President Ngo Dinh Diem of South Vietnam, dressed in his characteristic white suit, reviews a two-hour military parade on October 26, 1963, less than one week before he was to be overthrown and assassinated. (UPI/Bettmann Newsphotos)

Cardinal Spellman, Senator John Kennedy and Senator Mansfield. Over these years he had built up a reputation for personal bravery and integrity —matched by his stubbornness—and a preference for priestlike seclusion.

According to one story, an American once asked Diem's elder brother, Archbishop Ngo Dinh Thuc, why Diem had abandoned his earlier studies for the priesthood. "The Church was too worldly for him," Thuc is reported to have answered. Another anecdote is told by Denis Warner, the Australian correspondent. Warner said to a Vietnamese friend that Diem sounded too much like a priest to be brought back to Vietnam. "Not a priest," answered the Vietnamese. "A priest at least learns of the world through the confessional. Diem is a monk living behind stone walls. He knows nothing."

A year after Diem's return, Graham Greene, seeing the growing pressures on him, was to write in the *New Republic:*

> Diem is separated from the people by cardinals and police cars with wailing sirens and foreign advisers droning of global strategy, when he should be walking in the rice fields unprotected, learning the hard way how to be loved and obeyed—the two cannot be separated. One pictured him sitting there in

the Norodom Palace, sitting with his blank brown gaze, incorruptible, obstinate, ill-advised, going to his weekly confession, bolstered up by his belief that God is always on the Catholic side, waiting for a miracle. The name I would write under his portrait is the Patriot Ruined by the West.

Diem had returned to a fragmented and shattered country which no one else wanted. Everyone predicted that he would not last the year, but it turned out that he had been right and they had been wrong. Against vast obstacles Diem acted forthrightly and courageously in the early years of his government. He resettled nearly a million refugees from the North, most of them Catholics who had fled Ho's regime. When he decided to wipe out the gangster sects some of his advisers warned him against it; Diem seemed lonely and poorly prepared for conflict with such powerful enemies, and it was suggested that he make an accommodation. Instead, he crushed the criminal elements which had ruled Saigon through their control of gambling and prostitution and through their alliances with the French police; again *he* had been right and *they* had been wrong. In 1956, two years after his lonely arrival back in Saigon, there was much American enthusiasm for Diem; *Life* called him "the Tough Miracle Man of Vietnam," and the *Saturday Evening Post* labeled his country "the Bright Spot in Asia." The blurb for the latter piece read: "Two years ago at Geneva, South Vietnam was virtually sold down the river to the Communists. Today the spunky little Asian country is back on its own feet, thanks to a 'mandarin in a sharkskin suit who's upsetting the Red timetable.' "

Yet his early successes were misread by Diem and his family; they were not necessarily a blank check from the population, and they did not mean that Diem would always be right. He was successful in some of his ventures partly because of his timing. On his return from exile he was hailed as a man who had at one time stood up to the French; when he moved against the sects he was doing what most Vietnamese wanted, for they were tired of corruption and the sinister link between the law and Saigon vice.

But the challenges against Diem and his country were particularly cruel, unlike those faced by any other ruler in a new nation. Perhaps if he had governed another country in a less critical area, and one not as badly splintered and without such a tortured recent history, he might have emerged an entirely different figure. But the pressures of Vietnam simply forced him into the bosom of his family.

It was a large and forceful family. There had been Ngo Dinh Khoi, Diem's eldest brother (who was killed by the Communists); there was Ngo Dinh Thuc, the archbishop of Hué, who was venerated by Diem, first, because he was a priest, and second, because he was the only surviving elder brother; there was Ngo Dinh Nhu, the intellectual and Palace strategist, and closest to the President; there was Ngo Dinh Can, the unofficial governor of Hué, who ruled central Vietnam like a feudal war lord; and there was the youngest brother, Ngo Dinh Luyen, ambassador to England

and formerly emissary to several other European countries, who was considered something of a playboy by the austere Diem.

Within the family, Nhu and his wife were the most powerful, largely because they lived in the Palace and were with the President all the time. In family decisions they often acted in concert with Thuc. Brother Can, who was considered by many Vietnamese and Americans to be the most realistic of the family, often clashed with the Nhus, and the only debates which took place in the National Assembly came when Can's deputies clashed with Nhu's deputies.

Diem held a deep-rooted suspicion of almost everyone but members of his own family, who shielded him from the outside world; he had a strong sense of his own moral righteousness, and therefore of his inherent right to rule. Some of these qualities were once virtues; they helped him to survive in the first years of what was, to all intents and purposes, a condemned government. But eventually these traits became accentuated and excessive; they made Diem a prisoner; they came to haunt both him and the people who had helped put him in office; and in the end they led to his downfall. He, who could never have been corrupted by worldly goods, became corrupted by power and pride.

Diem was a shy man. He had taken his vows of chastity when he was quite young, and he was ill at ease in the presence of women, always a little afraid even of his sister-in-law. He was a prodigious worker who labored sixteen or eighteen hours a day, taking his work to bed with him and waking up in the middle of the night to continue. He hated to delegate responsibility; he tried to run the country by himself and with his family —even down to the granting of visas. Consequently the administrative machinery of Vietnam became increasingly snarled year after year, and any attempt at regional initiative was frowned upon.

Diem and Ngo Dinh Nhu considered themselves the most able military tacticians in the country. They established strategy and moved divisions and regiments and battalions around, often without telling superior officers in the field. In addition, the brothers often switched priorities on major projects whimsically, so that the country's resources were constantly being squandered.

Like his brother, Diem believed he had a unique knowledge of the war being fought, but American and Vietnamese officers in the field, who were charged with the responsibility of trying to fight it, disagreed strongly. Again and again, commands dictated by the Ngo brothers indicated a lack of understanding of the military needs in a given situation; to make matters worse, their confidence in their strategy had been systematically bolstered by fraudulent after-action reports filed by frightened commanders in the field.

Despite the growing sense of alienation among his former aides and friends in the Government, and the bitterness these officials felt toward the Nhus, many of them retained a considerable amount of grudging respect for Diem, even when they were plotting his overthrow; there was still affection for his vitality and for his considerable charm. "Kill him the moment you take the Palace," one officer once told another as they were preparing for a coup, "or else he will start to talk and he will talk you out of it. I know him."

As the years went by, Diem became less and less of a conversationalist and more and more of a monologist. Toward the end, a visitor was lucky to leave his office after a six-hour interview. Sometimes the talks lasted ten hours, with no break and with the visitor allowed to ask only one or two questions. One old friend who saw Diem in 1963 was shocked by this stream of words; he said later that he felt that Diem was talking in a desperate attempt to keep the visiting American from questioning him—as if they both understood what the questions would be about. Charley Mohr, then of *Time,* became adept at handling Diem as a result of shepherding a long list of *Time* VIP's into the President's office. The Mohr theory was based on the fact that Diem chain-smoked; every time the President lit a cigarette, Mohr would immediately ask a question. Robert Shaplen of *The New Yorker* saw Diem in 1962 and wrote: "His face seemed to be focused on something beyond me and beyond the walls of the Palace; the result was an eerie feeling that I was listening to a monologue delivered at some other time and in some other place—perhaps by a character in an allegorical play."

It is always a strange sight to observe a man paying homage to himself; I had occasion to do so on one of the national holidays. There are many holidays in Vietnam, for that troubled country celebrates liberation from a long series of oppressions, but October 26 is a special one: it commemorates the day in 1955 on which elections were held and the population was allowed to choose between Diem and the puppet playboy Bao Dai. The people voted overwhelmingly to elect Diem, though the election was typical of those which were to follow in that the number of votes cast greatly exceeded the number of names on the electoral rolls.

The wide avenue along the Saigon River had been readied days ahead of time, and traffic had been routed away. Armored amphibious personnel carriers, which were desperately needed in the Delta because of the wet season, had been up in Saigon practicing for weeks, despite the anguished pleas of American advisers. In many areas the war had come to a virtual halt because vital units were practicing for the parade. With so many troops present in Saigon, the possibility of a military coup increased, and counter-security precautions were in full force. The threat of assassination was also present, so only carefully selected units were permitted to march. Uniforms were issued to the elite and predominantly Catholic Presidential Guard only on the morning of the parade, and members of the unit were carefully inspected before and after dressing, so that no unauthorized ammunition could be hidden away. In addition, their weapons were checked several times during the morning. Other elite units went through the same careful scrutiny. The day before, men with mine detectors had gone over the area where Diem would be. At key points throughout the city were presidential tank units, their crews in full battle gear, their motors running, their radios on.

Reporters who had applied for seats two weeks in advance and had submitted photographs of themselves were issued special passes. We were told to be in our seats very early in the morning. At 7 A.M., on our way to the parade, we noticed a curious phenomenon; the police were turning away thousands of people. It seemed unbelievable, but it was true; the public was not to be allowed to watch the ceremonies. The parade ground stretched for several blocks on each side of the presidential reviewing stand, and that entire area had been blocked off. Only select people were permitted in the area: foreign visitors, special guests, wives of official members of the Government, and hordes of security men. But the public at large could only see the paraders gather at the start. This gave an odd aura to the entire ceremony: one felt as if he were watching a movie company filming a scene about an imaginary country.

After the parade Ambassador Nolting was beaming over its success. Jim Robinson of NBC, who was in the process of being expelled from the country, pointed out that the public had been barred, but Nolting refused to believe him.

The parade itself revealed much about the country. Off to the south flew several formations of fighter bombers. They were not permitted closer because they had been forbidden to fly over the city since two of Diem's best pilots had bombed the Palace in February of 1962. In the parade itself were long lines of Nhu's blue-suited Cong Hoa Youth; they were, in fact, civil servants allegedly loyal to him, but few of them were young, and few of them, as it turned out, were loyal. Madame Nhu's Paramilitary Girls were there too, goose-stepping smartly, and armed with the finest new American carbines and submachine guns. Scattered throughout the crowd were scores of police and security men. Diem was there, but the Nhus were not; this was part of a family policy which prescribed that for security reasons Ngo Dinh Nhu, Madame Nhu and Ngo Dinh Diem should never appear together in public. Even when they flew to Hué for family meetings they went in separate planes.

Diem arrived after most people were in their seats, received several salutes, made a quick tour of the short parade route, heard his own personal song played ("President Ngo should live forever"), and then sat impassively. He was small, strangely young-looking in appearance, with a duck walk which bordered on a bustle. From a distance he looked somewhat like the Little King in O. Soglow's comic strip. A few minutes after the parade had started, it was all over. After weeks of preparation the armored personnel carriers could go back to fighting the Vietcong; the Government was through with honoring itself for the time being.

The Government and the population lived side by side in what was at best mutual apathy and indifference. In those days the most encouraging thing that could be said about Diem was that he stirred no strong emotions among his weary people. At one time they had respected and even liked him, but much of that good will had eroded as he became more identified with his family. The population did not hate Diem the way it hated his brother and sister-in-law, but it no longer trusted him or his government. If apathy was what the Communists wanted, the situation in Saigon was ripe for them.

For his part, Diem had little instinct for his people. He operated not out of a sense of partnership, common bond and mutual identification, which had proven so effective for the Communists and for men like Prince Sihanouk of Cambodia, but out of a sense of duty, of religious feeling and a corresponding feeling of righteousness. The political result of all this was a leader who felt that he represented God to his people, who felt that he could do no wrong and had discharged his obligations if he remained morally and spiritually correct. Before becoming President, Diem wrote in an article: "The state is founded on the people; the mandate of heaven held by the sovereign is revocable if he proves himself unworthy thereof." He added: "A sacred respect is due the person of the sovereign . . . He is the mediator between the people and Heaven as he celebrates the national cult."

This curious sense of righteousness that was inflicted on his rather easygoing and tolerant people was not matched by any corresponding ideology on their part. There was almost no attempt to persuade the population to identify themselves in any way with their government. "A little good old-fashioned demagoguery," one American once said wistfully, "would do this government a lot of good."

Diem's ascetic life, his observance of his codes and his remarkable luck in escaping death several times and in finally achieving the presidency confirmed his belief in his divine role. Anyone who doubted him on any question was likely to be judged not on the merits of the disagreement, but on the fact that he defied and therefore blasphemed. Similarly, anyone whose personal life was judged to be morally inferior to his own was, despite other qualifications, dismissed as a person ill prepared to rule or lead.

Eventually, Diem's people knew him only as an outdated photograph; his trips to the countryside became increasingly rare, and more and more like inspection tours—the local officials alerted days in advance, the town carefully policed, and on the day of the visit the population lined up for hours in advance, standing at attention in the hot sun and wondering what all the fuss was about.

Diem's increasing aloofness brought him into continual conflict with American officials. They would urge him to change, to reform, to broaden the base of his government, to permit a political opposition. Each time there was a conflict the hard line would be taken by the Nhus, who opposed all compromise. The Nhus did not really trust the Americans; despite all our pledges, they did not believe that the American commitment to them, the family, was absolute enough. In these tugs of war the Nhus inevitably won; they understood Diem better, they were Vietnamese, they were his family and they knew that its survival came first.

The conflict came to a head during the abortive military revolt in November 1960; the paratroopers had in fact accomplished their coup d'état—and then they sat around negotiating terms with Diem. He promised a new and different government, but while they picnicked and dallied for one crucial night, Diem called in loyal troops and crushed the rebellion. There were several by-products of that evening. One was that a coup d'état would be far more difficult the next time, and that the Vietnamese would be more wary of attempting one. Another was that Diem's reputation for integrity became tarnished in the minds of many Vietnamese. He had promised to change the Government—virtually at gun point, to be sure, but a promise was a promise—and then he reneged.

Inside the Palace almost everyone had wavered and had suggested accepting the paratroopers' terms. Only Madame Nhu had rejected the idea of compromise and had insisted on fighting to the end; she had been right, Diem decided later, and her influence around the Palace rose sharply. "Up until then," she told me during an interview in 1963, "they had not taken me that seriously. But then they began to notice me, and began to worry when I said things."

Though the Americans did not sponsor the coup—if they had it would have been carried through during the hours when the paratroopers wavered—the Nhus considered them accomplices. At one point U.S. officials offered Madame Nhu safe-conduct to the embassy; in her mind this convicted them of participation. The Nhus were later able to use this incident to gather increasing power.

The ultimate result of the paratrooper rebellion was paradoxical. Diem's best and allegedly most loyal troops, led by a young officer who was so close to him that he virtually considered him an adopted son, had rebelled over the political oppression in Saigon and over the military conduct of the war. They were not glory or power seekers; they failed, in fact, because they did not seize power, because they did not know exactly what they wanted politically, because, in other words, they were too naïve. Therefore, the final lesson that Diem learned was not that there were some true anti-Communist patriots who opposed him and that reforms were desperately needed; it was, rather, that conciliation was the way of the weak and inept. This was a lesson which was to haunt him in the Buddhist crisis.

The Palace became more suspicious than ever, and as Diem turned closer and closer to his family, the regime became less and less popular; the Government, once tolerated, became actively disliked. Everything that went wrong in Vietnam was blamed on the Nhus. Ngo Dinh Nhu controlled the secret police apparatus; therefore he had to bear the brunt of the hatred for a regime under which midnight arrests were becoming increasingly frequent, all political opposition was outlawed and dissent had been quelled. Madame Nhu, proud and vain, who had outlawed first divorce and then dancing, was delving into men's politics with sharp and ill-concealed arrogance, and she became the target of even more intense hatred. Nhu was primarily interested in control of the population; Madame Nhu was primarily interested in political power, and the population knew this.

The Vietnamese traditionally believe in strong families, and Diem was nothing if not a traditionalist. (In late 1963, when American officials in Vietnam were discussing what type of man would be the best alternative to Diem, one of them was asked for his ideas about a candidate's necessary qualities. "Well, first of all he should be an only child," he said.) As Diem was the first to realize, the Nhus were largely responsible for his ascension

The family of Ngo Dinh Nhu in traditional Mandarin dress. Madame Nhu is second from the left, with Nhu himself immediately to the right of her. They are surrounded by their four children, who range in age from three to eighteen years. (UPI/Bettmann Newsphotos)

to the presidency in the first place. Back in the uncertain days of the early fifties when Diem was in exile, it was the Nhus who had lobbied successfully with other nationalists in favor of Diem. Nhu had formed his own party, the Can Lao, which was later to become a vast secret source of power in the country, and with it he had created the shaky little base which supported Diem when he returned in 1954. Henceforth Nhu and his wife were Diem's most ardent workers, for they felt they were working just as much for themselves. Thus, the test used by the Ngo government in evaluating a man became not what he had done for Vietnam, but what he had done for the Ngo family.

Moreover, Diem greatly admired his brother. Nhu was Western-educated, which Diem was not, and the President considered him a true intellectual. Nhu could make long and impressive ideological speeches, and he had devised his own political philosophy for Vietnam ("personalism," a confusing counterideology to Communism, which no one else in Vietnam ever understood). Diem considered Nhu the perfect Vietnamese: he was dedicated, he worked as hard as Diem himself and he was an intellectual.

I once asked a Palace official which of the brothers he considered more influential. The Vietnamese thought for a minute and then said, "Nhu, because he can always influence Diem, but Diem can never influence Nhu."

Ngo Dinh Nhu was a born intriguer. He delighted in spending vast amounts of time and energy to trick people into doing the simplest and most normal tasks. Though eventually this peculiar trait proved to be his undoing, it served him well for a long time; not only did he survive countless intrigues in Vietnam, but his reputation as a schemer discouraged many other plots. He was an arrogant, vain man, sometimes privately a little contemptuous of Diem, whom he considered to be his intellectual inferior. He told one reporter that he considered himself "the unique spine of the anti-Communist movement" in South Vietnam, and that the program would collapse without him. He once boasted to Charley Mohr and Dick Clurman of *Time* that he was the "only serious strategist of guerrilla war" in modern times, and then spent an hour describing his unorthodox techniques. (His plan called for Government troops to squat in Communist-base areas; these tactics were in fact used by hapless Vietnamese commanders with an unparalleled lack of success.)

In late 1963, when the head-on collision with the Americans appeared imminent, Nhu had apparently put out feelers to North Vietnam about the possibility of discussions. One American official who knew him well said that this sounded very much like Nhu: the man probably believed that he could work out some form of coalition government with the Communists, and that in the inevitable, concomitant double cross he would come out on top. "Just the idea of playing with the Communists would fascinate Nhu and make the negotiations worthwhile," the official said.

Nhu made no attempt to conceal his lack of interest in the needs of the

Vietnamese people; he was an intellectual and an aristocrat, and they were not. Stanley Karnow, now of the *Saturday Evening Post,* recalls a long conversation with him after the abortive paratrooper coup. Karnow had been asking Nhu about charges of corruption, and Nhu had offered to show Karnow his bank accounts. "But even if you're not involved in corruption," Karnow said, "people believe you are, and that in itself is a political reality." To this Nhu answered, "I don't care what the people think."

Nhu had a thin, chiseled, handsome face; if Hollywood had cast a movie on Vietnam and the Ngo dynasty, it would have been perfect type-casting to have Nhu play himself. He was not an extrovert, and he performed poorly in front of crowds; when reviewing his Cong Hoa Youth he would raise his hand in a Fascistlike salute and they would raise theirs in response, but his heart hardly seemed to be in it. He was a violent anti-Communist, but he was fascinated by the Communists and their methods. He came to mimic their techniques, and again and again to adapt them to his own needs; indeed, the Can Lao Party was modeled after the Communist Party. He also tried to create the equivalent of Communist cadres, and his long, boring speeches were filled with references to them.

Madame Nhu shared her husband's fascination for the enemy and believed that the Government would do well to adopt some Communist methods—particularly in regard to the foreign press. She once suggested to a press conference that the foreign correspondents form a committee to decide each day on "a common line to follow." She proposed Joseph Alsop* as a man who would be helpful in determining the line. The other correspondents decided that this might be a wise choice from her point of view, but felt that their editors might not be receptive.

The obvious result of the Nhus' fascination with Communism was a government which in many ways was patterned after the Communists'. One Frenchman who also knew the Hanoi government very well called South Vietnam "the only Anti-Communist People's Democratic Republic in the world," while a member of the Vatican delegation once said, "All they need to do is change the flags, and overnight South Vietnam would be a Communist country."

Under Nhu, the men who rose to power were of a kind. They were from the same geographical area and of the same religion as the Ngo family; more importantly, they were men who were at home in the daily intrigue of Saigon, men who concentrated more on petty Palace conspiracies than on the long-range needs of the country, men who had little sense of the needs of the peasants, but a highly developed feel for the Palace winds, men who understood the vast security systems of the country and who had little compunction about telling the brothers anything they wanted to hear. Thus the family became surrounded by officials who

*Joseph Alsop was a syndicated columnist during the Cold War era who strongly supported the American military effort in Vietnam and frequently lashed out at critics of that policy.

resembled Nhu and Diem in all minor and petty qualities, but who lacked the major talents of the two brothers.

Eventually South Vietnam became, for all intents and purposes, a Communist-type country without Communism. It had all the controls, all the oppressions and all the frustrating, grim aspects of the modern totalitarian state—without the dynamism, efficiency and motivation that Communism had brought to the North. It was a police state, but it was unique in that its priorities were so haphazard; as a result, it was hopelessly inefficient. It was likely to pick up people for the wrong reasons; it had a strong enough police force to shake the loyalty and allegiance of the population, but not efficient enough to make them truly afraid.

To a large degree all of this could be traced to the Nhus: to them, running a government was largely an intellectual exercise; the form and fun of it mattered as much as the result.

Madame Nhu in particular ruled by impulse. The traditional sentimental songs were one of the few things that the average soldier, clutching his cheap transistor radio, enjoyed in his pathetic life. But to Madame, such songs were the product of a weak and decadent society, not sufficiently anti-Communist, and she banned them all. The Vietnamese generals, proud men engaged in an exacting war, were treated at the Palace like house servants, lackeys in her personal control from whom she demanded the most complete and petty kind of obedience.

Madame Nhu was a strikingly beautiful woman, and she was well aware of it; yet she looked too perfectly manicured, too much like someone who had just stepped out of a beauty shop, to be leading a country at war. Her speeches rang with appeals to sacrifice, but there was nothing about her which gave any indication of sacrifice. To me she always resembled an Ian Fleming character come to life: the antigoddess, the beautiful but diabolic sex-dictatress who masterminds some secret apparatus that James Bond is out to destroy. She liked power, and it showed; once in an interview she told me, "People say I am a woman of intrigue, but that is not true. People who intrigue are people without means, and I am a woman of means." She hated the American press, but she loved all the trappings of the personal interview: the long list of American correspondents going through the elaborate procedure of requesting a private audience; the personal letters addressed to her explaining precisely what they wanted to ask; the correspondents finally arriving—and being kept waiting; her own dramatic entrance, and their paying homage before asking their questions; tea being served by little male servants who bowed and scraped so low that the gesture resembled some form of medieval torture. (In this connection it is interesting to note that public ceremonies at which her Paramilitary Girls performed were always highlighted by jujitsu contests in which the girls defeated the boys.)

In contrast to Diem, who was shy and ill at ease in public, and Nhu, who often seemed indifferent, Madame Nhu had a real zest for the ceremonies

Madame Nhu taking target practice in style with her Paramilitary Girls, whom she referred to as "my little darlings." (Larry Burrows)

of leadership. She was the only one of the family who walked the way a dictator should walk—with flair and obvious enjoyment, trailed by a line of attendants—turning slowly first to the right, then to the left in acknowledging the crowd. It was always a virtuoso performance, and a reporter watching felt this was the way Mussolini must have done it.

Madame Nhu had complete faith in herself and her cause, and little use for anyone who in any way contradicted or doubted her. Her tongue was sharp and agile and it spared no one, not even the Pope. "Poor Pope," she once told Charley Mohr, commenting on the *Pacem in Terris*, "he pleases everyone on earth with this encyclical. But how is this possible? Even God is challenged by the Devil. If something pleases everyone, it can be exploited."

Madame was the true believer—that is, she had complete confidence in herself and, by extension, in the right of the Ngo family to rule. The responsibility of everyone else, Vietnamese, American, private and general, was to understand this and get in line. She also had the complete fearlessness of the true believer. If she had been in Saigon when the final coup took place on November 1, 1963, she would never have allowed the brothers to leave the Palace. (On the other hand, the new junta would have had a terrible problem in trying to keep howling mobs from lynching her. As it was, crowds smashed a giant statue that she had created in her own image, and ran howling through the streets with the pieces.)

Every Vietnamese, afraid of her and angered by her and her power and regulations, passed on every scurrilous rumor about her. They believed that she owned all of the six thousand tiny taxis which roamed Saigon's streets; they believed that she owned most of the downtown bars in Saigon; they believed all sorts of nasty rumors about her personal life. She herself was well aware of this. During a prolonged series of interviews for a *Time* cover piece, she told Charley Mohr, "If any man is promoted and he is not too ugly, it is immediately said, 'A protégé of Madame Nhu.'"

In August 1963, NBC had a television interview with Madame during the Buddhist crisis. When she insisted that the cameraman be her own staff member, NBC agreed, and soon after the tape had been received by the New York office they contacted the NBC man in Saigon, asking who had made the tape, "because they really must hate her." They explained that every time Madame had said something about having liked the Buddhists when she was a little girl, the Vietnamese cameraman had flashed to her long, tapered fingernails digging cruelly into the side of her chair.

It was typical of the decaying spirit of the times in Vietnam that men contented themselves with scurrilous attacks on the person of Madame Nhu, rather than with concern for the real problem: her power. For she wielded an enormous influence, in the same way that a strong-minded wife exercises control in a family business. She was a fiercely determined, extremely practical woman with none of the intellectual pretensions of the Ngo brothers; she was vigorous—two decades younger than Diem, a decade younger than her husband—vital and uncompromising. She felt that both men were too unworldly, too intellectual and too removed from reality; they needed, she felt, someone to watch over their interests. Diem, she told me in an interview, "is terribly scrupulous—much too scrupulous. He is always worried." Her husband, she added, "is very intellectual, but it is not really a handicap. Like all the Ngo family, he is very cultured."

Madame's greatest strength was her consistency and her determination. Her credo was very simple: the Ngo family was always right; it should not compromise and it should ignore criticism. Critics would be convinced sooner or later—and if they were not, they must pay the consequences. During the Buddhist crisis, for instance, she argued that the population would remain loyal to the President only if he stood up to the Buddhists and crushed them. What made her particularly strong in family council was that in effect she was the conscience of the family, that in their hearts the brothers believed what she was saying; as a result, she could destroy all opposition arguments advanced by the Americans or the one or two Palace aides who still maintained some independence of thought, because she always took the line that Diem and Nhu wanted to hear.

After Henry Cabot Lodge* had just arrived in Vietnam, his wife asked

*A descendant of a patrician New England family, Lodge had represented Massachusetts in the U.S. Senate, run for Vice-President on the 1960 Republican ticket with Richard M. Nixon,

a veteran American in Saigon to describe Madame Nhu and her power. The American gave an appraisal similar to the above. "Yes," the ambassador said when he had finished, "that's exactly what her mother told me when we talked in Washington."

Madame had an almost mystical feeling about the Ngo family, and she talked constantly of how cultured they were. She ordered Vietnamese press officers to refer to her as Madame Ngo, although Madame Nhu was the accepted usage. She once told me with a perfectly straight face that it was absurd to call the family a dictatorship; after all, she said, every member had a free voice at family councils.

Step by step Madame Nhu and her husband shut Diem off from the rest of Vietnam. Dr. Tran Kim Tuyen, head of the secret police network, saw the paratrooper coup as the final warning to the Government and at great risk he wrote a long, carefully documented report for Diem, analyzing what had happened and what it portended for the future. Dr. Tuyen traced much of the trouble to Madame Nhu, and he warned that if the Government were to survive, Madame's role and power must be curtailed. After Nhu had shown the report to his wife, the influence of Dr. Tuyen, who had been the most brilliant member of the Palace staff, was effectively ended.

All power emanated from the Ngo family, in part through their vast series of subsurface networks of peculiar nomenclature. (When Dr. Tuyen headed the secret police, he held the title of "Director of the Political and Social Research Service of the Presidency.") The generals with political influence and power were not those with long titles and distinguished records, such as General Duong Van Minh, military adviser to the President, or General Tran Van Don, commander of the Army of Vietnam. The military who counted were those who had command of troops in the areas around Saigon; they had power because they were trusted not to participate in coups and would, indeed, help stamp them out. Throughout both the military and civilian establishments, a main source of power was the Can Lao Party, controlled by Nhu: a man might be a colonel, but if he was not a member of the Party and, say, a major was, it was the major who really exercised power.

At one time there were thirteen different secret police organizations, controlled by different members of the Government. Many of these police did not know one another, and we reporters took advantage of this. Neil Sheehan* would send a young photographer named Nguyen Thai into otherwise impossible situations; Thai, dressed like a secret policeman—in

and served as President Kennedy's ambassador to the United Nations before his appointment as ambassador to South Vietnam in the summer of 1963.

*Saigon correspondent for United Press International (UPI), Sheehan was an old friend of Halberstam's from college and would in time follow in his footsteps covering the Vietnam war for the *New York Times*.

open sports shirt, simple slacks and dark glasses—blended in perfectly with the others and used the same kind of small camera they employed. Each secret policeman thought Thai was a member of a rival organization and he was always accepted as such. He took excellent photographs of situations from which other photographers were barred, and he became an important source of news about the secret police. (Ironically, his only dangerous moment came at a demonstration by medical students against the Government; the students, believing that he was an agent, took off after him, and he barely escaped.)

By 1961 the power of the Nhus was immense. Imagine Diem as the President of the United States; in such a situation Nhu would have controlled all the country's newspapers, headed the CIA, the FBI and the Congress, served as Attorney General and Secretary of State, and written all the reports the President saw. What Diem knew of the outside world was what Nhu wanted him to know; what he saw he saw through Nhu's eyes; the people he met he met only after Nhu had approved them. Once, in 1961, Diem called in a corps commander, hauled his maps out and described a major operation he envisioned just north of Saigon in D-Zone, a major Communist base. When Nhu heard that this major operation was being planned, he summoned the division commander and ordered him not to commit his troops because he did not want them to leave Saigon at that time. The division commander called his superior, the corps commander, who, in a dilemma, went to see Nhu and said he couldn't countermand Diem's plan. Nhu finally devised a solution; he ordered the corps commander to deploy a couple of battalions to D-Zone and then send in phony information to Diem. The operation took place as Nhu had ordered, and of course it was reported to the President as fully successful.

Nhu had created the Cong Hoa Youth in his own image. He ran the Army's security systems, and he pitted one faction against another. Madame Nhu had her groups too: the Women's Solidarity Movement, regarded as an apparatus for family espionage, and the Paramilitary Girls. It was also clear that Nhu planned to use the strategic hamlet program, which was designed to separate the peasants from the Vietcong, as a means of controlling the population, in particular the young people. When the war had ended successfully, Nhu would emerge as the most powerful man in the country.

This strange triumvirate ruled over a government that had no parallel. There were elections, though no opposition candidates were permitted; there was a legislature, but it was the rubber-stamp kind, whose only real function was to legislate between representatives of brother Can in the central region and brother Nhu in Saigon; there was a cabinet, whose ministers had responsibility but no power and who lived in mortal fear of Madame Nhu.

The election returns of South Vietnam would have staggered the imagination even of the Communists in the North. In the 1963 Assembly elections, Ngo Dinh Nhu, representing Khanh Hoa Province, received 99.98 percent of the vote, while Madame Nhu, running as a candidate from a district in Long An almost totally controlled by the Communists, received 99.4 percent. When I asked her about this later, she said, "I am becoming a popular figure, which is very encouraging because I have no public relations."

In 1961, at the very vital point in the history of Vietnam when the Americans made their major commitment and praised Diem at every opportunity in order to improve the relationship, political disintegration lurked beneath the unrest on the surface. The three main power factions in the country were all shaky. First, the family depended on its growing police power, which in turn was making the rest of the population increasingly unhappy and the Americans increasingly nervous. Second, the Army's loyalty was dubious, despite the elaborate lengths the brothers had gone to in order to control it. Promotion on the basis of personal loyalty rather than ability, the use of informers, the banishment of men of integrity and initiative, and the domination of all strategy had not made the Army more loyal; these methods had merely brought about a tenuous control, and badly compromised and diluted a military force which was in a fight to the death with a tough enemy.

The third source of power was the Americans, seen as a potential danger by the suspicious Nhus, who tolerated the Americans only as long as they did everything the family wanted. Therefore, the increase in the U.S. role was offset by stronger efforts to minimize American influence and to keep the Americans out of the vital area of policy making.

Thus, a government was fighting a complicated war, suspicious of its own army and attempting to minimize its effectiveness; at the same time remaining suspicious of its major ally and attempting to minimize its influence.

It was not a happy time in Vietnam, despite all the surface optimism. Some Americans thought the answer lay in separating Diem from the Nhus—that Diem was good and the Nhus were bad, and that therefore everything could be solved by dividing the two. But anyone who dealt with the Government knew that this was an impractical solution; as Ambassador Nolting told one friend, "Trying to separate the members of that family would be like separating Siamese twins."

Chapter 3

A Strange Alliance: The Americans and Diem

A short time after I had arrived in Saigon I was having lunch with Doug Pike, a member of the U. S. Information Service mission and one of the brightest Americans in Vietnam. Pike, who had spent a good deal of time in Asia, was a specialist on psychological warfare, and was making an ill-fated attempt to impress on both the Government and the American military the importance of psychological warfare in a struggle like this.

That day he was in a less than enthusiastic mood. He had just been to see an American general about coordinating some additional "psy-war" teams into the Government program. The general had looked at him coolly and displayed contempt for "psy-war." "We're here to teach 'em to kill Communists," he said. Pike argued for a few minutes, got nowhere, and then reminded the general that the French had killed perhaps a million soldiers fighting under the Vietminh banner during their war.

"Didn't kill enough then," said the general. "We'll teach 'em to kill more."

The nine years of the Diem regime were marked alternately by excessive optimism, constant mutual suspicion, continuous political unrest, vast American military miscalculation, economic aid that did not reach the peasants, training and preparation for the wrong war—and no preparation for what was the predictable war. After we had entered Vietnam we tended to disregard every lesson the French had learned; by the early sixties our generals had begun to sound like *their* generals; our self-deception had begun to match *their* self-deception.

Diem had misjudged the Vietnamese people's acclaim for the popular reforms he brought about when he first came to power, but the real optimists in this situation were the American military officials in charge of the Military Assistance and Advisory Group (MAAG) in Vietnam. The Communists had prepared their cadres in the South, but had not yet made their challenge. The Americans, just finished with the Korean War, were remarkably ignorant of the nature of the French Indochina war. They still retained the Korean War psychology; they believed that if the Communists struck it would be by a traditional border crossing, a stab at the Seventeenth Parallel. Therefore they trained the Vietnamese Army conventionally, and they virtually ignored guerrilla and counterguerrilla techniques. They were openly contemptuous of the French experience; to them, the French simply had not fought well enough.

Not only did the chiefs of the American mission consistently fail to take the enemy seriously, they did not understand the political aspects of the war. They fawned over those Vietnamese who conformed to their own image: crew-cut Vietnamese air-borne officers, fairly bursting out of their uniforms, parachute insignia on their chests, and dropping occasional words of American slang. "How good is the individual fighting man?" Peter Kalischer, then with *Collier's,* asked General "Hanging Sam" Williams in 1956. "Man for man," answered General Williams, "they're as good as the Vietminh now." He went on to tell Kalischer that the officer corps was being built up, and that American mobile offensive tactics had replaced the French doctrine of static strongholds.

This was to become a familiar tune in Vietnam. The Americans kept repeating it, but the plan never materialized. After seven years, in late 1963, with most of the lower Camau peninsula already under Communist control and the few remaining outposts nothing but suicide traps, Neil Sheehan and I wrote stories which pinpointed how this strategy was not being followed. A very able American lieutenant colonel, relatively new to the country, took exception to our stories, pointing out that he had just finished a long and detailed plan for doing away with the posts, and that his Vietnamese counterpart had accepted it. Neil told him that we had heard a lot of American officers say exactly the same thing, and that we would believe it when we saw the outposts come down. The colonel listened, and then nodded his head regretfully.

An indication of the American blindness to the military situation was this comment, in the summer of 1959, by Major General Samuel Myers, deputy chief of MAAG, who said, referring to the enemy by the name used during the French Indochina war, "The Vietminh guerrillas, though constantly reinforced by men and weapons from outside, were gradually nibbled away until they ceased to be a major menace to the Government. In fact, estimates at the time of my departure indicate that there were a very limited number of hostile individuals under arms in the country. Two territorial regiments, reinforced occasionally by one or two Army regiments, were able to cope with their depredations."

For four key years, from 1955 to 1959, the Americans and Diem marked time. They had failed to prepare for the kind of threat that even the most cursory study of the Indochina war would have shown was most likely. The Government had failed to extend its authority to the villages; prodded by the Americans, it had made a stab at land reform, but because of Diem's own conservatism and lack of interest, the program had failed badly and had given the enemy rich opportunities for political subversion among the peasants. Local Government militia in the villages were badly trained and were still depending largely on the old French outpost psychology.

In late September of 1959, two Government battalions were searching for an estimated forty guerrillas in the Plain of Reeds, southwest of Saigon along the Cambodian border. Instead, they were ambushed by two enemy companies. The fire fight lasted fifteen minutes; twelve of the Government regulars were killed, and the rest surrendered their weapons. The second Indochina war had officially begun, though few people realized it at the time. From this time on, the enemy was to be known as Vietcong, which means, literally, Vietnamese Communist.

The new Indochina war was not a spontaneous uprising from the South. It was part of a systematic and calculated conspiracy on the part of the Communist government in Hanoi to take over the South. But it was the most subtle kind of conspiracy, for though Hanoi directed the war, set its pace, controlled its overall strategy and on the international front articulated the propaganda aims of the Vietcong, it did not in those days send North Vietnamese troops to fight in the South. Rather, the *face* of the war was of a purely indigenous uprising: the troops were Southerners, and captured weapons were usually employed. Some of the Southerners might have been trained in the North and might have served with the North Vietnamese infantry before infiltrating back to the South in the early sixties to serve as battalion or cadre commanders in the new struggle. In this type of conspiracy, Hanoi was aided by the frontiers of South Vietnam: the incredibly rugged Laotian border, and farther south, the Cambodian —a vague and aimless boundary separating South Vietnam from a neighbor more sympathetic to the insurgents than to the established regime. The failure of the Government to attempt even the most fundamental antiguerrilla techniques made the nature of this terrain relatively unimportant. Had the Government been more effective, the borders might have been more significant; successful counterinsurgencies in Greece, Malaya and the Philippines depended, among other things, on isolation of the rebels. (In 1964, according to reliable intelligence reports, the Vietcong not only increased the number of infiltrators, but by the latter part of the year Hanoi was reportedly sending North Vietnamese into the South.)

The pace was stepped up early in 1960; the Vietcong started a systematic attack on Diem's village officials, designed to undermine what little Government authority existed. Forty village chiefs were killed the first week and many arms were captured. Two types of village chiefs were targets: the bad and corrupt, because in killing them the Vietcong looked like benefactors to the population; and the able, who represented threats to the enemy because they were effective representatives of the Government.

To the Vietcong, terror was an act of discrimination. They also made schoolteachers a prime target; hundreds were murdered. Between 1959 and the end of 1961 the Government was forced to close six hundred and thirty-six schools, either because of intimidation, or because the Vietcong were using them for propaganda. Again and again the story was the same: brutal murders, decapitation of village officials and teachers in front of an entire village; hidden Vietcong cadres coming slowly to the surface. These spotlighted the corruption of officials, and by wholesale murders demonstrated that a government which could not protect its own officials certainly could not protect its people.

The Government troops, trained and poised to repulse a crossing at the Seventeenth Parallel, were totally unprepared for an enemy who stole the countryside away at night. Diem, proud and aloof, refused to recognize that insurgency existed in 1959 and 1960, because that would have been a reflection on the Government. For a long time his administration would not admit that a war existed; the Vietcong movement was written off as isolated banditry. Government casualties soared (some estimates place the number of civil servants and teachers murdered between 1959 and 1961 at over ten thousand) and so did arms losses. This produced an ever-quickening spiral, for as Vietcong arsenals grew, so did their capacity to strike and to capture more weapons. "Ngo Dinh Diem," said one enemy propaganda tract at the time, "will be our supply sergeant."

In late 1960 some American officials were still pretending that the situation in South Vietnam was healthy, that the revolt was primarily the work of disorganized bandits. By mid-1961, however, the Government position in the countryside was extremely shaky. The Vietcong were threatening to take over the entire rural Delta, and they appeared to have all the drive and momentum. The Government Army was ill prepared to fight back; it was disorganized, it lacked the mobility to catch the elusive guerrillas; its morale was extremely low, for it saw the enemy as the successor of the erstwhile victorious Vietminh, and thus believed that it was fighting men who were ten feet tall. The Army lacked leadership and it lacked a will to fight. According to a friend of mine, "in those days, when you woke up in the morning you didn't know whether or not you would have a country left."

In October 1961 the Taylor mission set the stage for the major American buildup and for the second step in the American commitment to Diem. It came at a time when the Diem government, difficult and isolated in 1954, had become almost paranoiac in its touchiness. It was reduced to police-state methods for survival, and it had grown more and more suspicious of its major ally—particularly following the abortive 1960 paratrooper revolt, which the Nhus still believed was planned by the Americans. Increasing numbers of small groups of nationalists who had been drawn to Diem in 1954 and who had liked his early rule now found him impossible to work with. If they were talented, they quickly ran into conflict with the family; as a result, many of the best people around him were leaving. Of course their departure made Diem more suspicious than ever and tended to make him rely more and more on his family, particularly on the Nhu branch—which was exactly what the Nhus wanted.

Seeing former supporters turn against him, Diem relied increasingly on the Nhus and on police-state techniques for control. As a result, more and more members of his own government and the population turned against him; the more frequently this happened, the more Diem relied on police methods. The Army was rife with political favoritism and security networks; personal loyalty, rather than merit or bravery, was the key to promotion. This is not unusual for an underdeveloped country, but South Vietnam was an underdeveloped country fighting for its survival; it could ill afford such luxuries.

It was against this background that the Kennedy Administration was forced to make a deliberate—and once again limited—choice in late 1961. It could back out of South Vietnam entirely—which would virtually turn Southeast Asia over to the Communists and might have disastrous repercussions in the next presidential election. It could search for another leader—but because of Diem and the Nhus, no national hero had been allowed to emerge. Moreover, Diem was a tantalizing figure in that he always seemed better than his government. Was the Government corrupt? Diem was a paragon of integrity. Was the Government unjust? Diem always seemed a model of personal justice and honor.

Finally, 1961 was also the year of the Bay of Pigs, the Berlin Wall and the deterioration in Laos; a change of government might backfire, and the Administration could not stand another major international bungle at that time. It could send U.S. combat troops into Vietnam, but were the American people prepared to subscribe to such a war? Besides, American combat troops would create exactly the same situation as the French had; they would be white men fighting Asians on Asian soil, and they would turn the entire population in favor of the Vietcong.

There was one other alternative: the United States could step up its own commitment to a point just short of combat. It could help the country to help itself, could send in advisers, helicopters, fighter bombers, and pilot trainers and pilots. It could, in fact, do everything but give the Vietnamese the will and desire to win.

This decision was made, and the reasons were relatively simple: there was nowhere else to go.

The key man in making this choice was Maxwell Taylor. As such, he was in fact a representative of what is known in Washington as the "Never Again Club," a Korean legacy—a phrase meaning that its members never again wanted to place American combat troops on the mainland of Asia without atomic weapons. Above all else, Taylor wanted to keep American combat troops out of the Vietnamese jungles. He and others like him shared a feeling that this was not America's war. Thus, the commitment was in effect a booster shot, but it was one step short of actual combat, and it was made in full knowledge of the limitations of the government on which it was being superimposed.

In effect, the Taylor mission reported that the war could be won, and could be won under the existing government—provided that a huge retraining program oriented the Vietnamese military away from conventional warfare to new concepts of flexible counterguerrilla warfare. The study called for greater mobility of the Vietnamese Army by giving them helicopters and amphibious personnel carriers. It recommended aid programs designed to break through the frustrations of Diem's overly centralized and personalized government and to bring aid down to the peasants. It suggested a series of reforms: broadening the base of the Government; taking non-Ngo anti-Communist elements into the Government; making the National Assembly more than a rubber stamp; easing some of the tight restrictions on the local press.

Above all, the people and the Government itself had to develop a relationship of mutual trust. All of this, Taylor and his advisers hoped, would end what was perhaps the worst characteristic of the Government: corrupt local officials constantly telling peasants that they had not seen those abuses which were in fact taking place before their very eyes. For the Vietnamese peasant there was no redress from official bungling or corruption, because even when Diem knew an official had acted improperly or incompetently he would not replace him, lest he lose face. To dismiss a man would show that Diem had erred by choosing that official in the first place. Thus, while Diem was not corrupt, he tolerated corruption; while he himself was not necessarily cruel or unjust, he tolerated cruelty and injustice. Friends of mine who saw the Taylor report consider it a brilliant analysis of the ailments and symptoms of a very sick country.

The U. S. Administration and its representatives in the field believed that by all-out support of the Diem government we could change its attitude toward its own people and persuade it to make changes it had been unwilling to make on its own. The problem, however, was very simple: the Ngo family wanted American aid, American equipment and some American troops, but it did not want American advice.

It was emphasized by Ambassador Nolting that support of the Government must not be half-hearted. The ruler's peculiar psychological make-up—and therefore the character of the Government itself—demanded that support must be full and enthusiastic and without quibbling. Only this, Nolting was convinced, could influence Diem.

But there was a flaw to this argument. An unresponsive government which has been receiving considerable American aid and not listened to American advice, and which then is given even more aid because it has repeatedly failed in its mission, is not apt to be more amenable to suggestion later on. Predictably, the reverse took place: the Ngo government became more convinced than ever that it had its ally in a corner, that it could do anything it wanted, that continued support would be guaranteed because of the Communist threat and that after the commitment was made, the United States could not suddenly admit it had made a vast mistake.

Although seven years and two billion dollars of American aid had previously been spent in the face of steadily increasing enemy strength, the American material aid recommended by the Taylor mission—the helicopters and the men to fly them—began to arrive in January of 1962. At the same time the Americans began to talk about some of the promised reforms. Almost immediately Ngo Dinh Nhu unleashed a violent anti-American campaign in the controlled press. After a few days of this—plus sulking on the part of Diem—the Americans decided not to push for reforms; they would back Diem strongly and hope that the sheer force of military equipment would help to turn the tide. So, the Americans began to give in to the Ngo family on virtually everything. Having failed to get reforms, our officials said that these reforms were taking place; having failed to improve the demoralized state of the Vietnamese Army, the Americans talked about a new enthusiasm in the Army; having failed to change the tactics of the military, they talked about bold new tactics which were allegedly driving the Communists back. For the essence of our policy was: *There is no place else to go.*

When reporters began to file stories which tended to show that the policy was not working, its authors, President Kennedy and General Taylor, clung to it stubbornly. At least part of the explanation for this apparent blindness is that although they knew things were going wrong, they felt that the alternatives were worse. The psychosis of the American position had been evidenced by none other than Lyndon Johnson, then our Vice-President, who visited the nation in the summer of 1961 as Kennedy's personal representative. Johnson praised Diem lavishly as an Asian Winston Churchill. On the plane out of Saigon a reporter started talking to the Vice-President about Diem and some of his faults. "Don't tell me about Diem," Johnson answered. "He's all we've got out there." Of course the Ngo family understood this perfectly well; the Americans were their main support, and the brothers had long learned the fine art of handling American diplomats.

By the time Maxwell Taylor arrived in Vietnam on his first trip in 1961, the options available to the United States were already limited; to a remarkable degree we were the victims of recent history—not so much a history that we had made as a history that we had ignored. In early 1964, Dang Duc Khoi—the former information officer for the Vietnamese government who had fled the country in August 1963, a step ahead of Nhu's secret police—was asked about the possibility, suggested by the French, of a neutralized Vietnam. It was too late for neutralism, Khoi said. There was no such thing any more in Vietnam; the enemy was too real and the game had been played too long. "But I wish," he continued, showing as much bitterness as I had ever seen a Vietnamese permit himself in public, "that the French had been as interested in a neutral Vietnam seventeen years ago as they are now. Then we could have been neutrals."

He was right, of course; the vital decisions in Vietnam had been made long ago, back when it was still called Indochina.

Part II

THE WAR IN THE DELTA

Chapter 4

In the Field with the ARVN

When I first went to the Delta, I saw that this was what the war was all about. The soil of the Mekong River lies rich and flat and green just south of Saigon. This area comprises only about a quarter of all South Vietnam, but most of the peasants in the country live there, about 80 percent of the country's agricultural resources are there, and when I arrived, most of the war was taking place there. Unfortunately, a major part of the Government's military effort was going into the central highlands and also into the central coastal region, where the Ngo family came from and whose population they trusted.

The Delta is difficult country to fight in: it consists mainly of paddies, swamps, canals and bogs. It is marvelous outlaw country; historically it has served as the hiding place for bandits. Yet its natural richness, its abundance of fish, rice and other food makes it easy country for guerrillas; the Ngo family's attempt to starve the enemy into submission had about as much chance of success as an attempt to deny a glutton food in an American supermarket.

At the end of September 1962 the optimism which pervaded the American mission in Saigon was strikingly absent in the Delta. There the enemy was gradually utilizing the cadres he had built up painstakingly during the eight years since the end of the Indochina war; he was fighting well and showing drive, resourcefulness and ingenuity. The guerrilla war fluctuates constantly; in the Delta young American officers serving as advisers were immediately thrown into the most complex and difficult situations imaginable. Also, the limitations of the Diem government—the problems and handicaps it imposed on field commanders, and the kind of leaders it chose for key areas—stood out even more conspicuously in the Delta.

The advisory mission placed young American captains and lieutenants down at the battalion level. It meant that at every level the Americans had as a counterpart a Vietnamese officer, hopefully passing on this country's vast background of military experience, trying to make the troops more aggressive, cutting down on mistakes, fighting the war the way we believed it should be fought. We also had men at regimental and division levels—and sometimes with companies—all the way to the top at the

Palace. (It was the belief of the men in the field that it was at the very top that the advisory effort was failing, and that if the Palace had really wanted its own officers to listen, the word would quickly have come down and the American advice would have been followed.)

At that time the Delta was divided by the Bassac River into two military areas. In the lower half, the Twenty-first Division was operating in the toughest part of the country, a territory which included the entire Camau peninsula, an area under Communist domination since before the French Indochina war. Here Government troops were isolated, and they rarely controlled more than the ground under their feet at any given time. The Seventh Division was in a more vital spot, in the upper half of the Delta, where the provinces were the richest and most heavily settled; approximately 25 percent of the South Vietnamese people lived in this area. But more important than its population was the fact that this was an area up for grabs; the Communists were not as strong here as they were in the lower Delta, but they were making an effort, and up until that time they had possessed the military initiative. However, there had been some recent Government successes, and when I arrived in 1962 the two forces were virtually stalemated, the Communists matching their greater discipline, political mastery and fighting ability against the Government's superior weaponry.

In those early days of my Vietnam assignment I was trying to decide how to evaluate this perplexing war. How do you add up thirty minor engagements each day, almost all of them in places you've never been to, and with no substantive information to cast light on the significance of the situation? It was very quickly obvious to me that the story could not be covered from Saigon briefing rooms, despite all the multicolored arrows on the maps. The Seventh Division struck me as being as good a litmus paper of the war as any: the problems were all there, the Government had a fair chance and it was unlikely that things could go badly there and well elsewhere, or vice versa. Besides, My Tho, the division headquarters, was only forty miles south of Saigon on a good road, and we reporters could drive down, talk with friends and participate in operations.

This proximity proved invaluable on two occasions. The first was the major battle at Ap Bac, early in 1963, when all the reporters hopped into cars and drove down to the site, thereby seeing what the military was trying to conceal and getting out with the story far ahead of official channels. The other time came in July, August and September of 1963, when the Pentagon, which was down on me in particular because of my pessimistic reporting of the Delta, was trying to monitor my sources. During those months the public information officers were keeping a highly inaccurate record of where I had been and what operations I had been out on, but since I could slip quietly down to the Delta and talk unobserved to old friends among the American and Vietnamese officers, this surveillance was pointless.

By the end of September 1962 there was growing concern over the direction of the war in the upper Delta, despite the fact that the Seventh Division had turned in what Saigon considered impressive victories. These were six consecutive engagements in which a total of more than a hundred Vietcong had been killed. To a large degree these victories were the product of the infusion of American aid. Helicopters, fighter bombers and armored personnel carriers had given a shot in the arm to Vietnamese regulars, and nowhere was this more noticeable than in the Seventh Division. (To a degree the changes in the use of the helicopters mirrored the ever-increasing American involvement. At first they were nothing but transport aircraft designed to ferry Vietnamese troops into battle, carrying two light machine guns for self-defense. Then, in late 1962, the armed helicopters arrived, with four mounted machine guns and sixteen rocket pods; they were to escort the unarmed helicopters into battle and were not to fire until fired on. But this was too dangerous—it gave the enemy too many opportunities—and the rules of engagement were further broadened. By mid-1963 the armed helicopters were often serving as fighter planes, carrying out strafing missions.)

But the American officers felt that the victories were deceptive. When the Government troops in helicopters had come upon the Vietcong, the guerrillas, surprised and panicky, had been flushed out and then were mowed down either by the fighter planes or by the armored personnel carriers. But the Government troops still did not use their rifles, and those U. S. advisers who had dealt with the Communists before felt that this luck could not last, that the enemy would soon change its strategy. They also realized that the new equipment was giving the men a false sense of security, and in addition they were worried because the troops were not fighting at night, were not using counterambushes against the guerrillas, were not waging psychological warfare against the enemy. All that the Government troops had done so far was to seize a momentary advantage because of the new weaponry—and they had even failed to exploit this fully.

The Americans were also worried about the unwillingness of Colonel Huynh Van Cao, the division commander, to risk casualties in battle; this was in direct contradiction to American advice. In essence, American military strategy is based on infantry offense, on the theory that their forces will in the long run expose themselves to even heavier casualties if they do not attack continually. But the Vietnamese were hesitant about this for political reasons; it was known that commanders who suffered heavy casualties incurred Diem's wrath. For that reason Cao was doing most of his killing by air and artillery; militarily he was really trying to get something for nothing.

Lastly, the Americans were disturbed by the fact that despite these successful battles there were as many guerrillas in the Seventh Division area as ever before; the Vietcong were having no trouble in recruiting or in replenishing their ranks. When I first went to My Tho I talked with some of the senior officers about this. It was true, they said, and very disturbing. At the beginning of the year there had been approximately five thousand guerrillas in the tactical zone; in the following nine months Government forces had killed an estimated five thousand Vietcong, and yet there were still approximately five thousand guerrillas in the tactical zone. This meant that there had been no real change in the basic politico-military situation in the area.

On October 3, 1962, I made my initial trip to the Delta. Because that particular excursion made a lasting impression, and because what I learned on the first military operation I accompanied was later to prove significant, I shall describe that field trip in some detail.

When I arrived I asked one of the senior officers if we were in real trouble in the Delta.

"No, we're not in bad trouble here—not yet, anyway," he said, "but we've got us a lot of war. We'll give you plenty to write about down here."

Two days earlier, elements of a crack Vietcong unit, the 514th Battalion, had ambushed a group of Catholic volunteers and had killed forty of them. Now there were reports that the 514th had been seen in western Dinh Tuong Province, and the division was about to go after them.

Since this was my first operation, Lieutenant Colonel John Paul Vann, the division adviser and one of the brightest young officers in Vietnam— he was later to become a major source of controversy—assigned me to his best unit, a battalion whose adviser was Captain Ken Good, a thirty-year-old West Pointer from Hawaii. Good was exactly what an officer in his position should be: thoughtful, intelligent, diplomatic, decisive, brave and candid. Three months later he was killed at Ap Bac by a sniper bullet, and his death hit all of us very hard.

I can still remember certain details of that night: shaving (so that I wouldn't have to in the morning), and a careful check on essentials like my boots, extra socks and mosquito repellent. I felt like a boy preparing for the first day of school.

I shall always remember the scene at the small Tan Hiep airstrip at My Tho the next morning—that morning and the many mornings afterward when I went out on other operations. What greeted me was a miniature D-Day. The ARVN (Army of the Republic of Vietnam)* forces were lined up in small squads all over the airstrip. The men looked very tiny and patient and were in full battle gear, wearing helmets and carrying American-made weapons—all designed for bigger men. Jammed into packs were bags of caked cold rice and bottles of *nuoc mam*, the rotten-smelling fish sauce they use on food. They seemed to be unusually light-hearted; except for their attire they could as easily have been traveling *en masse* to Saigon for a well-deserved furlough as going into battle.

Vietnamese soldiers are among the most likeable people in the world.

*In other words, the ARVN was the South Vietnamese army loyal to President Diem.

Peasant-tough and peasant-shrewd, fooled by little, they evaluate what they see so simply that a bad officer never fools his men and a good officer is always loved. Now they stood at ease, some listening to their transistor radios (the great status symbol in Vietnam), some singing sentimental songs.

The Americans were the nervous ones, for getting the helicopters there on time, loading the troops into them and directing the copters to the right place was their responsibility. This sounds relatively simple until you discover that every rice paddy looks like every other one. Since the helicopters were a little late, I started to take pictures to keep busy, but in the midst of this activity I suddenly got the shivers; privately I hoped that the delay meant the mission had been aborted. But when I asked one of the officers about this, I suspect he understood my thought processes, for he smiled and said, "No, there's nothing at all wrong. They're on their way. You can relax—you'll get your story."

Suddenly the choppers appeared on the horizon, like a plague of giant grasshoppers coming out of the night. After they had landed there was no time for me to hesitate, only time to try to get into the right one, scramble aboard, hold on to my hat (the sign of a tenderfoot is that he is always losing his hat to the swirl of the helicopter blades), and follow the squad inside. These were old H-21 helicopters, tired remnants of the fifties, banana-shaped, bugged by mechanical problems, but surprisingly sturdy and durable. They were piloted by some of the toughest young men in the world, who might refer to their ships bitterly—"an accident looking for a place to happen," one officer called them—but who would take quick umbrage if any layman was critical of them.

The squad of soldiers was delighted to have me with them. In part this was probably because it meant that their Vietnamese officers would treat them a little better, but the fact that all Americans in Vietnam are regarded as mobile cigarette-vending machines might also have had something to do with my welcome. (Actually, offering cigarettes to the men was mere reciprocity, for the Vietnamese troops were usually more than willing to share their meager rations; they are among the most generous people on the face of the earth.) But beyond these considerations, I sensed the squad's pride in having someone else share this terrible war which had been going on so long, an American who would die if they died.

The soldiers kept grinning and reached out for my arm to feel the hair on it: completely smooth-skinned people, they are awed by the amount of body hair Westerners have, and one of their favorite games is to pull it. Other members of the squad were sitting on the floor of the copter, shaving; they did this by using tiny mirrors and tweezers, pulling out the few hairs on their chins one by one.

There were two ways helicopters flew over the Delta: very high or very low. We flew high for the first ten miles, then low, right above the treetops, for the last half mile or so. Pilots called this flying "map of the earth," and the advantage was very simple: the guerrillas could hear the aircraft, but because of the trees they couldn't see them until too late. It is an exciting, spine-chilling business.

We sped over startled farmers, one of the oldest professions scanned by one of the newest. Earlier in the war the Vietcong had told the farmers to run away when they saw helicopters; the farmers had run, and of course gunners had drawn the wrong conclusion and fired on them. But now the farmers had learned, and they froze whenever they saw the aircraft. Later I was to notice that they never looked at the helicopters; as far as they were concerned the aircraft did not exist.

Now, as we skimmed across the paddies, our gunner suddenly opened up with a burst, and a farmer fell down. Later the pilot asked him what he had seen, and the young man, who was very inexperienced, claimed that he had seen the farmer go for a gun. But the pilot and I had been watching too, and we were sure that the farmer had done nothing, that the youngster was nervous. The pilot reprimanded the soldier, but of course that did not save the farmer somewhere back in the paddies.

Almost immediately after this burst of fire we landed. The Vietnamese scrambled out into water that came up to their shoulders. I decided it would come to my waist, jumped out and felt it seep over my shoulders too, which meant a soggy ham sandwich for lunch and the end of my Minox camera. But there is one good thing about landing in a deep rice paddy: the shock is so abrupt and complete that for the rest of the day you won't bother trying to stay comfortable or clean or dry.

The land spreads out flat and open, but the villages are usually built about thirty yards inside treelines. These are the Asian equivalent of Normandy hedgerows; they offer excellent protection, and camouflage is one of the military arts that the Vietcong practice to perfection. When they arrive in a hamlet for the night, they will immediately prepare perfect defensive positions along the treeline. ("You can never tell our Air Force that," one Vietnamese colonel said. "The Air Force always wants to bomb the hamlet. You tell them, 'Bomb the treeline, the VC are always in the treeline,' and they pay no attention at all. The French were the same way; they always bombed the hamlet too.")

We started moving in small groups toward the treeline about a hundred yards away. This is the most dangerous part of an assault in the Delta, for you are out in the open and the treeline is an enemy haven. As you approach the edge of the woods it looks like a set designed by a camouflage expert. Indeed, it may very well have been, as "The Fall of an Empire," a marvelous documentary made by CBS, can attest. Some Russian footage in this film about the Indochina war shows a bridge and two French fighter bombers flying lazily above it. Nothing moves: there is obviously nothing but a little shrubbery beside the bridge. Then the planes pass on, and suddenly half the bridge seems to come alive; a battalion of Vietminh has been hiding right in front of the camera. This is a particularly chilling shot from a chilling film.

Moving in a rice paddy is a bit like trying to run in one of your own dreams—slowly, your feet stuck, feeling exposed and all alone. I found myself curiously winded, my throat was absolutely dry and I felt terribly tall, easily the best target in the paddy. Captain Good and another American, Captain Gary Werner, a PIO (public information officer), were split up farther down the line. It is not a good idea for Americans to bunch up, for they make too good a target; similarly, it is always wise to stay away from the radio man in such situations, for the Vietcong will often fire their first burst at him, hoping to get an ARVN officer.

As we approached the treeline, we began to hear firing off to our right. In combat all firing—at least at first—sounds close. I ducked down in the paddy again, and then looked around; all I could see was one of the cheerful little Asians who had felt the hair on my arm. In the helicopter he had seemed like just another faceless Vietnamese, his life as casually and momentarily entwined with mine as a cab driver's might be; now, suddenly, he was a sergeant responsible for my life or death, and for the lives of the other ten men in the squad.

In that first moment of panic, followed by embarrassment and shame about the panic, I made the discovery that eventually comes to some Americans in Vietnam—that this really was a Vietnamese war. For though the Americans were always talking about it being a Vietnamese war, in many ways it was not. Americans arrived in Saigon to find other Americans; they went to an American PX and American movies; they rode in buses with other Americans, and flew with other Americans in the field in American helicopters; often they slept in American quarters with fellow Americans, eating, more often than not, at American messes. This was the pattern for all but the small percentage of American soldiers assigned to battalions or in a combat-related role, and up to now it had been true for me. Now, all at once, the world reversed itself: certain Vietnamese were responsible for my life, and other Vietnamese had orders to kill me. I had spent more than three weeks in Vietnam and had to come to this paddy to learn where the war began.

We advanced, and reached the hamlet without encountering direct enemy fire. Once inside, we heard firing in the background. There was no resistance in our hamlet and we spread out quickly, ready to serve as a blocking force in case other units drove the Vietcong toward us. There were only a few women in the village, and several children—in Vietnam the children were everywhere—and one goateed old man looking like a Confucian sage or Ho Chi Minh. There were no young men in the village; there never were, I was told. At the first sound of the helicopters and battle they always fled because they were automatically suspected of being Communists and at the very least would be taken back to My Tho. The war shuttled back and forth for the young men; they hid from the Communists too, but this was harder because the enemy was always there, slipping in at night before there was time to hide. Later I learned that during the morning three young men had been caught in a field as a helicopter landed and had made the mistake of running. One was immediately brought down by automatic-weapons fire; the other two stopped in their tracks. They were not, it turned out, Vietcong at all. They were simply two poor peasants from the village, one an unemployed man with four children, the other a widower so poor he could not even afford to marry again.

Now in the village one woman told the Vietnamese captain that there had been no Vietcong in the area. The captain, nine years in his rank—paradoxically, an indication that he was probably a very good officer; those who were promoted quickly were the political ones—did not believe her. There was too much tension, he said, and he asked her a few more questions about the village and its income, and when the Vietcong were last seen. Where were all the young men? All the young men, the woman said, had decided to go to the next village because they feared the Vietcong were coming. By now the captain was convinced that the woman was lying and that she was probably the wife of a guerrilla; he told one of his staff officers to guard her so that she could not communicate with the other women, and went quietly to another hut. There he began to chip away at another woman's story, and soon he found holes in both accounts.

The interpreter was impressed by the captain. "He is very good at it," he told me later. "He starts talking about the crops and about his own problems—what his wife is demanding from him, the difficulty of living in the big city of My Tho, how he would like to come back to the country because there is nothing in the city like a buffalo ride. For the first five minutes he never mentions the war. In the end, they always talk."

The second woman did talk. A platoon of guerrillas had been in the village a day before, she said. They had been very confident and had held a party for the villagers; there had been much excitement over it. They said that they had just scored a major victory, having killed forty of the American imperialists (this was apparently a reference to the ambush of the Catholic volunteer company, in which forty Vietnamese had been killed). Then the Vietcong had exhibited some of the arms they had captured, and the villagers saw that they were American weapons.

One of the Vietcong had started serving tea, and another had given a sermon in the form of a fable. In it there were poor people who had no land and wanted to be free, but they had no guns; there were rich foreigners who had guns, but who were against the people; the foreigners gave these guns to bad people who were their puppets, and they paid the puppets; but the puppets would not fight, and so the foreigners themselves had to fight. But the poor people were brave and captured the guns, and now the weapons would be used against the foreigners and the puppets, and many of them would die because of it.

As he left the hut the captain cursed the woman who had talked, loudly and in rough Vietnamese; this was to guard her against reprisals, the interpreter said, since she had been good to us and there would be no troops there that night to protect her.

"It sounds like a pretty effective party the Vietcong threw," I said. We spoke in French; like many Vietnamese he felt he could speak more freely to the reporters in that language.

"Yes," he said, "the parties are very good. We do not give parties like that."

I asked what would happen to the first woman the captain had interrogated.

"What can we do?" he said. "She is one of them. She is a bad one. But taking her away will do no good; it will just make the others angrier. It is too late to work on her, and if we take her away, her children will definitely go over to the enemy. Do they teach about this at Fort Bragg?" he asked bitterly.

Those moments gave me a quick sense of what the war was about, but like many lessons it was obscured at the time. The sounds of battle were near and very real, and they were what I had come to hear, not an argument with an old lady whose teeth were stained with betel-nut juice. I was wishing we would move on to the battle—or at least near enough to see it, without being too close for danger. There was action less than half a mile away, and Captain Good was obviously anxious to move the battalion in that direction. But there were no orders, and he and the Vietnamese captain were both irritable. The Vietnamese were punctilious about sticking to plans instead of following their instincts.

Already by eleven o'clock the sun was punishing, and I brought the brim of my jungle hat down over my eyes. We cut a few coconuts and sipped the milk. There was never any fear of going thirsty in the Delta; the water was impure, but coconuts made life and the war a bit more bearable. We sat and watched the T-28's air-strike the nearby village. Later we found out that a Vietnamese Ranger company had been brutally ambushed at this village. They had landed in helicopters about a hundred yards from the treeline, where a unit of the 514th was perfectly camouflaged. Normally the unit would have opened up on the helicopters as they came in, but this time, with an impressive display of battle discipline, it held fire until the Rangers were about thirty yards from the treeline, their feet glued to the mucky bottom.

It was a swift little slaughter. Before they could even return a shot the Rangers suffered heavy casualties; a platoon was virtually wiped out in an instant. Even after recovery they had little option but to keep their heads down behind the dike walls and fire back as best they could. The only thing that allowed them to move at all was an almost perfect air strike by the T-28's, but this did not come until they had been under deadly fire for two hours. Finally Captain Jim Torrence, the American adviser with the company, sensed that the Vietcong were slowly slipping out, keeping their exodus covered with automatic weapons. By noon they had left, and the Rangers moved into the treeline. There were no bodies—not even any expended cartridges. The enemy was always cool, never leaving their dead behind; in part this was a matter of pride and in honor of their dead, but its purpose was also to shake the morale of the Government forces, to give them no satisfaction as to how much had been accomplished, so that there would always be doubt about any possible victories. Thirty Rangers had been killed and a few more wounded; virtually the entire platoon of an elite unit had been wiped out, an unusually high casualty rate for a Government-initiated action.

But almost obscured by the immediate sorrow and bitterness of this reversal was the fact that the guerrillas had changed their tactics: one small element of an enemy battalion had stood and fought. This was to prove of immense significance in the months to follow, for it marked the end of the post-buildup honeymoon in the Delta; it meant that the enemy had adjusted to the new heliborne tactics. But of course at the moment no one realized this; in our battalion we were only irritated by the failure to get in on the fight. For the rest of the day we played the game—which is to say, we chased the Vietcong unit. Overhead two light spotter planes kept circling in hopes of detecting the now-elusive guerrillas, or at least of drawing fire. But the Vietcong, knowing that a superior force was after them, were not anxious to make contact with the Government now.

We had a quick lunch in the village. One of the Vietnamese officers shared his food with me; there was little, but in the Delta sun one loses his appetite. The interpreter said that the captain had checked his company commanders and platoon leaders to make sure that the troops were behaving properly, and that they had paid for everything they had taken in the village. The conduct of ARVN troops in villages had become one of the major conflicts between the Government and the population. Too often the troops had stolen chickens or molested the people; in contrast, the well-disciplined guerrillas would work beside the villagers in the field, and they did not steal from them. It was generally agreed that the presence of American advisers had helped to keep the troops in line; however, Neil Sheehan had recently accompanied a special psychological-warfare team known as the Political Action Group, whose main purpose was to convert the population, and they had gone through a village, he recalled, handing out Government leaflets and stealing ducks.

After lunch we started eastward, moving along a main canal. Now I learned the special agony of pursuit in the wet season. The Delta is nothing but an intricate series of narrow canals linked with larger ones. There are no bridges as we know them; there are simply rounded bamboo poles which stretch from one side to another. The Vietnamese, who are all agile, had no trouble in crossing, but for an American, particularly this American somewhat out of condition and unsure of himself, it wasn't so simple. Four times that day I fell into canals to the delight of my comrades, and I soon forgot about the armed enemy we were chasing. By the end of the day I had mastered the trick—momentum at any cost—and was able to cross without incident. The Vietnamese troops took my new success with good grace, although I could tell they felt deprived of the diversion I had been providing. Soaked though I was, I failed to match the record of my colleague, Mert Perry of *Time,* who is the all-time champion Delta wader. Mert is a very heavyset, enormously likable man who simply is not built for bamboo. "I fell off so many times one day that it was like a USO show," he told me later. "Each time we got to a canal the entire company would run up to watch me cross. One burst of a BAR would have wiped them all out."

That afternoon, as we walked endlessly in the sun, two things made a deep impression on me: the difficulty of chasing guerrillas in that terrain, and the agony of the war for the peasants. Even the land which wasn't swampy or boggy was lush and rich, and an entire company could have been hiding within ten yards of any spot we passed. The canals, too, provide cover, for the Vietcong carry reeds for straws, and can slip under water and breathe for hours, suffering only from the leeches. The whole countryside is a natural hiding place: rice land mixed with thick brush,

David Halberstam accompanies an ARVN patrol in the Mekong Delta. (Horst Faas)

deep canals, sugar-cane groves, mangrove swamps, coconut groves. Unless the population was willing to tell the troops where the Vietcong had hidden, the Government had a nearly impossible task—and at that time the population wasn't telling; at best, the peasants were on the fence. One could hardly blame them; they did not like or trust the Government, and they were not going to risk their lives to inform for a regime which could not protect them.

The four-hour hunt that afternoon reeked of futility even to a novice like myself. The troops and officers obviously knew it too; from noon on there was usually little contact in this war. In those days it was largely a matter of following a script: one company reached its objective, another marched to its target—maneuvers were only carried out to please the people back at the CP (command post) with their arrows and their maps. The hopelessness of all this lowered the morale of the troops. About the only time the pattern varied in those days was when the Vietcong decided to shift the tempo. Sometimes, after staying one step ahead of the sheriff all afternoon, they would spring an ambush at twilight, just outside the Government base, hitting quickly when the ARVN were tired and lazy and dejected, and then slip off.

Once during that long afternoon there was a brief glimpse of the enemy, about five hundred yards away; there was a quick burst of fire, but almost immediately the guerrillas slipped into a cluster of trees. As usual, the enemy had set the pace and determined the time, the place and the odds. It would take a major Government initiative and offensive to change all of this, and so far it was not forthcoming.

The other thing that struck the novice observer was the way the war shuttled back and forth for the peasants: they endured the Government troops during the day, the Vietcong at night. In all my time in Vietnam I never grew accustomed to the resultant sights. That afternoon, as we walked through the village where most of the fighting had taken place, a weeping peasant came out and stood in front of the charred remains of his hut. In one hand he held a dead piglet, in the other a dead baby. His grief was silent; I could hear nothing. For a moment one of our lieutenants broke from the line, but the Vietnamese captain saw him and gestured him back. There was nothing to be done, nothing that could be said.

About a hundred yards away we came upon a dead peasant lying in the yard of his hut with a poncho spread over him. Two huts farther on, a desperately frightened old man of eighty was genuflecting in front of the American and Vietnamese officers and telling them that he had never heard of the Vietcong. How many times had this old man had to tell Government troops that he knew no Vietcong? How many times had he had to tell the Vietminh or Vietcong that he knew no Government troops? "The war," a young Vietnamese said to me bitterly later, "only lasts a lifetime."

The sun was at its hottest about three o'clock; then the weather broke and there was a feeling that the going would be downhill from then on. My uniform, which had been soaked and then dried in the sun over and over again, finally seemed permanently dry. By now the only sign that there had been any fighting were occasional dead catfish floating in the canals, killed earlier in the day by mortars or bombs. After crossing the main canal and joining up with another battalion which had been covering the far side, we sat down and took a break. Trooper after trooper came by with a live chicken strapped to his pack. The American officer attached to this unit followed, and we looked accusingly at him. He caught our glances and said defensively, "What the hell can you do? They go all day and they don't get anything in the way of chow, and they put up with all this"—he gestured around him—"I can't tell them no. They've got little enough pleasure as it is." He was right, of course, but our officers were wondering what the reaction was in the village from which the chickens had been stolen, as well as the effect on the morale of the troops in our battalion who had been denied chickens.

After the break we marched single file for three more miles, until we met the rest of the division. It had been a rough day and the troops were tired and hot; about thirty ARVN had been killed, two helicopters had been shot down and one American gunner killed. The latter would give the guerrillas a boost; it was relatively early in the days of the helicopters, and victories over these craft helped to prove to their own people and to the peasantry that they could stand up to what they called "the iron birds."

At large cost we had found and hurt the 514th—to what extent, no one was sure, but the estimates were of at least ten dead. The operation was over; it was just past six o'clock. "Time to turn the country over to the VC," one young American officer said sardonically. The American advisers were bitterly opposed to this kind of office-hours warfare. They wanted to harass the enemy continuously, not just by day, in order to exploit the superior weaponry and potentially superior mobility the Government had. Theoretically it was easy to agree; pursuit seemed logical and militarily valid. But I was tired and worn out, and I was also glad to be alive. I would have made a very proper ARVN officer.

We sat around, waiting for trucks, and some logistical genius brought over warm beer. The American officers asked me what I thought, and I told them I was more interested in what they thought. Well, they said, this was what the war was like—hot and frustrating and unrewarding, days filled with violations of even the most obvious kind of military common sense, days spent hoping desperately for the break which would make the enemy fight.

Back at the base I learned just how much of a tenderfoot I was. My neck was red, but my feet were a dismal pasty white; they looked like the feet of the dead. I had come to My Tho with just one set of footgear, and I had to wear soaking-wet boots for the next five days. From then on when I went into the field I brought two pairs of boots, combat; one pair of shoes, civilian; and one pair of shoes, shower.

That night Lieutenant Colonel Vann and some of the officers recapped the operation. They were concerned about the fact that there had been such a good chance to knock out a unit of the 514th, that the knockout hadn't been executed, and that the psychological reaction of the peasants in the area where the battle had taken place couldn't have been anything but unfavorable.

There was much more to worry about, we learned later. The operation I have described took place on October 6, and until then the Seventh Division had been working well. But unbeknownst to all of us, that day really marked the beginning of the end in the Delta. President Diem, concerned about the loss of the Ranger platoon and what he considered to be excessive losses in Government-initiated actions, called Colonel Cao to Saigon. That night the American advisers of the two offending units were summoned to Cao's headquarters and they patiently went over the action with Cao. Early the next morning Cao set out for Saigon with a well-rehearsed explanation. According to Cao's account (told to Vann, and later confirmed to me by Vietnamese sources), he arrived at the Palace before breakfast. All morning he watched people file in and out of the President's office. Lunch came, but not for him. Finally, late in the afternoon, he was summoned by the President.

Cao never had a chance to give his carefully prepared briefing; instead, Diem began one of those monologues for which he was becoming increasingly well known. Cao was reminded—as if this was necessary—that there was a good chance he would soon be a general. But certain problems had arisen recently: he was taking far too many casualties, more than any other field commander. He would have to be more careful; he was listening too much to his American advisers. Diem further issued a very simple warning: if Cao wanted a promotion, he would have to be more prudent. This threat came at a time when the Americans were working desperately to make Cao more aggressive, but of course he obeyed Diem.

My next trip was on a mission to Dinh Tuong Province. A friend in the operations room warned me, "Bring your sun-tan lotion. It won't be anything but a long hot walk tomorrow." The American officers were disturbed; for months, with some measure of success, they had organized a joint planning group which emphasized traditional staff techniques and the use of military intelligence. Before that time the tendency had been for helter-skelter dashes into the countryside, operations based more on whether the local province chief was a friend of the division commander than on whether any of the enemy were in the area. Such operations might not produce any dead Vietcong, but they might encourage recalcitrant villagers to pay their taxes to local officials.

Now tactics had reverted to the old methods again. "They've just thrown away six months of work," one of the operations officers said. The

Government would be operating in terrain where it *might* find the enemy, but there were other areas where enemy companies could be almost definitely pinpointed. In addition, even if the enemy were sighted, "that battle plan is almost guaran-damn-teed to let them escape to the last."

Next day's operation was a farce: short marches, long stops, interspersed with shorter marches and even longer stops. I was with Captain Raymond Whittaker of Sumter, South Carolina, a Negro officer and a patient man. At the start he was as gentle as he could be about the day ahead, but he gave little impression of hope. We landed in open fields from helicopters and made the brief, tense walk to the first village. But we found there only a few women and a vast amount of Vietcong propaganda material. Whittaker listened for several minutes while his Vietnamese counterpart translated the propaganda sheets in detail. "It says the Vietcong are going to win the war," Whittaker finally said laconically. Then some of the men brought over an old woman who was questioned briefly and who told us that one hundred Vietcong had been in the village the night before. She pointed in the alleged direction in which the alleged guerrillas had vanished. "It's always one hundred VC, and they always went thataway," Whittaker said.

The troops sniffed through the village, picking up what they could. The atmosphere was relaxed and seemed to have nothing in common with the tension of my first mission a few days before. The women even gave the soldiers some pineapples. This could have been dangerous. A few months earlier, troops had been treated well in another village and the women had given them little cakes. Eight of the men had eaten them and had become violently ill two hours later. Thanks to helicopters they were quickly evacuated, their stomachs pumped out and their lives saved. Colonel Pham Van Dong, their commander, had thought this very funny. "So when the population is very good to you and gives you all the cakes, you must perhaps be a little more careful," he said.

The village was our first "goose egg"—the term for any mission which draws a blank, and referring to the zeros on the map—and we moved on to our next objective. En route the troops were bunched up, and a sense of sloppiness pervaded the outfit; there was no point man, no flanking unit, no search along the line of march, nothing but a methodical crunching ahead. I looked at the troops and then at Whittaker, but he gave me a distant I-don't-ask-about-the-skeletons-in-your-closet-buddy-so-don't-ask-about-mine look, and turned away. At about eleven-thirty, when we reached our second objective—a village by the river—the troops immediately settled down for lunch. They set up no defensive perimeter, and their single recoilless rifle was pointed toward the command post. A Vietnamese friend of mine, a photographer, came over and I asked him what the troops thought about this mission. "The troops told me I should have stayed home and saved myself the walk," he answered. "They say they have been here many times before and know all the old women by now, and that they will never find the Vietcong here. They say they have come here often enough to be fathers of the little children. But there are worse places to be, and now they will have lunch."

"We will be here a long time today," the Vietnamese photographer said. "The men say that their captain does not like to fight. They say he is a political officer, but they do not mind because it means that not so many of them have to die. So they take it easy." Take it easy they did: from noon until three they took a siesta. It always staggered the Americans; again and again, combat operations came to an almost complete halt at midday. We used to hope that the Vietcong observed this tradition too.

It was hard to get any sense of war at moments like these in the field. These troops, sprawling casually in front of me, their weapons carelessly tossed aside, some sound asleep, could be as brave as any man could ask. But as soldiers they were only as good as their leadership, and too often their officers were sloppy and indifferent. The troops themselves were mostly peasants, not city boys from Saigon raised in an atmosphere of insidious comfort and affluence. Instead they had grown up knowing nothing but war; from the time they were born they knew that they would have to fight for one side or the other. In the Vietcong they would make no money, but would probably become deeply committed to its cause; by fighting for the Government they would at least draw some pay and could spend more time with their families.

They were not the best-paid warriors in the world; though they were the allies of the richest nation on earth, and fighting a war which deeply affected that affluent nation, they made less than Saigon's taxi drivers—perhaps fifteen dollars a month, plus a small allowance for their wives and children. They were inordinately cheerful about life; because they were Buddhists and because of their lack of knowledge of anything but war, they were fatalistic about life and death. If a soldier lost a friend he wept —not for his friend but for himself. They carried weapons made for men twice their size and never complained. They passively accepted fraudulent operations and corrupt officers. Their ability to bear suffering was beyond the comprehension of any Westerner; I saw many dying Vietnamese, but I never saw one cry.

The Vietnamese soldiers were small by American standards, a little over five feet tall and weighing perhaps one hundred pounds, but they were wiry and looked like little wrestlers. They could walk for miles, and their feet were like iron. Because their pay was so small, they had become accustomed to life without money. Their wives near headquarters would sometimes take unexpended cartridges from their husbands and barter them in the market for food. It was a short-sighted way of surviving, of course, because the bullets inevitably ended up in the hands of the Vietcong, but the Vietnamese peasant has never been able to afford the luxury of thinking ahead.

At three o'clock the siesta ended and the American advisers, restless and irritable, got ready to move out. But all afternoon we stayed in that same little village while the Americans grew more and more tense and the Vietnamese became more and more serene. We drank tea, we ate coconuts—and we did not move. "What do the troops say?" I asked the photographer. He came back in a few minutes. "The troops say we will spend the night in the field. They are not surprised at what has happened; they say it could be worse—because it is not raining. One of them says this is better than the mountains because there are no coconuts and chickens there, and it is much warmer here. I think they are all very tired of this war."

We ate a second meal in that same village, which increased the tension. Finally, after dinner, we set off again. After cutting through some tree clumps we reached a nearby river; there we boarded landing craft and motored upstream about ten miles. Trucks were supposed to meet us at a small village, but they didn't arrive. As usual the troops were right; we spent the night in the field.

A few of us stayed in the house of the district chief. We slept on flat wooden beds, and fought the hard surface and the mosquitoes until dawn. In retrospect the worst thing about the whole operation was that we were more tired by our night of rest than we were by our day of chasing the enemy. When I returned the next morning to My Tho and talked to the other American officers, I discovered that other units in the operation had behaved in the same way.

Chapter 5

Finding an Elusive Foe

We never saw much of the enemy. We saw his handiwork—the ravaged outposts, the defenders with their heads blown off, their women lying dead beside them—but more often than not the guerrillas only showed themselves when they had superior strength. The first lesson that an American adviser in Vietnam learned was that the enemy was good; if he stayed on a little longer, he learned that this was wrong: the enemy was *very* good. He learned that the Vietcong concentrated on only a few things and that they did them well; that they made few mistakes; and that —in sharp contrast to the Government forces—they rarely made the same error twice. The American officers also learned that the enemy had a reason—political, psychological or military—for almost everything he did. Even when he appeared to be doing nothing, we learned belatedly that this did not mean he was inactive, only that he was content to *appear* inactive.

If they paid attention, Americans also learned that the enemy was absolutely sincere; he was willing to pay the price for the difficult task he had set for himself, and he had a far better sense of these difficulties than the authorities in Saigon. If he was underrated in Saigon, this was certainly not the case in the field; there it was widely known that we were fighting his war on his terms.

The Vietcong had no illusions about the type of war in which they were engaged. It was a war of revolution, and they knew the weaknesses of the Government as well as their own strengths. The American military thought of them as men carrying weapons, but the fact was that they were most effective at night indoctrinating the peasants—when they carried no weapons and wore no uniforms. The misery of the people was their ally, and they played on it. Where Americans often parroted slogans about improving the world of the Vietnamese peasant, the Vietcong, who had risen from this misery themselves, knew that lip service was not enough. To them the war was entirely political; its military aspects were simply a means to permit them to practice their political techniques. They made every grievance theirs: long-standing historical antagonisms, whether against Asians or Caucasians, became *their* grievances, as were economic inequities, the division of land, the arbitrary system of tax collection— even the ravages of disease.

56

As the Vietcong achieved military success through their political techniques, the Government and the Americans responded with increased weaponry and more troops. But this did not mitigate the grievances; indeed, the increased number of troops often meant more bombings, more deaths and more suffering. The strategic hamlet program* was an ill-fated attempt to correct this imbalance, but it strangled in Vietnamese mismanagement and also because, for all their talk of "winning the people," the American mission never understood the war as the enemy did.

The Asian Communists had developed their guerrilla style by fighting Chiang Kai-shek, and a previous generation of Vietnamese had refined it in the war against the French. Guerrilla warfare is virtually an art form, and the Vietcong were more than craftsmen at their trade; they were artists. So knowledgeable and successful were they that when American officers prepared for their tour in Vietnam, they read not the writings of the French or American tacticians, but the writings of the enemy. The United States was there because the Vietcong had proven stronger than our allies; we were fighting a war among his people and on his soil, where he had been successful for twenty years.

The Vietcong, of course, were not the Vietminh; it was not that simple. For one thing, the American role was not comparable to the French; we were, after all, fighting to get out, whereas the French had fought to stay on. Yet the heritage and the legacy and the enemy's impetus were very much the same. To much of the peasantry the Vietcong was the same as the Vietminh; it dressed the same way, it used exactly the same tactics and techniques, and it operated in exactly the same manner.

The Vietcong never used the word Communism. Once Paul Fay, Undersecretary of the Navy, came to Saigon and delivered a rip-roaring speech on how to teach the peasantry about the evils of Communism. A CIA friend of mine who heard the speech said, "God, wouldn't that be lovely! These people have never heard of Communism, but if we went around preaching against it, they might decide that it's a pretty good thing and want some of it."

Just as the Vietcong resembled the Vietminh in the peasants' eyes, the Government troops too often acted like the soldiers in the same uniforms who had fought during the days of the French: patrolling the hamlets during the day, grabbing village chickens for lunch and disappearing after 6 P.M., so that just in case some villager was inclined to help the Government, he would have no protection at night when the Vietcong arrived.

---

*Initiated in early 1962, the strategic hamlet program was designed to deny the Vietcong access to the South Vietnamese peasantry by gathering peasants from several neighboring villages into one large, fortified hamlet, where they would also receive modern services, including schools and health care. But the plan soon proved a dismal failure: the guerrillas had little difficulty infiltrating the hamlets, American aid earmarked for the support of social services usually found its way into the pockets of corrupt South Vietnamese officials, and the peasants deeply resented being uprooted from their ancestral homelands. By 1964 the program was essentially abandoned.

Inevitably the Government forces played into the enemy's hands. The Vietcong would prophesy that the Government troops would come, that they would be led by Americans, that this would mean bombings from planes piloted by Americans and that as a result villagers would die. Sooner or later there would be a battle, there would be strafings of the village and there would be troops with American advisers. Then at night the Vietcong cadre in the area would arrive in the village and dispense medical aid, and of course they would gain more recruits.

The guerrillas had prepared for this kind of fighting long in advance. At the end of the Indochina war they had carefully set to work developing cadres, gathering ammunition and preparing weapon-storage points, digging secret, cavelike hideaways and tunnels, and training cadres to take over the schools. They had had another advantage: in the embryo years of the new nation they were the dissenters. It was the Government's job to deliver; their role was only to sit by and criticize. In underdeveloped countries a new government starting out with a tiny number of trained people must somehow develop a competent administrative staff. It cannot meet—at least no new government has—the vast expectations of a newly independent people: glittering hopes in education; in the standard of living; in reforms, agriculture and health.

Such new governments are inevitably clumsy. The Diem government was no worse than most, but in South Vietnam the problems were greater than in most other newly independent states. The French had left behind a civil-service system fraught with corruption; Diem was a poor administrator; what little talent there was in the country was quickly siphoned off to the military—where, if it was really outstanding, it was ignored. Too often the only contact the villagers had with their government was corrupt local officials who showed up often enough to collect taxes, but not often enough to provide services.

In contrast, the Vietcong did not have to provide; they merely promised to. They would divvy up the land holdings of absentee landlords; this cost them nothing and won them the peasants' allegiance. Suspecting that the Government would take their land back, the peasants would simply not inform on the Vietcong, and often they and their families were active agents. The fact that when victory had been won the Vietcong intended to collectivize the land, as they had in the North, was something else; there was no need to bring that up now.

In addition, the Vietcong had years of experience behind them. As one American intelligence officer told me, "The trouble with this war is that everywhere in the countryside the enemy has some political commissar who's been fighting revolutionary warfare on the winning side for twenty years, with all the training and professionalism that entails, and up against him we've got someone who, if he's trained at all, was trained by the Americans or the French, and who has been on the losing side." Because competent officials who were a threat to the Vietcong were killed, there was a tendency toward fence-straddling on the part of local officials. While sending in enthusiastic progress reports to the capital, they tried not to see what the enemy was doing; in effect, they had come to a gentlemen's agreement with the Vietcong and were thus providing a vacuum in which the guerrillas could work.

The Vietcong started indoctrinating their people when they were very young—the younger the better. They offered them adventure and excitement, and they advertised themselves as the enemies of oppression, as the heralders of a better world—but they always based their appeal on the most fundamental issues. If land was the grievance in one community, their pitch was based on land reform; if bad local government was the source of unhappiness, the Vietcong would execute the offending village official while the peasants watched. To a young boy growing up in the total deprivation of an Asian back-land, only dimly aware of the inequity between his life and that of other, wealthier Asians, the enemy's call was persuasive—particularly when, say, a member of the Vietcong ran the local school.

Soon the youngsters would be involved as bearers for troops or as messengers, earning advancement only on merit and being fully committed every step of the way. There was a thoroughness in the enemy's political indoctrination which was completely missing on the Government side. Before a youth was permitted to hold a Vietcong rifle he would first undergo long political and psychological training. He *believed*. His, he was sure, was a righteous cause: he was liberating his people; the Government was cruel and owned by the Americans; his war was to liberate his countrymen from the Americans—just as his father had liberated half of the country from the French. Also, it was part of the Vietcong's mystique that they were the poor robbing the rich, so for this reason they often went to great lengths to capture weapons when they could more easily have smuggled them into the country; it gave them a sense of pride and self-reliance.

Only when the enemy was convinced of a young man's political commitment and complete indoctrination was he allowed to begin his military training. Here again there was an insistence on excellence. A weapon was priceless and significant; when it came into his hands for the first time a ceremony was part of the promotion. On that day the recruit became a man.

This, then, was the enemy's raw material: tough, indoctrinated men, willing and ready to die; men of great physical endurance who had known few softening distractions in a lifetime of hardships. The leadership was equally good. The battalion commanders were usually men who had fought in the Indochina war; though they were mostly from South Vietnam and usually from the specific area in which they would serve, they had been given additional training in the North. The best of a good army, they had been fighting for years and had risen on ability alone—and they knew that they would lose their jobs if they made mistakes.

The Vietcong also had a sense of military cunning that few Americans took into account. During these twenty years they had fought constantly against an enemy which had superior equipment and air power. By necessity they had learned to be careful and shrewd, and how best to exploit their limited resources. In order to survive they had to be wily; to be careless, sloppy or indifferent meant sure death. They could never rely on an air strike or on armored personnel carriers (APC's) to bail them out of trouble; rather, there would be air strikes to wipe them out and APC's to crush them. They had to be elusive. "Their commanders," an American captain once told me, "have a sixth sense about their flanks. It is almost impossible to surround them."

If the Government troops failed to train, so much the better; the Vietcong trained regularly. They studied the techniques of U.S. helicopter pilots, and before a major attack they built mock models of the Government emplacements on which to practice the assault. Within Vietcong units were groups specially trained for each phase of an attack: troops for the first wave, troops for the demolition of key points of the defense, troops for gathering up weapons, troops for covering the escape.

In this war the ambush was a vital ingredient; it involved relatively little man power and it often inflicted heavy casualties. Always there were preordained escape routes. In addition to killing Government troops and capturing weapons, the enemy achieved a psychological advantage through the ambush: it scared Government troops, made them less anxious to leave their bases and slowly helped to dry up Government access to the countryside, thereby allowing the Vietcong to move around that much more freely. Frequently an attack was made only to set up an ambush; thus, the attack might be a minor part of the operation, the major objective being to ambush the Government relief columns. For this reason there was little enthusiasm on the part of Government troops to come to the aid of their less fortunate colleagues under attack.

By nature the Vietnamese are afraid of the night and of the jungle. Very early in a young man's career the Vietcong broke his fear of the darkness; the guerrillas were taught that the night was their friend, the enemy of the white man and his airplanes. To operate in the dark became a way of life with the Vietcong: they lived, taught, traveled and fought at night. The same was true with the jungle; by force of necessity the Vietcong came to know and use the tropical forests, as their countrymen under the Government flag would never do.

The Vietcong's military commanders were completely under the control of their political commissars. Every decision was based first on political needs, only secondarily on military ones. "If we give them a licking in a certain area," said one American officer, "we can almost bet that within ten days or so they'll knock off a good-sized outpost in the same neighborhood—just to show the flag and let the peasants know that they're still in business."

The first time you met a member of the Vietcong there was a sharp sense of disappointment. He was not, it turned out, very different; he was simply another Vietnamese. When you saw him he was usually either kneeling and firing at you or he had just been captured—or, more often than not, he was dead: the bodies were always lined up, their feet in an orderly row. The guerrilla wore little, perhaps a simple peasant pajama suit, perhaps only shorts. He was slim and wiry, and his face would remind you of your interpreter or of that taxi driver who drove you to My Tho. Only the haircut was different, very thin along the sides, and very long on top and in front. It was a bad haircut, and like the frailness of the uniform and the thin wallet with perhaps only a few pictures of some peasant woman, it made the enemy human. But one's sympathy did not last long; this was the same face that had been seen by the outnumbered defenders of some small outpost before it was overrun.

There were not many operations in which the Vietcong were caught; few prisoners were taken in this war. One of the few exceptions to this that I ever observed took place in April 1963, when I accompanied the new armed-helicopter units in the upper Camau peninsula on what were known as Eagle flights. An Eagle flight was risky business; it meant that a small number of elite troops circled above the paddies in the choppers, looking for likely targets. When an objective was sighted the helicopters dropped out of the sky, virtually on top of a hamlet, and the troops made a quick search, probing and scouting. If the enemy was there, other regular units, waiting in the rear with other helicopters, would be thrown in quickly. But dropping swiftly out of the sky and exploring the unknown with a handful of troops was sometimes terrifying; the helicopters have the visibility of a press box, but you were watching a war instead of a football game. When you plunged earthward, little men sometimes rushed to different positions, kneeled and started firing at the press box while your own tracers sought them out.

On that day in April the 21st Recon Company, a particularly good outfit composed largely of troops who had fought with the Vietminh during the Indochina war, was with us. We were scouting a Vietcong battalion, moving along a line of villages which we thought the battalion had been using as its main line of communication in that region. But this was the upper Camau, almost completely enemy territory, where one could find a Vietcong squad in virtually every village.

It is perhaps deceptive to use a word like "battalion" here; when such a unit attacked a given point it might number three hundred men, but immediately afterward it would break up into small groups slipping into neighboring villages and awaiting the signal for the next operation. A single large force would make too good a target for the Government; besides, by splitting up, more men could indoctrinate more peasants, and no single village would have to take on the task of feeding three hundred extra mouths.

At about eight-thirty in the morning we saw some movement in a village below, followed by a few light crackles around us. It was ground fire; the bait had been taken. We came in low over the village and saw some men scurrying to positions. Three of the helicopters, including our own, dropped their troop load while the others circled and strafed some of the positions. We were making our advance on the treeline under fire when we saw a man in a black suit desperately running across the open field. It was the dry season and the fields were covered with sun-caked mud. Suddenly a helicopter descended almost on top of the man; he stopped and held up his hands. The Vietnamese commander ran over to him. There was no weapon on this Vietcong; neither was there any of the bowing or scraping that local guerrillas posing as farmers sometimes employed.

The captured man was angry and defiant, and at first a little scared as well—until he saw me and spat at me. The commander slapped his face very hard and said something in Vietnamese. Later I was told that the captain had said to the prisoner, "The Americans are very kind. They do not kill, and they are always telling us not to kill you, but I am not so kind and I will kill you. You will see." The interpreter thought this was very funny. "You know, the enemy takes these young boys and they tell them how fierce you Americans are, and so they are all convinced that the Americans will eat their hearts for breakfast as soon as they are captured. The captain is right; you have no real taste for war." The Vietnamese commander interrogated the captured guerrilla and told us that he was well indoctrinated. "They are taught well to hate," he said a little apologetically.

It is true that the Vietcong were better at hating than our Vietnamese, though at times Government troops could be very cruel. Once, south of Bac Lieu, Vietnamese Marines had fought a particularly bitter battle but had captured a number of Vietcong prisoners. According to a Vietnamese friend of mine who was there, the enemy were very cocky and started shouting anti-American slogans and Vietnamese curses at their captors. The Marines, who had lost an officer that day and were in no mood to be called lackeys of the Americans, simply lined up the seventeen guerrillas and shot them down in cold blood. "They had to believe their own propaganda," my friend said.

The captain said that the guerrilla was probably from an elite battalion operating in the area. "I think maybe he was a squad leader." Then the officer turned and spoke briefly and intensely to the guerrilla. He was telling the prisoner that they would kill him unless he talked—and perhaps they would kill him by throwing him out of the helicopter. "The captain is very smart," said the interpreter. "It will be the guerrilla's first helicopter ride and he will be very scared." They tied up the guerrilla and placed him in the helicopter (later we were to find out that he had indeed been frightened but did not crack), and the captain and I walked back across the open field to the village. We could hear a good deal of firing, and as always I hunched over as much as I could, but the Vietnamese officer strolled casually. He carried a small swagger stick, and he looked as if he were a large landowner inspecting his plantation. I was impressed.

By the time we reached the village the troops had rounded up two more guerrillas. They did not even pretend to be farmers; they had not surrendered until they began to take fire not only from the ground, but from some of the nine other helicopters in the area. The captain was convinced that there were other Vietcong somewhere in the village, that there had been at least five or six of the enemy stationed there. But he also suspected that the others had excellent hiding places and that we would not find them. "They are probably dug in under this village somewhere," he said. He checked his watch. Time was important because the helicopters had been aloft for a long while. He told his men that they had five more minutes to search the village, then turned to the prisoners and started to talk to them. One, about nineteen years old, gave him a look of defiance and turned away, but the other, who might have been twenty-five, gave the captain a curious look. "Maybe," the captain said later, "he is a little more tired of the war and the propaganda. We shall see. The other will not talk." He was right; the next morning the elder one confessed that they were members of a battalion which had hit two outposts in the Camau the week before and had come here to rest. This guerrilla was tired; he had been fighting too long—for seven years—and he wanted to leave the Army.

At the appointed minute the troops were back. They had found an American carbine, and the captain was surprised because it was more than he had expected. The weapon had been found in a false thatch in a roof. The captain was pleased. "Good troops," he told me. "When they search they want to find something, and when they fight they want to kill."

Then the helicopters returned and we all jumped in and prepared for the next assault.

The next two villages produced only some crude grenades made by an old farmer. "The local guerrilla," said the Vietnamese captain. These were the lowest of the three types of Vietcong: they farmed in the day and fought at night, and they had the worst weapons. When I first came to Vietnam their arms were all homemade; by the time I left they were using French equipment and even some American M-I's. But even in April 1963, in a village where there were no other weapons, a homemade grenade or a rusty rifle had great power.

The local guerrillas were a vital part of the Vietcong apparatus. They gave the village a sense of Communist continuity, they could provide intelligence on Government activities and serve as a local security force for a traveling commissar, or they could guide the professional Vietcong troops. This last was particularly important to the success and mobility of the guerrillas; everywhere they went they had trained, local guides to steer them through seemingly impenetrable areas. Because of these local men the enemy's troops could often move twenty-five miles in five hours —which meant that a raiding force attacking at night was almost impossible to find by daylight. These local guerrillas were also part of the propaganda network, for in a village they might be the only ones with a radio. (Sometimes it was only the shell of a radio, but the local man would pretend he could hear news and would give out information of Vietcong victories.)

We flew back to the base to refuel, and then returned to the area. Shortly before noon we hit pay dirt. Out of one village came a flock of Vietcong, running across the paddies, and there was intense fire from the treeline. While five of our ships emptied their troops, the rest of the choppers strafed the area. Soon the guerrillas broke from their positions and ran for a nearby canal, where they might find hiding places. We came hurtling down on them at a hundred miles an hour, just a few feet off the ground. We were still drawing fire, but it was more sporadic now.

We bore down on one fleeing Vietcong. The paddy's surface was rough and his run was staggered, like that of a good but drunken broken-field runner against imaginary tacklers. We came closer and closer; inside the helicopter I could almost hear him gasping for breath, and as we bore down I could see the heaving of his body. It was like watching a film of one of your own nightmares, but in this case we were the pursuers rather than the pursued. The copilot fired his machine guns but missed, and the man kept going. Then there was a flash of orange and a blast of heat inside the ship, and the helicopter heaved from the recoil of its rockets. When they exploded the man fell. He lay still as we went over him, but when we turned he scrambled to his feet, still making for the canal, now only about fifty yards away. While we circled and swept toward him again he was straining for the bank, like a runner nearing the finish line. We had one last shot at him. Our copilot fired one last burst of the machine gun as the guerrilla made a desperate surge. The bullets cut him down as he reached the canal, and his body skidded on the hard bank as he collapsed.

We turned and circled again. All over the paddies helicopters were rounding up Vietcong soldiers. We landed near the village which other members of the Recon company were searching. The troops were gentler with the population than most ARVN soldiers I had seen; in front of one hut a medic was giving aid to a wounded guerrilla.

"I have never taken this many prisoners before," the Vietnamese captain said. There were sixteen of them. He turned to one of his men. "Show the American the poor little farmer," he said. They brought in a wiry young man. "This one says he is a farmer," the officer said. He pushed the young man in front of me and flipped the prisoner's palms over. "He has very soft hands for a farmer," the captain said. "He has the hands of a bar girl in Saigon. He is not a very good soldier yet. In a few months, though, he might have been very good."

The prisoner was beginning to tremble. The conversation in a foreign language obviously frightened him, and I was sure that this was why the captain was using English. I asked the captain what kind of enemy we had surprised. "Territorial," he said. This was the middle rank of Vietcong guerrillas; we called them provincial guerrillas. They operated in groups of up to one hundred and were often attached to the hard-core units to beef up their strength for a major attack; they would also hit smaller outposts.

"The leadership was not very good," the captain said. "If it had been a hard-core unit, there would have been more fighting and more dying. I think we surprised them."

Before we took off again, I walked over to the canal. The little soldier's body had actually crossed the finish line; his shoulder was over the bank, his blood was still running into the canal and there was a look of agony on his face.

The helicopter pilots and the Vietnamese captain decided that they had enough fuel for one more strike. The pilots were in very good humor, pleased with the day's bag. As we skimmed over the countryside once more, they boasted of how they had made the Air Force look sick again. There was a running battle between the helicopter pilots, who were Army officers, and the Air Force over the respective merits of the helicopter and the fighter plane.

We hit one more village and encountered no resistance. But as I was walking toward the treeline I suddenly heard shouts and cries all around me. I was terrified, for I was unarmed and about fifty yards from the nearest soldier. Suddenly from deep bomb shelters all around me more than twenty women and children came up; they were wailing and pointing at me. Clearly, they were scared. Judging from its defensive preparations, this was a Vietcong village, and for years these people had heard propaganda about vicious Americans like me. As far as I was concerned they were dangerous too, and we stood looking at each other in mutual fear.

I yelled out to Major James Butler, asking him what to do. Butler suggested that I try to give a good impression of Americans. "Protect our image," he said. Later he congratulated me on being the first *New York Times* correspondent ever to capture a bunch of Vietcong women. I gladly turned them over to the Vietnamese captain.

The troops were remarkably restrained in what was obviously a Vietcong village. At times the quick change in Vietnamese behavior was amazing. One moment they could be absolutely ruthless; the next, they might be talking to a prisoner as if he were an old friend. The enemy was different, however; I was told by those who had been captured by them during the Indochina war that they were not so tolerant. This was hardly surprising; much emphasis was placed in their indoctrination on teaching them to hate. They were the have-nots fighting the haves, and even after capture their feelings rarely changed.

We flew back to Bac Lieu. It had been a good day. There had been few Government losses, and there was a chance that from all those prisoners we might learn something important. Everyone was tired and relaxed and happy. If nothing else, the day seemed to prove the value of the Eagle flights. Only Mert Perry of *Time,* who had also come along to observe the new strategy, seemed a bit depressed. It had been a good day, he agreed, and in one way the Government had done very well. But after all, he pointed out, it was a pretty limited business, and in the long run it might backfire. There was no follow-up; no one would be in those villages tonight working with the people. These peasants had seen helicopters and they knew that Americans flew the helicopters; they had seen killing and they had seen their men disappear. The conclusions that the villagers would draw were obvious—particularly if the Vietcong were there to help them. Every man taken today, Mert said, probably had a brother or a son or a brother-in-law who would take his place after today.

We listened to Perry in silence, for we knew that he was right. The Government had scored a quick victory, but in Vietnam, victories were not always what they seemed. It was an endless, relentless war to which ordinary military rules did not apply. We went to bed that night a little less confident, knowing that although for the moment the enemy was paying a higher price, he was still out there somewhere in the darkness, living closer to the peasants and ready to seize the initiative once more.

Chapter 6

Disaster: The Battle of Ap Bac

After the Diem-Cao meeting the entire momentum of the Seventh Division came to a halt. The joint planning staff, which the Americans had worked patiently on for a year and a half to set up, became a sham; Cao started to plan operations entirely on his own. Any attempt by the Americans to teach the Vietnamese the importance of military intelligence became futile. Despite improved intelligence about the whereabouts of the Vietcong, thousands of men were launched in operations aimed at areas free of the enemy. Escape routes were deliberately left in the planning of every operation lest the Vietcong be forced to hold their ground and fight, thus inflicting more casualties on Government troops. Assaults on treelines were preceded by prolonged artillery barrages in order to alert the guerrillas. Cao's prudence was almost phenomenal; in fourteen division operations, from the time of his October meeting with Diem to December 22, 1962, when he was duly rewarded for his loyalty and obedience, only four of Cao's regular troops were killed. During this same period hundreds of Civil Guard and Self-Defense Corps (village, or local, militia) troops were lost while defending static positions.

Although none of us fully realized it then, this was the decisive time in the Delta. A guerrilla war is seen first-hand by the local population; for this reason, not only must a successful force in such a war prove that it has political benefits to offer the peasantry, but it must also prove that it can protect them. In such a military and political situation there is sometimes a crucial moment of truth, which is often unperceived by fairly knowledgeable observers: the moment when the local population senses which side is winning. During those months in the fall of 1962, I and others, although realizing that the war was not going well, did not fully comprehend—because the lack of Government momentum did not affect us as directly as it did the peasants—just how badly things were going. We talked in terms of stalemates, but I have since become convinced that there is no such thing in a guerrilla war. One side has the momentum and the other doesn't—it is just that simple—and the first people to be aware of this momentum are the peasants.

Moreover, guerrillas almost always try to attain their objectives—both military and political—with as little fuss as possible in order not to warn their opponent. In the Delta the Vietcong had had all the momentum in the early part of the war. In those days the Government forces were unprepared to challenge the Vietcong, and the peasants sensed immediately that the guerrillas would probably be victorious in the end. Then came the American buildup and the infusion of aid, which gave the Government forces a new vitality and mobility. For a time in the spring and summer of 1962, when the Government was challenging the Vietcong control of the upper Delta, the peasants moved back on the fence and our intelligence began to improve.

But in the fall of 1962 the slowdown came; the Government failed to utilize its mechanized equipment and other resources, and it squandered its momentum. Government battalions were not hunting and chasing and punishing the enemy; the Vietcong were allowed to lead more leisurely lives, and Government troops were not straying from the district capitals. Once again the first to realize the implications of this change of tempo were not the American intelligence officers in Saigon, or even in My Tho, nor the reporters, nor the optimistic officials in the Pentagon; it was the peasants living in the areas being fought over who knew that outposts were being overrun, knew that the guerrillas were moving about freely, knew which side was more willing to fight. The Vietnamese peasants are extremely realistic people, and they have a keen sense of the directions of the winds.

In My Tho in early February 1963, a young captain came over to me and said, "Do you want to see what this war is really like?"

I remember this incident quite well, though I wrote nothing about it at the time. It was not the kind of story I was eager to write. I was an American, and I was looking for operations and victories and captured weapons, not for small outposts which had been silently overrun and which would never be heard from again.

We flew in a helicopter to a small Self-Defense Corps* post about forty miles away, which had been overrun that morning just before dawn. There we found the bodies of twenty of the SDC, almost all of them shot through the back of the head, which meant that many of them had been asleep at the time. This kind of incident was to become a familiar one in Vietnam; at the time its significance escaped me, but if I could have read the handwriting on the wall, I would have reported it.

The widows of the troops, frightened and bewildered, were wailing and asking for help. What little security they had enjoyed in life had just disappeared. They were surrounded by swarms of suddenly fatherless

*A paramilitary branch of the South Vietnamese army, the Self-Defense Corps was supposed to protect local villages and outposts from Vietcong attacks. However, its members were poorly trained, grossly underpaid, and, above all, hampered by the difficulties of defending a static position against a mobile foe who launched surprise attacks at night.

little children—the more isolated the hamlet, it seems, the greater the number of children. The American captain walked among the dead, making a point of showing me those corpses which had been badly mutilated by the enemy. We had an interpreter with us, and he talked to the women. "They want some troops to come here," the interpreter said. The captain told him to tell the women that he would try. "How can you promise anything in this goddamn country," he said bitterly. Then he asked the interpreter to tell the women that he was sorry about what had happened. He seemed embarrassed about saying this.

There was an old man among the remaining villagers, and through the interpreter the captain began to question him.

Were any of the SDC missing?

Two were missing.

How long had the fight for the post lasted?

There had been no fight.

Did the men from this post ever go out and patrol?

The old man said he was sorry, but he did not know about any patrols. (On the way back to My Tho, the captain said cynically, "They go out at night, walk down the path, take a leak, and then call it a night patrol.")

Did he know how many Vietcong there had been and what unit it had been?

At this the old man simply turned away. One could not blame him; the Vietcong were very strong in that area.

Later the captain said, "This happens every night. Half the time they get it in the head. Sometimes it's treachery, a plant inside, but not always. Those boys weren't out of that outpost once in the last two months—you could tell by looking around. Why should they go out? What can they find? What the hell do they protect?" The captain had been in Vietnam for only five months, but it was long enough for him to be angry at the way the war was being fought. He told me that the outpost had lost fifteen weapons, including a BAR*—enough arms for a platoon. "They hit places like this every night," he said.

In early December of 1962 we had learned that Cao would get his star; he was to command the Fourth Corps, which was responsible for the entire Delta. The announcement of this and other promotions was one of those sleeper stories; vitally important to American interests but virtually unnoticed in the United States—reports like this rarely make even the back pages. The news media and the American public are far more interested in stories about battles and casualties.

Cao was the most political-minded and most ambitious of all division commanders, and he was the least respected by his Vietnamese colleagues. Like Diem, he was a Catholic from central Vietnam—indeed, also

*BAR stands for Browning automatic rifle—a large, gas-powered machine gun capable of firing 250 to 300 rounds per minute.

from Hué, site of the Ngo ancestral home. His religion and his birthplace made him a member of that elite group trusted for military command in the Saigon area. The personal loyalty to Diem that he had demonstrated in the past had gained him a key position ahead of many Vietnamese considered far more capable and more experienced.

The Seventh was strategically located: only about forty miles from the capital on a main road, this division could help to depose—or to rescue—the chief of state in a matter of hours. Cao had earned this trust by coming to the aid of the beleaguered Diem during the 1960 paratrooper coup. In part this was because of genuine respect for the President; in part it was opportunism. Cao had hitched himself to Diem, and clearly he realized that he would rise or fall with him.

Cao was a vain man, apt to speak of victories in first person singular ("I kill fifty Vietcong today") and to exaggerate the enemy's casualty figures outrageously. Reporters finally devised the "Cao Formula": one took his figures, subtracted the announced Government casualties in the same action, then divided by three for a figure approaching reality. He was forever announcing that he had killed high-ranking Vietcong officials during battles; it was estimated that he had "killed" eight Communist zone chiefs the previous year. He also felt that he was the only officer who truly understood guerrilla warfare, and as a result believed that he could plot Vietcong movements four or five days in advance. He was invariably wrong, but the idea fascinated him.

Like many high-ranking Vietnamese officers, Cao was extremely skillful in handling visiting American officials. When General David Shoup, commandant of the Marine Corps, arrived in My Tho on a brief visit, he was greeted by the Seventh Division band playing the "Marine Hymn," and by a huge sign reading: "The United States Marine Corps: From the Halls of Montezuma to the Banks of the Mekong River." Shoup was duly impressed. Before the arrival of Brigadier General Jerry Kelleher, chief of operations for Military Assistance Command, Vietnam, Cao grabbed Lieutenant Colonel John Vann, his U.S. adviser, and asked him what Kelleher's particular interest was. "Night patrolling and night fighting," Vann answered. When Kelleher arrived, Cao devoted a large part of his briefing to the importance of night fighting, emphasizing that his division needed to do more. "Then why don't you?" demanded Kelleher, leaving Cao speechless.

Like too many other politically appointed Vietnamese officers, Cao, who was a member of Nhu's Can Lao Party, had heard few shots fired in anger. He seldom visited the battlefield while fighting was going on, and he had almost no idea of how his troops reacted under fire. He was fond of saying that his men were the best trained in the world; they were, in fact, poorly trained, and they needed instruction desperately. He rarely saw the province chiefs in his area, and he scheduled operations on the basis of whether a chief was being cooperative politically.

Cao's appointment showed once again how little influence the Americans had in Vietnam. Indeed, American intervention on behalf of a Vietnamese officer was likely to hurt him. The three officers generally regarded by our military mission as outstanding were at this same time all shunted into insignificant positions. Duong Van Minh was given the title of military adviser to the President; General Tran Van Don lost command of the troops in the First Corps and became Army commander—which meant that as a kind of official greeter he had to go out to the airport and meet all visiting Americans; Colonel Pham Van Dong, who was considered by many Americans the outstanding field commander in the country, was made an inspector of the strategic hamlet program. The demotion of Colonel Dong from deputy corps commander in the Delta was a particularly hard blow to the Americans. They had been so impressed by his leadership that they had urged Diem to make him a general. Diem, however, did not trust Dong, and many people—including Dong himself—believed that the American recommendation had hurt his chances.

Curiously, troop command, which was sought by so many competent Vietnamese officers, went to one man who was unhappy in the role. In the Seventh Division, Cao was replaced by his former chief of staff, Colonel Bui Dinh Dam. Colonel Dam was a nice little man and a good staff officer, but the last thing he wanted was direct responsibility. He was terrified of battle, of airplanes and of Cao. In his subsequent days as division commander he was so frightened at the prospect of losses, particularly helicopter losses, that he almost never employed the aircraft except when absolutely necessary to ferry him back and forth from My Tho to the command post. During these rare rides he would always sit alone, nervously fingering his rosary. He was not an imposing figure.

Cao had pushed Dam's appointment, since in effect it would keep the division under his control, by telling Diem that Dam was as loyal as Cao himself. It was indeed an intriguing way of choosing an important officer for a key role in the war. Yet, Dam's faults notwithstanding, there was a general sigh of relief among the American advisers as the year 1962 ended and the new shifts were made. The Americans felt that they could exert more influence on Dam than they could on Cao.

Just how large the improvement was they found out very soon. Late in December very reliable intelligence had reported the location of a Vietcong company in western Dinh Tuong Province, just south of a village called Babeo. This was in the same vicinity where the Rangers had been mauled on October 6. It was a singularly tough area. Located on the edge of the Plain of Reeds, about fifteen miles northwest of My Tho, there was little access to it. "You can get into a fight any time you want to up there," one American adviser said. Its villages were lined with foxholes, and beneath some of the huts were bomb shelters. Now, on December 28, heavy enemy concentration was reported in Babeo. Colonel Vann, working with Colonel Dam and hopeful of exerting influence as soon as possible on his counterpart, urged the Vietnamese officer to strike immediately, preferably on January 1, 1963.

Dam, who was extremely considerate of the people around him, did not feel that American helicopter pilots should have to get up at 4 A.M. after celebrating New Year's Eve. He had a point, and the operation was set for January 2. The target area was just north of a small village called Ap Bac. This was to become a notorious name in Vietnam, and the event was to be scrutinized, debated, reviewed, investigated. The Americans in Saigon were, in fact, to do everything but learn from it.

When reading about Ap Bac it is important to remember the context in which the battle took place. The mercurial elusiveness of the Vietcong had become more and more exasperating and frustrating to the American advisers. Over and over again one heard the same sentence (which was to change as the Vietcong became stronger): *If we could only make them stand and fight.* The U.S. military were desperately eager for a traditional set-piece battle into which they could throw the Government's vastly superior material resources. At that time a Vietcong battalion averaged a little over two hundred men, equipped with a few automatic weapons. Only eight months later the same battalion was apt to average between four hundred and five hundred men, with—thanks to Government generosity—perhaps eight to ten machine guns, a large number of BAR's and several recoilless rifles.

Ap Bac was to be as close to a golden opportunity as there ever was in Vietnam; instead, it was a battle which demonstrated on a grand and dramatic scale all the tiny failings of the system, all the false techniques, evasions and frauds which had marked the war in Vietnam. It was also typical of the atmosphere existing at that time in Vietnam: having suffered a stunning defeat, the American military headquarters referred to it as a victory. Also, headquarters officers became angry not with the system which produced the defeat, nor with the Vietnamese commanders who were responsible for it, but with the American advisers who observed and criticized it and with the American reporters who wrote about it.

After the battle, when a Vietcong after-action report fell into Vietnamese hands, it was learned that the enemy had had a strong notion that an attack was imminent. Ironically, the guerrillas had been encamped at a point about two miles west of Ap Bac; fearing that an attack was coming there, they had moved eastward to the village itself—right into the pocket of the Government attack.

The Vietcong after-action report also revealed a hitherto unsuspected guerrilla capacity to monitor the Government radio; the enemy knew when each Government unit crossed the line of departure, when and where the reserve was placed, what orders were given—and those which were not obeyed. There was even some glee expressed in the Communist report about the delay and difficulty in getting the ARVN troops to attack.

In the beginning our luck in the Ap Bac operation seemed very good. The Government force was three-pronged: a battalion of the Eleventh Regiment was to be landed to the north by three helicopter lifts; in the meanwhile, two task forces of Civil Guard troops, each of battalion size, would move up by foot from the south. In addition, a company of armored amphibious personnel carriers would assault from the west. This combat vehicle, commonly called a 113, is the closest thing to a tank in the Delta; if properly employed it can be an awesome weapon in this kind of war. It moves well through wet rice paddies, and it can deliver sustained fire against an entrenched enemy. Moreover, in those days the Communists had little in the way of antitank weapons.

If a reserve force was needed, it would be landed by helicopter in one of the many paddies to the west. The east was deliberately left unguarded because it consisted of relatively open rice land; if the Vietcong tried to flee across that barren terrain, they would make an excellent target for aircraft and artillery.

The planned assault of the three attacking forces looked something like an open claw. Inside this claw was the Vietcong's 514th Battalion, reinforced, according to our intelligence, by local guerrillas with at least three machine guns and a dozen or more BAR's. In the area there was also a vast and thorough network of foxholes. Most of the enemy were regular troops, disciplined and extremely accurate with their limited firepower. Since automatic weapons were highly prized by the Communists, the men handling the BAR's and machine guns were superbly trained. "When you recapture a BAR from them," an American captain told me, "it's a sign that you've wiped out an entire heavy-weapons squad. You usually get three or four bodies as well."

The Vietcong had moved into the Ap Bac treeline because their battalion commander was wary of a heliborne force. Such evasion was typical of guerrilla tactics; they fought only when they had superior forces, and even then only when *they* could pick the time, terrain and circumstance of battle. When the Eleventh Regiment battalion landed to the north on the first of its three helicopter lifts, there was no shooting; only the third lift drew fire. The Vietcong did not want to tip off their position or join battle until necessary, for, unlike the Government force, they could not reinforce their troops, and they were only equipped for a one-day battle. Then, probing to the south, the guerrillas ran into Task Force A; gliding off to avoid an encounter, they moved slightly to the west, where they ran into Task Force B. At each point of contact, brief but fierce fire fights took place. After the second of these, the Vietcong moved back reluctantly to the treeline at Ap Bac and dug in. At last the standing battle the Americans wanted was about to take place. Analyzing his decision in the after-action report, the Vietcong commander wrote: "It is better to stand and die than run and be slaughtered."

Now Colonels Dam and Vann decided to land the reserve force to the west side of the village treeline. It was here that some of the most publicized aspects of Ap Bac took place, more dramatic than some of the weightier implications of the battle, for nearly all the helicopters ferrying in the reserve troops were hit. One managed to unload its troops but was so badly damaged that it could not take off again; a second, returning to the landing zone to help the first, also suffered direct hits and was unable to take off. A third helicopter then returned, drew heavy automatic-weapons fire, crashed and burned. All told, five American helicopters went down in the combat area, three of them when they returned for their downed companions. (Eventually this reopened an old debate on helicopter tactics. Some Americans—Vann among them—claimed that under such circumstances we were throwing good money after bad; others, like Brigadier General Joe Stilwell, Jr., chief of the support group and an officer particularly sensitive to the pilots' morale, felt that it was important for them to know that their own people would back them up.)

What else was happening made a dismal scene as well. All the flaws and lack of training came back to haunt the Government troops as the Vietcong stood and fought. The reserve troops that the now-crippled helicopters had ferried in suffered heavy casualties as they spilled out of the aircraft. Those who survived were almost immediately pinned down in paddies by heavy fire from the treeline, for the enemy, well armed and well camouflaged, had a clear field of fire.

The two task forces were only half a mile to the south, and the company of 113's, the perfect combat vehicle for this situation, was a little more than a mile to the west. But on this day they were useless. With the Americans desperately asking for help, Colonel Dam ordered the 113's to the site of the downed helicopters. Unfortunately, the commander of the mechanized unit was Captain Ly Tong Ba, a key Diem appointee. He was a complex officer; most Americans felt contempt for him, but others were quite impressed. He was a Southerner and an aristocrat, intelligent, quick, at times appallingly arrogant, something of a spoiled child. If he did, in fact, have some good days, this was not one of them; at this moment he refused to move his APC's. American officers trying to spur him on drew only curt remarks; he was a Vietnamese and they were Americans, and they could not tell him what to do. Overhead, Colonel Vann, circling in a light spotter plane, radioed Ba's unit that Dam had ordered it to advance. But Ba refused to move; he would not even send out a reconnoitering party to choose the best place to cross the canal—something that should have been done long before.

Finally Captain James Scanlon, an American adviser with the unit that had been pleading with Ba to attack, scouted a path for the unit himself and found a route from the crossing site to the treeline about a mile away. But even when Ba finally agreed to move, it took the armored unit four hours to reach the site of the battle. (After it was all over, Vann clocked the unit while it returned over the same stretch, and found that the carriers covered the same distance in fifteen minutes.)

When the 113's finally arrived at the open fields west of Ap Bac, they turned in a singularly futile performance. Despite the fact that these carriers were mounted with .50-caliber machine guns, recoilless rifles and light machine guns, they did not put a dent in the enemy's fire power. At times they cowered behind the downed helicopters; their gunners were firing without raising their heads, and often their tracers streamed off vainly into the sky. Ba fired the .50 in the command carrier for a few minutes, then relinquished it to a sergeant; within minutes the man was killed, and thereafter Ba had even less desire to fight than before.

In the meanwhile, Scanlon and an American sergeant named Bowers, who had landed with the reserve and had been pinned down with the helicopters, had to carry the wounded into the 113's by themselves. Following this, Scanlon, whose bravery was typical of that shown by many Americans that day, slipped behind the wall of the rice paddy where the troops were crouching. He found them thoroughly disorganized, holding their weapons over their heads and firing blindly. When he tried to rally them to attack a machine-gun post, the Vietnamese turned away from him. Scanlon found a young Vietnamese lieutenant who spoke English— or rather, as Scanlon was to recall later, who knew English "except when I asked him to attack." Although Scanlon then made the same request in Vietnamese, the officer pretended not to understand.

The armored personnel carriers, which had been designed by the United States for just such a situation, proved utterly inadequate. They failed because an ally did not use them properly, and because the officer commanding them felt no obligation to listen to the advice of his ally or to the commands of his superior. The carriers made a few sporadic stabs at the treeline but never a unified assault. Consequently, they suffered six casualties, though they never came close to the enemy, because the Vietcong were able to concentrate their fire on single vehicles.

To the south the situation was even worse. There, in a command post several miles from the battle zone, the province chief, Major Lam Quang Tho, a political appointee in command of the province's troops, refused to allow his units to budge. Theoretically, in a situation like this a division commander had authority over a province chief, but in reality it was purely a matter of who had more influence at the Palace. The Ngos were delighted to play division commanders and province chiefs off against one another; the conflict would keep both parties vacillating and insecure. As a result, province chiefs were in effect independent commanders.

Certainly, that day Major Tho was strikingly independent. On his own he turned the two task forces into blocking forces; in case someone just happened to chase the Vietcong out of the treeline, forcing them toward the south, Major Tho would be there waiting. Yet Tho had the best tactical position that day, for both task forces were only a short distance from Ap Bac and would have been able to slip up on the enemy's flank. Unlike the reserve force to the west, which was bearing the full brunt of the Vietcong fire power and which would have had to attack across an open field, the units to the south would have been protected by the treeline itself as they advanced.

Three times that day, according to both Vann and Dam, the latter ordered Tho to attack to the north with his task forces. Each time Tho refused. Four times a young lieutenant commanding Task Force B asked for permission to attack; each time it was denied. (It was incidents such as this which kept alive a spark of hope among reporters that under some circumstances the war could go better.) Like Captain Ba, Major Tho was never court-martialed or even investigated for his disobedience at Ap Bac.

By midafternoon, when it became increasingly apparent that the regular units would not attack, let alone overrun the Vietcong, the commanders and advisers decided to ask for the reinforcement of an air-borne battalion from Saigon. But here again the American advisers ran into the Vietnamese system, and this resulted in the third fatal mistake at Ap Bac. The decision to call on the air-borne battalion was made at 2:30 P.M., which meant that it would probably arrive just before dark. The Americans believed that in the meantime there would be little change in the battle lines, and therefore their idea—with Colonel Dam's concurrence—was to use the air-borne battalion to try and block the one open side, the east, in order to bottle up the Vietcong for the night. While the terrain there was too open for the Vietcong to move safely during the day, the canal system would permit them to get away under cover of darkness; it was a foregone conclusion that they would try to slip away at night. But Vann and Colonel Daniel Boone Porter, the corps adviser, hoped that if the air-borne battalion plugged the gap, and if flares were dropped all night long and the area was bombarded with artillery, they could contain the Vietcong until the next morning.

This was hardly a foolproof method; nevertheless, the enemy had taken a heavy pounding all day from Government fighter bombers and armed helicopters, they probably had a fair amount of wounded and they might not be as mobile as usual. General Cao, however, who was now the corps commander and who was at the command post with Porter, disagreed with this plan. He decided to drop the air-borne to the west, behind the reserve force. The Americans protested vigorously; as Vann said later in discussing this decision, "They chose to reinforce defeat rather than to try for victory." Cao was adamant; obviously he had suffered more casualties than he wanted (the final figure was sixty-one dead and one hundred wounded) and he was determined to break off the fight.

Thereafter, to all intents and purposes, the battle was over. Ironically, the air-borne battalion landed at dusk, as estimated, and in the resultant confusion a fire fight costing several lives took place between them and the reserve force.

A bitter parody of Ap Bac, written by one of the helicopter pilots to the tune of "On Top of Old Smoky," went:

> The paratroops landed
> A magnificent sight
> There was hand-to-hand combat
> But no VC's in sight.

Several days later, when Cao's decision came under increasing scrutiny, he attempted to blame Dam for the decision, claiming that Dam was in command and that he, Cao, had only *suggested* the landing to the west. In the presence of General Le Van Ty, the Vietnamese Army commanding general, Vann defended Dam and said that he had been overruled by Cao. Cao's behavior was hardly a surprise; when I showed up at the command post a few days later, he made a special point of saying to me, "This is the first operation of the Seventh Division since I left it. It is now under a new commander." That same night the inevitable happened: the Vietcong escaped. They policed up their brass and left only three bodies behind. Their battlefield discipline had been excellent. Madame Nhu, who had been told that the battle was a victory and that the only problem had been caused by an American colonel flying around in a small plane contradicting American advice, never forgave me for quoting our advisers on how well the Vietcong had fought.

In Saigon the reporters heard about Ap Bac in the middle of the afternoon. Peter Arnett, Mert Perry and I started checking around. At first all we could learn was that three helicopters were down and that a heavy fire fight was going on. Finally, at 6 P.M., we were able to put together a fragmentary story. But none of us was satisfied, so we went out to Tan Son Nhut air base to talk to the tired, tense and bitter helicopter pilots as they came in.

Later, General Harkins and the public information officers seemed surprised at the extent of our knowledge about the battle; how they expected to keep such a disaster secret when it had taken place within fifty miles of Saigon is puzzling. However, it was typical of the American command in Saigon that, though we filed stories about Ap Bac for three days, none of the military or State Department information officers ever bothered to go down there; the reporters went every day.

That evening we got a very good story from the pilots about the helicopters' part in the battle, and returned to Saigon to file. We showed far less initiative, however, than Neil Sheehan of UPI and Nick Turner of Reuters, who had hired a car immediately and driven down to My Tho that afternoon. There Sheehan pieced together a much fuller and more basic account of what had happened, and of the failure to attack. Ironically, Arnett's and my stories received much wider use—because they were concerned mainly with what interested Americans the most, the downed helicopters—than Sheehan's piece, which was about more disturbing and significant aspects of the battle.

On January 3 we flew down to the command post at Tan Hiep airstrip, where I asked Vann what had happened. "A miserable damn performance," he said, "just like it always is." The Americans' bitterness was compounded by the frustration of watching a perfect opportunity squandered, by the loss of three Americans, including Ken Good, and by the death of so many Vietnamese. It was still early in the morning, and no

Government troops had set foot inside Ap Bac; yet the advisers knew instinctively, like a good fisherman whose line has gone slack, that the Vietcong were gone.

Arnett and I went to Ap Bac in a helicopter. We circled the area for several minutes. The parachutes lay like tiny handkerchiefs in the paddies, the dead still sprawled there, and the tracks of the armored personnel carriers told the story more clearly than any after-action report. Below us, Sheehan and Turner, who had arrived before we did, were walking through the village with Brigadier General (now Major General) Robert York.

"What happened?" Sheehan asked York.

"What the hell's it look like happened, boy," York answered. "They got away—that's what happened."

There was almost no hope of any pursuit. On the field to the west of Ap Bac, Captain Scanlon was again having trouble with the Vietnamese —this time to get them to load their dead into a helicopter. Most of the loading was being done by Americans, and only when Scanlon threatened one soldier bodily did the men come out of their trance. Sheehan helped them. "I saw all those bodies covered with blankets, with their little feet sticking out, and I did something I hadn't done in years," he told me. "I crossed myself."

Moments later, while General York and Sheehan and Turner were waiting in the open paddies to hitch a ride back in the helicopters, the final bitter touch of the nightmare occurred: from a distant CP [command post], Major Tho began to fire artillery into the village. There was no forward observer, of course, and by the time the barrage ended, five Government soldiers had been killed and fourteen wounded. Sheehan and York hit the marshy ground as shells landed within fifty yards of them.

When Arnett and I flew back to the CP we found a brass-plated, white-helmeted honor guard paying tribute to General Cao, who had not bothered to visit the battlefield. General Harkins was also there, about to leave for Saigon, and we asked him what was happening. "We've got them in a trap," he said, "and we're going to spring it in half an hour." We looked at him, completely bewildered. The enemy was long gone, the Government troops were so completely disorganized that they would not even carry out their own dead, a province chief was shelling his own men—and a trap was about to be sprung? As on so many other occasions in Vietnam, we never knew whether Harkins believed what he was saying, or whether he felt that it should be said.

The battle of Ap Bac was followed by a second battle—a press battle. Two days later Admiral Harry Felt,* Harkins' superior officer, arrived in Saigon on an inspection trip obviously precipitated by Ap Bac. At the airport Sheehan asked Felt if he had any comment. The admiral replied,

---

*Admiral Felt was commander of the U.S. Pacific Fleet and thus had overall responsibility for the American military effort in Vietnam.

"I'd like to say that I don't believe what I've been reading in the papers. As I understand it, it was a Vietnamese victory—not a defeat, as the papers say." He turned to Harkins, who said, "Yes, that's right. It was a Vietnamese victory. It certainly was." As they turned away Harkins apparently identified Sheehan, for Felt turned around and said, "So you're Sheehan. I didn't know who you were. You ought to talk to some of the people who've got the facts."

Sheehan, who can hardly be described as a shy young Irishman, answered, "You're right, Admiral, and that's why I went down there every day."

However, Ap Bac had created a sharp reaction in the States, where a combination of a lack of public interest and official optimism had left most people unprepared for bad news. Suddenly the fact that three Americans had been killed and five helicopters downed aroused the interest of the American public in the failures that were taking place. "People keep writing me," Ambassador Nolting said several days later, "asking, 'Fritz, what's going on out there all of a sudden? I thought we were doing so well.'"

On the second day after the battle, a group of Vietcong troops in the vicinity of Ap Bac was actually flushed out. When Government officers refused to provide a promised blocking force, Vann finally rounded up every available American, including clerk typists, water purification men and cooks, and formed his own blockade to help capture some of the enemy. Ironically, because I was covering this incident I missed a conference which was symbolic of the whole dispute between the American press and its government. Roger Hilsman, then Assistant Secretary of State for Far Eastern Affairs, was in Saigon and had expressed the desire to meet reporters informally. During the discussion some of the reporters, particularly Charley Mohr, tried to explain why the Government was failing in its mission, and of Nhu's basic hostility to the United States. Hilsman implied that the reporters were naïve, that the important thing was not to be liked, but to be tough and get things done. It was an acrimonious session.

Our reporting about Ap Bac brought us immediate criticism from the mission. Every army, the line went, had its defeats; why build up Ap Bac? But time after time we had watched the ARVN turning in sloppy performances, regularly disregarding both American advice and common sense. We had filed stories on these skirmishes but had found it extremely difficult to present the true picture to our readers; a typical piece would end with a little note saying, "The Vietcong got away," which hardly did justice to the situation. To us and to the American military advisers involved, Ap Bac epitomized all the deficiencies of the system: lack of aggressiveness, hesitancy about taking casualties, lack of battlefield leadership, a nonexistent chain of command. The failures at Ap Bac had been repeated on a smaller scale every day for the past year, and if not corrected quickly, they boded even greater trouble for the future.

Many advisers felt that Ap Bac gave the American high command tangible evidence of what they had been reporting for months, and there was much hope that something positive would finally happen. One captain even told a reporter that he was sure Harkins would make a strong case with the Government over the failure of Ap Bac. The adviser was so emphatic about this that the correspondent went to see John Mecklin, the head public affairs officer, to ask whether it was true that Harkins planned to make a formal protest to Diem.

Of course there was no protest, formal or informal. The set policy, or at least the interpretation of it by the high American officials there, was to get along with the regime and to convince the American people that the war was going well. A fuss over Ap Bac, which had such basic implications for the military, political and diplomatic status quo in Vietnam, would almost surely incite Diem, and this, given the nature of the Government, was sure to be useless. Moreover, it would be hard to maintain the picture of a successful war at home if disputes between American and Vietnamese officials were reported. Thus, the reaction of the American mission to Ap Bac was just as important as the battle itself, for eventually the mission focused not on what had gone wrong and why, but on the men who had talked and written about it.

In an attempt to counter the bad publicity about Ap Bac, Nolting ordered the release of a four-month-old captured Vietcong document. This stated that the Vietcong had underestimated American intentions in Vietnam and that the Communist timetable had been slowed down. But I and my colleagues felt that in general this document was a much more accurate and perceptive description of the war and the forces at play in it than any American statement we had ever read. It predicted that the Americans would become bogged down in a frustrating, unrewarding war; it described prophetically the built-in contradictions of the American-Diem relationship; and it noted that though the Government had a vast military superiority at the time, the Vietcong retained "absolute political superiority." We were all a bit chilled by its acute analysis. None of us wrote the stories that I believe the mission anticipated; for example, Mal Browne* borrowed the American mission's favorite phrase at the time and noted that the Vietcong appeared "cautiously optimistic."

While American officials turned on the reporters—thereby abdicating hope for any new leverage with Diem by telling him in effect that it was all right for him to do whatever he pleased—the rewriting of history was taking place. General Cao was telling Americans, particularly ones with new faces, that seven Russian advisers had been seen in Ap Bac. In Saigon the Government-controlled papers were already attacking Vann, who, they said, had given contradictory orders to Vietnamese troops from a

*Malcolm Browne was the Associated Press correspondent with whom Halberstam shared a Pulitzer Prize in 1964 for their reporting from Vietnam.

plane above Ap Bac. According to this version, the troops had done the proper thing in all the confusion by staying where they were, thus showing considerable bravery. Sheehan, whose reporting on Ap Bac had shown particular enterprise and initiative, was also singled out. One paper ran a photo of him in uniform, with a banner headline exclaiming: "The American Adviser Sheehan; What Does He Really Want?" There was no story —just the headline and the photo—but henceforth Sheehan was known among us as The-American-Adviser-Sheehan, and was repeatedly badgered by the question, "What do you *really* want?"

There were others who did not believe that Ap Bac was a victory for the Government. In the Vietcong after-action report—which was much more detailed and accurate than the Government's—they analyzed the Government errors, pointing out that the battle was a major psychological setback for the ARVN, and that the effect it would have on the population would benefit the guerrillas enormously.

Then, in order to gain a further psychological edge, the Vietcong commander took his troops back into Ap Bac a week later, flew the Vietcong flag from several rooftops, and sent Cao a letter daring him to come back and fight. The Americans pleaded with the Vietnamese for an operation. The photos taken by a reconnaissance plane were studied, plans for an operation were drawn up, and in Saigon two Marine battalions were placed on alert for several days. But there was no operation. Cao refused to engage the enemy; he wanted no more part of the 514th Battalion.

Three months later Cao finally returned to Ap Bac, this time with five thousand men—one of the largest operations in Vietnamese military history—carefully telegraphing his moves so that there would be no major contact. In a preliminary scouting expedition the night before the operation, a Civil Guard company ran into a battalion of Vietcong, probably in an ambush. A Government regimental commander immediately ordered two companies of his regulars to close with the guerrillas. They were moving toward the trapped company when Dam, now even more conservative under pressure from his corps commander, told them to break contact. The next day the huge operation went forward and the troops found no sign of the Vietcong. In the meantime the Civil Guard company had been decimated.

Chapter 7

Collapse in the Delta

For Lieutenant Colonel John Vann, the battle of Ap Bac and the subsequent Vietnamese and American reaction to it were a bitter disappointment. Many Americans considered him one of the two or three best advisers in the country. In September 1962, when General Maxwell Taylor had come to Vietnam on one of his frequent trips, he had lunched with four advisers of different rank who were generally considered outstanding; Vann had represented the division advisers.

Vann was a man of curious contrasts. Thirty-seven years old, one of the younger lieutenant colonels in the Army, he was clearly on his way to becoming a full colonel, with a very good chance of eventual promotion to general. He was clearly about to take off in his career—one of those men who reaches his mid-thirties and suddenly begins to pull away from his contemporaries.

Yet most Army officers of this type tend to be sophisticated and polished, usually with a West Point background, often from second- or third-generation Army families—in contrast to some of their colleagues who excel as combat officers, but who find other aspects of the Army a bit baffling. Vann, however, could hardly have been more different from the traditional gentleman-soldier. There was little polish to him: he was a poor boy from Virginia, who always reminded me of a good old Appalachian South redneck—and it was literally true that on operations his neck and arms always turned an angry red.

Vann had risen by sheer drive, vitality and curiosity. After one year of college he had enlisted at the age of eighteen, and became a B-29 navigator at the end of World War II. In 1950 and 1951 he commanded the first air-borne Ranger company to be sent to Korea, specializing in actions behind enemy lines and against North Korean guerrillas who were trying to harass UN forces behind our lines. After Korea the Army sent him to Rutgers to teach the ROTC units there; he learned as well as taught, going to night school and receiving his B.S. degree. Then he was assigned to Syracuse University (the Army is very good about encouraging its people to pick up extra degrees), where he got an M.A. in business administration and all the credits necessary for a Ph.D. in public administration. He also attended the Army's Command and General Staff College.

Vann is a blunt, essentially conservative, at times almost reactionary man. One of the ironies of Vietnam was that at a time when the Pentagon and other elements unhappy with our reporting were claiming privately that the foreign correspondents in the country were a bunch of liberals who opposed Diem on ideological grounds, much of our information came from men like Vann.

Vann had volunteered for duty in Vietnam. Once there, he had shaken a desk job; then, knowing that he was to replace Colonel Frank Clay in the Seventh Division, he had gone on as many helicopter missions in the Delta as possible while preparing to take over. By the time he left Vietnam he had participated in more than two hundred helicopter assault landings. As a result, he knew as much or more about his area of Vietnam than any other adviser—or indeed than any Vietnamese officer—that I ever met. He also *walked* through one operation every week, and even ordered his Air Force liaison officer, Major Herb Prevost, to walk with the field soldiers regularly. Hence, Prevost became that rarity in Vietnam: an Air Force man who knew something about the effect of his weapons and about the political complexities of the war.

Once a week Vann also visited the three regiments and seven provincial capitals within his bailiwick, driving to some, going by light plane to others. His Vietnamese counterparts, Cao and Dam, who hated traveling by light plane and frequently became airsick, were delighted to have him take over these inspection tours. He frequently stayed in these local headquarters as a guest of the province chief; invariably the chief would send a girl up to the room—an attempt, Vann suspected, to get something on him and thus give the chief some leverage if there should ever be any conflict.

Vann endlessly interrogated the missionaries and priests in his area, and any time a reporter saw him, the reporter was likely to be questioned closely about what he had seen in other parts of Vietnam.

Vann also tried to set an example by his personal courage, and his walking in the field on major operations had a considerable effect on the Vietnamese troops, who had never seen any of their own officers above the rank of captain in the field. But the walks had another purpose: they were a futile attempt to shame Vietnamese officers into walking in the paddies too. What Vann, and many others like him who tried similar tactics, failed to realize was the power of the mandarin legacy: the whole point of being a major or colonel was that you *didn't* have to go into the field, and therefore the distinction and class separation of such officers from their juniors was much sharper than in a Western army, and the prerogatives of a high rank were more fondly cherished.

What the Americans were attempting to do, by setting examples like this, epitomized our entire problem in Vietnam. They were trying to persuade an inflexible military ally, who had very little social or political sense about its own people, to do what the Americans knew must be done, but this would force the Vietnamese officers to give up the very things that really mattered to them and that motivated them in the first place. How could anyone make the Vietnamese officers see, almost overnight, that the purpose of promotion was not primarily to separate them from the misery whence they came, but to get them to inspire or lead others?

Vann also insisted on driving his own jeep unescorted after dark in an attempt to change the Vietnamese belief that the night belonged to the Vietcong. Moreover, he ordered all his advisers to go out on at least one night operation or patrol each week; this well-intentioned directive failed, simply because many of the advisers could not persuade any troops to go with them. Eventually, at Cao's request, the colonel rescinded the order.

If Vann had any shortcoming, it was one typical of the best of the American advisers in Vietnam: the belief that the adviser's enthusiasm, dedication and effort could, through diplomatic guidance of his Vietnamese counterpart, successfully buck the system. This naïveté was the result of favorable encounters with other systems, and an overly optimistic view that in time of war common sense will prevail and allies will be inclined to agree on basic goals. This hope was doomed in Vietnam; the system was stronger than the men bucking it, particularly in the pressure of the fighting in the Delta. Tantalizingly, there was always just enough of a glimmer of success, or a transitory victory or just plain luck, to make the advisers keep trying.

Over a period of time Vann and a few officers like him taught most of the foreign correspondents the essentials of guerrilla war: why the outposts were a detriment ("They know where we are, but we never know where they are"); the danger of using the wrong weapon ("This is a political war and it calls for discrimination in killing. The best weapon for killing would be a knife, but I'm afraid we can't do it that way. The worst is an airplane. The next worst is artillery. Barring a knife, the best is a rifle—you know who you're killing"); the dangers of the American material commitment ("By giving them too much gear—airplanes and helicopters —we may be helping them to pick up bad habits instead of teaching them to spend more time in the swamps than the enemy"); the importance of the weapons exchange ("I don't think the Vietcong have any problems of recruiting; I think for varying reasons they can get all the people they want. Their problem right now is getting weapons; that's the only thing limiting the size of their units and the nature of their attacks, so unless we stop arming them we'll be in a very serious situation").

In February 1963, in the midst of the dry season, the Seventh Division was still virtually inactive. It had refused to fight at Ap Bac, and now it was refusing countless other opportunities to engage the enemy at a time of year that favored the hunter rather than the guerrilla. Our intelligence had improved, and knowledge of the enemy's whereabouts vastly exceeded the Government's willingness to act on it. For weeks the officers in the advisory group waited and fumed about the sham operations that the division was launching. Finally, in the first week of February, Vann sent a long and detailed message to American headquarters. In it he noted that there were now ten points where the Vietcong were known to be located in company strength or more; about thirty-five areas where they were known to be located in platoon strength or more; and that despite this intelligence the Vietnamese refused to act. It was a very strong and fully documented indictment.

When it reached Saigon, the message created a major controversy. President Diem was already angry with Vann because of the press coverage of Ap Bac and had urged General Harkins to remove him. Consequently, Harkins was less than enchanted with Vann; in addition, he held Vann partly responsible for the press coverage of Ap Bac. The general felt that somehow Vann should have been able to manage the outflow of news better. He was so angered by Vann's latest message that he called a meeting and designated a staff officer to investigate the report. If there were any mistakes in it, he wanted Vann relieved.

The officer spent eight hours checking the intelligence reports at My Tho. On his return to Saigon another staff meeting was held, and the officer announced that the only thing wrong with Vann's paper was that all of it was true. Harkins still wanted to relieve Vann, claiming that his relationship with Colonel Dam must be unsatisfactory. After the meeting, however, several other generals on the staff persuaded Harkins that if Vann were relieved it might seriously damage the morale of the advisory group, and that when the reporters found out about Vann's dismissal it might create a major scandal. (As a matter of fact, Vann never told any of the reporters about this; I only learned of it weeks later from another staff officer who was still angry about the incident.)

Harkins is a West Point man who served with distinction as a staff officer to General George Patton during World War II. He had been chosen for this post in Vietnam by General Maxwell Taylor, who had written the victory plan for Vietnam. Harkins was also known in Army circles as a good diplomat, a man who could be counted on to get along with a difficult man like Diem. His boiling point was relatively high and he was not likely to pound the table, speak indiscreetly to reporters or veer from the policy line. His appointment was, in fact, a substantive *part* of the policy; the hard line against Diem had been abandoned and the soft line, the tactic of smothering Diem with kindness and keeping our own people in line, was put into effect with Harkins' appointment.

The private instructions that Harkins received from Taylor are a matter of conjecture, but almost certainly they must have included the suggestion that Harkins turn his cheek to a great deal of Vietnamese mendacity. Thus, when Vann challenged the direction of the war in his area—the Seventh Division—he was raising doubts about the effectiveness of our whole policy and questioning the role of the man who had been specifically chosen because he would go along with the policy. If the Kennedy Administration, knowing that it was a tenuous policy at best, had selected as its instrument someone more likely to draw a line, there is a chance that

General Paul Harkins (right), who headed MACV (Military Assistance
Command, Vietnam), with U. S. Ambassador Frederick Nolting. The two men
were in charge of the American Mission in Saigon during most of the Kennedy
era. (François Sully/Black Star)

the story of Vietnam might have been slightly different—but of course this
is pure conjecture.

Harkins had other problems. He had spent a lifetime in conventional
war situations and had no particular preparation for a complex and delicate political war, where the most important voices often spoke in the
softest whispers. He was probably more willing to settle for the straight
"kill" statistics characteristic of traditional military situations than for the
circumstances which produced those statistics. One's impression was always that MACV's figures reflected what MACV* wanted to hear. There
was no differentiation, for instance, between Government forces killed on
offensive operations and those killed in static, defensive points, though this
would have been one of the truest indicators of how successfully the war
was being conducted. An estimated 70 percent of the total casualties—and
this remained a constant, according to American advisers—were inflicted
at static points, thus proving that the attempt to mobilize the Government
forces had failed.

Another factor was against Harkins: his age. He was born in 1904 and
was in his late fifties during his years in Vietnam. The problems which
existed in Vietnam in those days—the legacy of a colonial war, racial

*An acronym for Military Assistance Command, Vietnam. MACV was the agency charged
with coordinating the work of American military advisers in South Vietnam and with distributing military aid.

tension, poverty, anti-Western feeling—were alien to the experience of a military man whose formative years had been spent in far less complex situations than those created by nationalism emerging from vast colonial empires. (In this connection, I believe that part of the truly remarkable admiration for President Kennedy in much of the underdeveloped world came from the feeling of these peoples that because he was young, he *understood.*) In contrast, Lodge, though virtually the same age as Harkins, had been in politics all his life and immediately sensed the turbulence of the situation on his arrival.

The middle-aged Western military man, regardless of his nationality, has been trained in military orthodoxy and has little feel for a war practiced by guerrillas; in such a situation he clings to whatever traditional evaluations he can—such as statistics. In reality, however, statistics mean next to nothing in this kind of war and inevitably give an erroneous impression by favoring the side with the most equipment. (I remember a sharp argument between Sheehan and an American senior officer. The latter cited the high rate of Vietcong casualties and claimed that this proved that the war was being won. Sheehan insisted, however—and most guerrilla war authorities support him—that this was simply a sign that the war was being lost and that the Government was losing control of the war and the population. In a successful counterinsurgency, he insisted, when you are doing well the casualties do not rise; they drop, and the war simply goes away.)

Shortly after Vann filed his report, pointing out the ARVN's failure to follow intelligence in the Delta, MACV and Harkins were to receive one more thoroughly documented warning. Once more it was from an impeccable source: Colonel Daniel Boone Porter, Vann's immediate superior and the corps adviser who was responsible for the entire Delta. Porter is a mild, professorial sort: there was always a briefcase under his arm, and he looks as if he was on his way to give a lecture on the use of the English language. But people who knew him said that he had been a fire-eater in the past; moreover, he was reputed to know as much about basic small-unit infantry tactics as any man in the Army. He was a dedicated, hard-working soldier, and those who knew him, Vietnamese and American alike, swore by him. Charged with the responsibility for the entire Delta, Porter had seen the vast disparity between Vietnamese potential and accomplishment; similarly, the optimism of his superiors conflicted with the danger signs he saw in the field.

In February 1963, Colonel Porter submitted his final report before going home. Friends who read advance copies warned him that it was unusually strong and suggested that perhaps he sweeten it by noting some of the progressive steps taken: the increased number of operations, better communications, better care of equipment, and so on. Porter declined; he had already noted some of the improvements in an earlier report, he was deeply concerned over current trends and he was going to write what he felt.

Harkins was so upset by the report that he ordered all copies of it collected. At a meeting of senior advisers, according to one officer who attended, the general said that Colonel Porter's report would be "sanitized," and that if there was anything of interest in it afterward, it would be made available to them. The report was never seen again. This was highly unusual; most senior officers' reports were immediately made available in Saigon for other officers to read.

Unfortunately for us reporters, Porter was extremely close-mouthed about this whole affair; none of us learned of the incident until long after he had left Vietnam.

At about this time Harkins received still another report on the Delta, this time from a general on his staff. A friend of mine who saw it after it left MACV headquarters said that all along the margins of it were notes in Harkins' handwriting which said simply, "Vann," "Porter," "Vann again."

Meanwhile, in April 1963, an angry Vann was on his way home from Vietnam, his tour completed. Unlike most Americans who were unhappy with our role in Vietnam, he was not just a dissenter, but a dissenter armed. A business statistician by education, Vann had spent long hours documenting the failures and errors of the war in terms of meaningful statistics. He could point out that during his tour in the Delta the number of small outposts had not only not decreased, but that despite their vulnerability and the fact that they sharply reduced mobility, there were actually more outposts than on his arrival. He could prove that, as everyone had suspected, the province chief's political relationship with Diem had a direct bearing on the number of troops he received. Long An, for instance, a heavily populated province immediately south of Saigon, in which the majority of the Vietcong incidents in Vann's zone had taken place, had fewer troops than Kien Phong, a thinly populated province in the Plain of Reeds, which had less than 10 percent as many incidents. As a result, by the end of October 1963 the Vietcong were virtually in complete rural control of Long An.

After spending a month with his family, Vann showed up for duty at the Pentagon in mid-May 1963. There he found that no one seemed to be interested in Vietnam or in his opinions on it, though he had just returned from perhaps the most critical and certainly the most controversial area in this country's only war. Although men of division-adviser rank were normally de-briefed in Washington, the three ranking Delta experts, Colonels Porter, Ladd and Vann, were not asked to give their views. When Vann began a search for the de-briefing officer, he was told that it was "Saigon's wish" that he not be interrogated.

So at first the Colonel gave informal talks to a few friends, but as word spread he slowly found himself in increasing demand among higher officers. Finally General Barksdale Hamlett, the Deputy Chief of Staff of the Army, heard Vann's briefing, and at the general's request the item was placed on the agenda of the Joint Chiefs of Staff for July 8. Vann was advised by some of the generals who had already heard him talk that he must be more moderate, and that in particular he must be careful not to be critical of General Harkins, the personal choice of Maxwell Taylor, the Chairman of the Joint Chiefs of Staff.

By a curious coincidence the Chiefs had just heard another briefing on Vietnam by McNamara's* special adviser on guerrilla warfare, Marine Major General Victor Krulak. Krulak was to play an important role in Vietnamese affairs as a special investigator, and according to him the war was going well. At this point Krulak had just returned from a brief trip to Vietnam and had written an extensive report, which was extremely sanguine about the strategic hamlet program. According to one member of Harkins' staff, the report had been prepared with the close collaboration of the MACV; in any case, Krulak was simply telling the Pentagon what it wanted to hear. Vann's feelings were well known, and when his appearance before the Joint Chiefs was scheduled, Krulak's office began to telephone Vann's superiors for a copy of his report. Vann was warned by several high officers to stall and not to let the report be seen by others until the last possible minute. His briefing was set for 2 P.M. on a Monday; at about 9:45 A.M. on the morning of the briefing he sent a copy of the report to Krulak's office.

Vann arrived very early for the briefing and waited outside the office of General Earle Wheeler, the Army Chief of Staff, in case there were any late developments or questions for him to answer. According to his wife, "He was as shined and polished as a man can get—John was really prepared that morning. There wasn't a wrinkle near him."

What follows is Vann's report of the incident, but it has since been confirmed by a member of Wheeler's staff.

At 10:45 A.M. there was a telephone call to one of Wheeler's aides in the waiting room outside the general's office. The conversation went like this:

"*Who* wants the item removed from the agenda?" asked the aide.

After a silence the aide said, "Is it the Secretary of Defense or the Chairman's office?"

There was more talk at the other end. "Is that an order or a request?" Wheeler's aide asked. Then, after listening to the reply, the aide said, "Let me get this right. The Chairman *requests* that the item be removed." He then added that he would check with General Wheeler and call back. Hanging up the phone, he turned to Vann and said, "Looks like you don't brief today, buddy."

In a few minutes the aide returned, dialed a number on the phone and said, "The Chief agrees to remove the item from the agenda."

*Secretary of defense under Presidents Kennedy and Johnson, Robert S. McNamara had been head of the Ford Motor Company before coming to the Pentagon. Enamored of efficiency, he became known for his attempts to apply the methods of cost-benefit analysis to military procurement and for shaping the American policy of gradual escalation in Vietnam.

And so the Joint Chiefs did not have to hear Vann's briefing, nor did anyone else during the brief period that he remained in the Army while waiting for his papers to be processed.

For whatever reasons—perhaps because he was not a general, perhaps because he lacked expert advice in how to handle and exploit a protest of this sort, perhaps because it was not an election year, or perhaps because no one was that concerned over the state of the war in Vietnam in those days—Vann's retirement caused little stir at the time. There were a few stories and interviews—one in the *Times,* an excellent story in the New York *Journal-American* and a good interview in *U.S. News and World Report*—but they were sparse, so the Pentagon was really never forced to explain why Vann had left the Army.*

By April, what Colonel Vann had predicted was already happening. The ARVN had shown that they were afraid of contact with the main Vietcong units, and the unchallenged enemy were becoming bolder and bolder. Better armed than before, they were picking fights with Government troops, something they had avoided six months earlier. It was a never-ending cycle: the more cautious the ARVN became, the more the Vietcong were able to move freely; the greater the guerrillas' freedom, the easier it was for them to slip up on large Government outposts and capture weapons; the better armed they became, the more the population was impressed and the Government forces intimidated—thus, a full circle.

Under these circumstances other faults came more into focus. Local officials and commanders became dependent on lying their way out of situations. For instance, because Diem did not want the ARVN to risk casualties and because Colonel Dam had reported that the war was going well, it became impossible for Dam to meet the enemy challenge. To do so would have required taking casualties, and then Diem would have demanded to know why there need be casualties in an area which, according to Dam, the Government had long controlled. Thus, potentially good men became prisoners of their past mistakes, and in the early months of 1963 the Vietcong took over the Delta countryside virtually unchallenged.

Even Government victories were badly tarnished. On July 21 we were told of a great Government victory in the Cho Gao area, northeast of My Tho, where a large force had clashed with the 514th Battalion. According to the original reports, three hundred guerrillas had been killed, and so the next day the PIO's [Public Information Officers], very eager to have us down there, laid on a press junket via helicopters. It turned out that in a prolonged battle fifty-eight, not three hundred, guerrillas had been killed and that twelve weapons had been captured. Eighteen Government

*John Paul Vann returned to Vietnam in early 1965 as a civilian official supervising American military advisers in the central highlands. After rising to a rank equivalent to lieutenant general, he died in a helicopter crash in June 1972 at age forty-seven while on his way to a battle then raging at Kontum.

regulars had been killed, fourteen of them in a single company which had made a very difficult infantry assault across an open rice paddy.

It was clear that despite Cao's claim of wiping out the 514th, it was still very much in operation. Nevertheless, there was an official ceremony celebrating the victory, in which Colonel Dam rose and gave a humiliating little speech about what a great commander Cao was, and how this victory was all his. (Of course neither of them had been on the battlefield.) Then Cao spoke: it was not his victory at all, but that of President Ngo Dinh Diem, who had personally ordered him to destroy the 514th Battalion.

The battlefield told a somewhat different story—despite Madison Avenue Cao's attempt to dress up the scene for the television cameramen by having his men prop the dead bodies of the Vietcong in empty foxholes. The fact that only a dozen guerrilla weapons had been captured meant that most of the enemy had managed to escape. Indeed, American intelligence later confirmed that the 514th was at normal operative strength several days later. In addition we learned that only one unit had made an assault and that apparently the 113's had failed to overrun the treeline.

We also noticed at the time that some of the American division advisers were not taking part in the festivities. Later, after the coup, when the advisers talked more freely, we were told that once more the battle plan had been drawn up with a deliberate escape hatch for the Vietcong, that the 113's did not assault, and that Cao himself had been terrified throughout the operation and had refused to commit units which might have blocked the enemy's escape. In fact, we were told, Cao had been so jittery that early in the day the artillery fire had gotten on his nerves; he had ordered it stopped, and refused to rescind this command throughout the day. Another rare chance to annihilate a hard-core enemy unit had deliberately been turned down. "We didn't wipe them out," an American adviser said later, "we just scratched at them."

Three weeks later there was another loudly proclaimed victory at a place called Go Cong—a victory that had many of the same elements as Cho Gao. On this occasion a Vietcong battalion had struck a district post, then moved down the main road and set an ambush for the relief column. However, the Vietnamese roared up the highway in 113's and caught the vast Vietcong force in an open field. Usually the Vietcong were more careful, by preparing an exit route along treelines, but this time they were too cocky and the 113's had a field day rolling over their positions. But in the middle of the battle, with the Vietcong being routed in confusion, Colonel Dam told the armored unit to break contact with the enemy. As usual the Americans protested, but Dam was adamant; he had inflicted heavy casualties on the enemy, had suffered few himself and was not going to press his luck. Turning to the chief American adviser of the armored unit, Dam said, "Call your ambassador and your reporters and bring them here."

As the adviser later said, "All they cared about was the ball score."

In Saigon, Go Cong was nevertheless hailed as a considerable Government victory. After all, the friendly troops had reacted quickly and well. But a friend of mine, a non-American who was an expert on guerrilla warfare, took me aside and told me why he felt it was hardly a victory, why in fact it was a sign of imminent disaster. The action had taken place very near a district capital outside of My Tho, he noted, and at least five hundred Vietcong had participated. Yet this large a force had been able to gather near a major center in a heavily populated area, without one single peasant warning the Government. Therefore, my friend said, it was not a victory, but rather a grim lesson in making it clear which side controlled the population and could move freely in the countryside. The war, he said, was closer to being over than anyone realized.

In those days, anyone who expressed doubts about Vietnam's future was immediately inundated with facts about the strategic hamlet program, which was an attempt on the part of the Government and the United States to create fortified villages where a number of social and educational services would be provided to the peasants. It was the key, the American command said, "to winning the people," and it would counteract all the failures of the war. If the critic expressed worry about the peasants' feelings toward the regime, he was assured that under the strategic hamlet program injustices were rare, that the basic needs of the people were being met and that this was "democracy from the bottom up." If one mentioned the military failures in the Delta, he would be told that the program was making all the difference in that area, that it was way ahead of schedule. Progress was there, the American official would say; it might not be readily discernible, but it was there.

Yet common sense evoked suspicion: the idea that the hamlet program, a difficult and complicated undertaking, would succeed so easily where so many other contrivances had failed; that a government unable to handle its people and with a reputation for appointing police-state hacks to key positions would suddenly appoint talented, vigorous and honest men to administer the program; that an administration which had such a quixotic attitude about the priorities of the war could handle a vast and complicated program like this and make it work—all this was difficult to believe.

Though a similar program had been tried unsuccessfully before, under the French—the people had been herded into *agrovilles*—in theory the strategic hamlet program was as good an answer to the problems of Vietnam as anyone could think of in those days. It was not a cure-all—though in the bankruptcy of the American-Diem relationship it was treated as such—but a complicated, chancy idea, and if the executors of the program were smart, tough and lucky, it might provide part of the medicine needed for a very sick country.

The hamlet program was designed to help the peasant to help himself and to separate him from the guerrilla. It assumed that the peasant wanted to help himself—unfortunately this was not always the case—and that his sympathies were with the Government side, all things being equal. The program was designed to provide the peasant with both the arms and the desire to defend himself, by giving him services which he had lacked in the past and whose absence had made him susceptible to Vietcong propaganda. The program was an idea as much as an entity, and when it fell apart completely in mid-1963, it was not from lack of weapons.

The hamlet program was better suited for the central coastal region and for the highlands than for the Delta. In the coastal and plateau regions the peasants lived in small, clustered villages which lent themselves to the type of defense proposed; there was little need for relocation; withholding food from the enemy was more feasible because of the limited resources of such regions; and communal use of the land was traditional because of the limited amount of rice acreage. Also, the Government had put its major effort into these regions because the Ngos were more interested in them.

The Delta was quite a different story; yet the difference was never recognized in high American councils. It took only the most superficial knowledge to realize that the programs which worked farther north were unsuitable in the Delta. For one thing, the Delta guerrilla found it easy to live off the land. Even more important was the fact that the population of the Delta was not clustered into convenient little groups; it was spread out aimlessly and endlessly over this rich soil. Therefore, all too often this meant relocating people from an area which they loved and had held for many generations, to a region for which they cared not at all—in order to fight an enemy they did not really consider their enemy. By and large the population of the Delta had been on the fence, but the very act of relocation turned thousands of peasants against the Government.

Even so, under certain circumstances the hamlet program might have provided a partial answer in the Delta. But the plan wasn't bolstered by the honesty, efficiency and skill it needed; instead, all the weaknesses of the system were brought out. Of the thirteen province chiefs in the Delta, few were from the South or had any understanding of the Southerners' temperament and affection for their land, and only two of the chiefs seemed to have grasped the psychological concept of the program—that a mystique had to be created to make the peasant *want* to come into the hamlet. One hundred such people, not one hundred kilometers of barbed wire, could resist the Vietcong.

The dream envisaged remained only on paper, for Mr. Nhu saw it as a means of population control instead and put his people in charge of the program. Province chiefs competed with one another over the number of hamlets they could build. The more hamlets they built, the more they were in favor with Nhu and the more U.S. aid they received; consequently, one problem for the American mission was the tendency of Vietnamese officials to divide a hamlet in half and count it as two, thereby getting twice the aid. Each chief engaged in a mad scramble to build hamlets faster than the next: "If you stand still long enough down there, they'll throw a piece of barbed wire around you and call you a strategic hamlet," one American said.

But the success of the program in the Delta rested largely on the strategy of building hamlets slowly, starting with one secure area and then slowly branching out and gathering other villages into a protective umbrella, thus creating a sense of mutual protection through the interlocking units. But this type of construction never took place. Instead, hamlets went up helter-skelter, lacking any overall, Delta-wide plan of priorities. Vast numbers of troops who should have been on mobile duty were tied up building and defending hamlets, so that eighteen months after Maxwell Taylor had described the desperate need to increase the percentage of mobile troops, there were more of them in static positions than ever before.

As a result of this rush of construction, both Americans and Vietnamese boasted loudly that the program was far ahead of schedule and that it would be completed sooner than expected. The American military high command was a willing partner in this self-delusion; it was only too glad to listen to favorable statistics. In April, when an American general visited a Delta province, he was given an enthusiastic briefing by a Vietnamese officer to the effect that seventy-two hamlets had already been built and that many more were on the way, while in reality only thirteen were really secure. When an American told him this, the general became angry at the American officer and immediately accused him of lying. But the numbers games went on, while beneath the surface the hamlet program in the Delta was an inflated, jerry-built structure. Inside the villages—which could not protect themselves from attack in any case—the people were either passive about having been shoved around or actively angry about the broken promises of medical and educational services. "Sometimes all you found representing the Government inside these hamlets were the Cong An—the local police officials working for Nhu—usually ill trained, men who were there because they were related to someone in Saigon, who were ignorant and tough, and who abused the population. No wonder the Vietcong looked like Robin Hoods when they began to hit the hamlets," one high civilian official in the Delta told me.

In 1964, a year after the plan had failed and Diem had fallen, an amazingly frank report on the hamlet program by USOM (the local term for the Agency for International Development) said, "From the very inception it was apparent that many of the provincial officials did not fully understand the concept and were so frightened by the pressures from the President and his brother that they would employ any measures, from forced labor and confiscation to false reporting, to achieve the quantitative goals set."

Thus, in June and July of 1963, when the Vietcong began to assault the Delta hamlets, they were attacking what was essentially a paper program. With the exception of Kien Hoa, where the province chief understood the meaning of the program, they encountered only a thin defense—a few local militiamen, most of whom lacked the will to resist and many of whom had been infiltrated earlier. In many hamlets the local workers had not been paid as promised; in others the sons of officials had been exempted from service. Because of hundreds of such abuses, the discontent and lack of commitment made the enemy's task easy. Rather, the Government's presence was too often felt by the fear it generated among the peasants. The Saigon *Post*, which is an English-language paper run by the Vietnamese, said plaintively, on January 10, 1964, when for the first time since Diem's fall free speech was allowed in the Vietnamese press:

> Yet these indirect causes are forgivable. What cannot be forgiven is the sad but commonplace case of abuse by district chiefs—more often by their chiefs for security. Name a single Delta province where the deputy's name is not whispered with fear among the peasant population and with a furtive, over-the-shoulder glance.
>
> On the answers to these questions depend whether the peasant will look to the Government for protection of his person, his rights and his property, or to the Vietcong. And we must not forget that as long as there is one aggrieved peasant, there are ten potential Vietcong sympathizers and as many potential recruits. And every new case of abuse will widen this gap between this essential war factor and the Government.

Even in Kien Hoa Province the Vietcong forged a remarkable record. During a long period of time in 1962 and early 1963, when they were laying low militarily, they had steadily and successfully built up shadow governments in the villages and hamlets of this province, and recruited peasants. An American officer in Kien Hoa told me that between April and June 1963 the guerrillas were able to recruit two thousand men, and to form and equip two new battalions of six hundred men each, besides expanding to full strength the single battalion which had previously operated in the province.

Thus, the strategic hamlet program never really affected the Vietcong's ability to handle the population, for it never separated the guerrillas from the source of their greatest strength: young men.

The Vietcong approach to the program as a whole was extremely clever and once again showed their understanding of the nature of the war. The Americans and the Government had hoped that the hamlet concept would force the Vietcong to attack the people; this would enrage the population and encourage them to defend themselves against the guerrillas; at the very least it was thought that it would turn the peasants against the enemy and put them on the side of the Government.

But it did not work out that way. The Vietcong were not hungry, and they did not need to prey off the villagers. Since they were usually local Southerners, often from the region in which they were bivouacked, they knew the area well—and they had infiltrated the hamlets. When they attacked, they attacked only the symbols of the Government: the armory or command post of the hamlet, the hamlet chief or the youth leaders (who were particularly hated because they were Nhu's men). They rarely harmed the population, and so the people of a village, who saw that the Government had not kept its promises and could not protect them, often sided with the Vietcong after a raid.

With Vann gone, the pressure on his successors in dealing with the press was enormous in June and July; knowledgeable American advisers would often just turn away from reporters when asked about conditions. As the situation deteriorated in an atmosphere of military secrecy during these months, we became dependent on lower-echelon officers for first-hand observations, and on American civilian officials connected with the hamlet program—the latter being under less pressure to conform than their military counterparts.

During those two summer months we watched the Vietcong winning by default in the Delta. A year after the American buildup of weaponry and personnel had reached its peak, it was clear that the Government had lost the initiative, that the enemy had benefited more from the weapons than we had, that his capacity had increased more than the ARVN's the past year, and that with the failure of the Government civic program the guerrillas' tactical position was also superior.

The implications of all this were extremely serious. The American buildup, which had been prompted by a deteriorating situation in late 1961, had lost its edge and momentum; the Communists had learned to react, and thanks to the outposts the enemy had been able to use the Government as a supply store. In 1962 the Government's main strength had been its main-force units and their weaponry; now even this advantage was gone. By July 1963 some of the enemy battalions had over five hundred troops; the 514th, which had caused so much trouble, had six hundred trained soldiers and 57- and 75-mm. recoilless-rifle sections, 81- and 60-mm. mortar sections and .50-caliber machine guns. By August the Government battalions which, with the exception of the Marine and air-borne units, rarely had more than three hundred and thirty effective troops, were no match for the Vietcong main-force units. Not only were the guerrilla units bigger, but they used their weapons better and had better NCO's. As a result, though the Government still had a superiority in artillery, it was now openly afraid to tangle with the enemy. In a war which was so largely psychological and in which the opinion of the populace was so important, this was disastrous.

Colonel Pham Van Dong, one of the most knowledgeable men in the country, and who had commanded a regimental combat team under the French, returned in dismay to Saigon from a tour of the Delta in July. "It's just like the Indochina war, only worse. The VC are preparing for hard-hitting mobile warfare, with battalions as well-equipped as the Government's, and perhaps bigger," he said. A Vietnamese general allowed Sheehan and me to see the private figures of the Vietnamese Joint General

Staff; even such statistics as these—which I distrusted as being too optimistic—showed that the trend was going in the wrong direction. Whereas the Delta figures for the last six months of 1962 had been relatively favorable in comparison with the past—thanks largely to the impact of the new American gear—there was a sharp drop for the first six months of 1963. This indicated that the enemy had learned how to counter the new techniques. According to these figures, Government weapons losses had risen about 20 percent and Vietcong weapons losses had dropped about 25 percent. One of the most important statistics indicated that the Government had lost eighty crew-served weapons (meaning BAR's, machine guns, mortars or recoilless rifles), an increase of about thirty; in comparison, Vietcong losses of these vital weapons had dropped from one hundred and fifteen to fifteen. These figures are important, because each side gives up these weapons reluctantly; their loss is a very good indication of the effectiveness of each opponent's first-line fighting. If there is a tide in the war, the exchange rate of such weapons will reflect it immediately.

On August 15, 1963, the *Times* published my long piece. It began: "South Vietnam's military situation in the vital Mekong Delta has deteriorated in the past year, and informed officials are warning of ominous signs. Essentially, these military sources say, a Communist Vietcong build-up is taking place in the Delta. They find it particularly disturbing because it has persisted since an American build-up twenty months ago." The story went on to state that the Vietcong were engaging in "a sizable military offensive" and were preparing large, beefed-up battalions for mobile warfare.

No story I ever wrote drew a more violent reaction. The President of the United States was angry, his generals were angry and his civilian officials were angry. At a press conference Dean Rusk* specifically criticized the story. I still have the cable the *Times* sent me about his conference:

RUSK AT FRIDAY NEWS CONFERENCE TOOK EXCEPTION TO REPORTS OF DETERIORATING MILITARY SITUATION IN VIETNAM STOP HE CITED DECLINE IN SABOTAGE AND PROPAGANDA INCIDENTS AS WELL AS LARGE-SCALE ATTACKS AND SAID ADDITIONAL AREAS WERE COMING UNDER GOVERNMENT CONTROL WITH STRATEGIC HAMLET PROGRAM MOVING FORWARD STOP DOES THIS WARRANT STORY FROM YOU?

I answered that unfortunately our story still stood and that I was sorry that Rusk didn't believe it.

In Washington some officials in the Pentagon compared my story to Vann's written brief (I had not seen Vann or heard from him in four

*Secretary of state under Presidents Kennedy and Johnson, Rusk was a hard-line opponent of Asian Communism who became a principal architect of the Johnson Administration's buildup of American forces in Vietnam.

months, but our views on the Delta were basically the same) and felt that the similarity might be incriminating—that perhaps he had been leaking intelligence to me.

In Saigon, where Military Assistance Command Vietnam was receiving all kinds of jolts about the story from higher command, the job of disproving it fell to Major General Richard Stilwell, the operations chief of MACV. Disprove it he did, according to his lights. He later assured me that he had lost a good deal of sleep over it. In a briefing several days later, to a room filled with visiting reporters, he attacked both the story and me by name, and he produced a lot of figures that showed how well the war was going in the Delta.

There were also attempts to contradict my story through a few visiting reporters who were then writing remarkably optimistic views of the war in Vietnam. One of the most important of these was written by Miss Marguerite Higgins, then a reporter for the New York *Herald Tribune.* Miss Higgins, who had been in Vietnam for a brief time, wrote on August 28:

> . . . But as of the moment General Harkins and his staff flatly contradict published reports that South Vietnam's U.S.-backed fight against the Communists—particularly in the rice-rich Delta—is "deteriorating" and that a Vietcong build-up is taking place to the point where the Communists will be able to conduct mobile warfare with battalions as well equipped as the Government's.
>
> "What is mobility?" interjected one of the general's corps advisers. "Mobility means vehicles and aircraft. You have seen the way our Vietnamese units are armed—fifty radios, thirty or forty vehicles, rockets and mortars and airplanes. The Vietcong have no vehicles and no airplanes. How can they be mobile?"

Presumably Miss Higgins was quoting a corps adviser in the Delta. In any case, the statement seems to me particularly revealing, for it sums up the incredible arrogance of the upper-level American military establishment in this crisis, and shows how little the Americans had learned from the French. To be sure, the Vietcong did not have mobility by Western technological standards. But they had an Asian ability to filter quietly through the countryside unobserved, to move twenty-five miles a night on foot, or in sampans with excellent local guides, to gather and strike quickly and then disperse before the Government could retaliate. That was the only kind of mobility they had, but it was a far better kind than the Government's, and too many American generals never understood it.

About that time I saw Denis Warner, the Australian correspondent, who told me: "The American generals are talking about the Mekong Delta just the way the French generals talked about the Red River Delta in 1951 and 1952. I bet I could go back to my old notebooks and find the same quotes from the French generals that the Americans are telling now."

Part III

THE FALL OF THE DIEM REGIME

Chapter 8

The Buddhist Revolt Begins

Early in the spring of 1963 I was privately criticized by experienced colleagues for not writing more about the political problems of Vietnam. I had been concentrating on the Delta; that was fine, my friends said, and it was good that I went out on operations, but such stories only indicated one facet of the country's malaise.

I agreed with my critics, but the fact was that the political situation in Vietnam at that time was difficult to describe, for there were few pegs for stories. (In the vernacular of the trade, a "peg" is an event which provides a vehicle or an angle for a reporter to write about a trend that has been developing slowly.)

In all the time I had been in Vietnam there had been no major new developments—no attempted coups, no mass rebellions—simply a hardening of attitudes. The essence of the political situation was that Vietnam was a country ruled by a clumsy and heavy-handed government, whose population had a latent sense of discontent. The resentment was palpably there—anyone could feel it—but it did not lend itself to daily reporting; there were no elections by which it could be tested, no criticism in the newspapers, no deputies standing up in the Assembly to speak.

There was no organized opposition, simply and only because there was no focus of protest. All the outspoken, anti-Communist, anti-Diem leaders had left the country or were imprisoned; the intellectuals who remained were harried and divided, talking ineffectually in hushed voices in private homes; even those Catholics who wrote what verged on criticism of Diem in their little papers were quickly silenced by the Government. Thousands of political leaders were in prison, and opposition to the Vietnamese government was only expressed surreptitiously.

This state of affairs ended with the Buddhist crisis, which began in the spring of 1963.

On May 9 I received a phone call from the Vietnamese Director General of Information, who said that there would be a special press conference that afternoon. When I asked why, he said that the Vietcong had murdered nine Buddhists in Hué. I was immediately suspicious, because it was highly unusual for the Government to take the initiative in press matters; when it did, it was usually trying to conceal something rather than enlighten us. Other reporters were equally cynical, and it turned out that our doubts were justified. The conference had been called because Nick Turner of Reuters had gotten wind of the real story, and this had frightened the Vietnamese bureaucracy.

At that time, few of us knew much about Buddhism in general, or its Vietnamese particulars, other than that it was the major religion in Vietnam and that about 70 percent of the population subscribed to it. (Later, during the actual Buddhist crisis, there was a concerted effort on the part of the Nhu family, and forces sympathetic to it, to belittle this percentage —Madame claiming that it was only 15 percent—but this was belied by a Government brochure handed out by the Vietnamese embassy in Washington, which said that the nation was 90 percent Buddhist. Actually, about ten and a half million Vietnamese called themselves Buddhists, although about half of these were basically ancestor worshipers and half were practicing Buddhists; of the rest of the country's fourteen million people only about one and a half million were Catholics.)

There had been persistent reports of discrimination and some persecution of Buddhist priests in the central coastal region, and it was known that many Buddhists felt that if they were to get ahead in Vietnam they had to become Catholics—which produced a group of converts known as "1955 Catholics." But we reporters knew little else; to us the Buddhist monks were strange little men in orange robes—distant, faceless little Asians. Like other Americans in Vietnam, we were concerned with the war. After eight months there, I knew no Buddhist priests, knew little about Vietnamese Buddhism and had never been in a pagoda.

I missed that first press conference; I was tired after eight months of digging for stories and was on my way to Hong Kong for a two-week rest on the day the conference was called. It was good to be getting away; let the others put the story together.

They did. The incident had taken place in Hué, near the Seventeenth Parallel. The lovely old imperial capital of Annam, Hué lies on the bank of the Perfume River, in the central coastal region of Vietnam, and it is the most Oriental city in the country. It was still the home of Ngo Dinh Can, the President's brother who was the feudal overlord of the central region; more important, it was the see of Archbishop Ngo Dinh Thuc, Diem's most respected and eldest living brother. Because of Thuc's position and because of his strong role in the family, the Church had become much involved in temporal affairs—so much so that Ngo Dinh Can had reportedly complained to some Buddhist leaders and to the military that he was tired of demands by Thuc's young priests for troops and trucks to work on one Church project after another.

But Hué was also the center of Vietnamese Buddhism and Buddhist teaching. In precolonial days the greatest flowering of Buddhism in Vietnam had taken place there, and much of this aura lingered on in the form of a longing for the past. In this region approximately 80 percent of the population was Buddhist; moreover, in contrast to the rest of Vietnam, where Buddhism was fragmented and disorganized, it was militant, well organized and extremely well led in Hué. And whereas in most parts of the country there was a modicum of religious tolerance, in the central coastal region, and particularly in Hué, the very strong religious feelings had practically brought the Buddhists and the Catholics to the verge of a religious war. Correspondents talking to young Catholic priests in Hué were stunned by the venom with which they described the Buddhists and their religion; talking with Buddhists, the same correspondents came away frightened about what would happen if a Buddhist government ever took over in Saigon. It is hardly surprising that even after the fall of Diem, whose family exacerbated the tension, this religious conflict has continued, with both sides claiming that the Government is favoring the other.

As far as can be determined, what provoked the Buddhist crisis in Hué was a series of coincidences. Several days before the outbreak, Archbishop Thuc had celebrated his twenty-fifth year as bishop. It was a great occasion, and both the Government and Vatican flags were flown from rooftops and church steeples. Diem attended the festivities, and when he saw the flags, which violated a Government law proclaiming that only the Vietnamese flag could fly in public, he issued a statement calling attention to this ordinance.

Unfortunately, Buddha's birthday—his 2587th—came only a few days after this announcement, and the Buddhists in Hué wanted to fly their flag too. The Government prohibited this, and also denied a Buddhist request that their leader, Thich Tri Quang, be allowed to speak on the local radio. The Buddhists, aroused and well organized, marched on the radio station, where they were turned away. At this, thousands of angry, militant Buddhists massed in a square in the middle of the city, and the police could not break up the demonstration. Finally, Government troops were brought in; the major in command ordered them to fire, and they shot into the crowd. No intermediate step, such as firing over the heads of the crowd or using tear gas, was taken. Nine people were killed, and an armored car rolled over some of the victims.

The first official version of the incident was the Government's; it stated that a Vietcong agent had thrown a grenade into the crowd. But this account was slowly discredited as more details became known; a group of West German doctors, working in Hué as part of an exchange program, produced eyewitness and photographic evidence that supported the subsequent Buddhist version. The Government quickly buried the victims without performing any autopsies, and stuck steadfastly to its grenade story—one more example of its policy of blaming anything awkward on the Vietcong. Conflicting reports continued to filter in; the American consulate in Hué reported to Saigon that the Buddhist version was correct and that the Government's was completely inaccurate.

During all of this I sat in Hong Kong, admiring the scenery and being glad that I was out of Saigon. Bob Trumbull, then the *Times'* chief correspondent in Southeast Asia, with headquarters in Hong Kong, and a wise and thoughtful man with more than two decades of experience in the area, said, "This is the kind of thing which gets going in Asia and then keeps on building. It sounds like the students in Korea. Vietnam may be ripe for it."

But Charley Mohr, who at that time was the *Time* bureau chief in Hong Kong, came closest to putting his finger on the situation. "It's the same old story. Diem can't admit he's wrong, and so the Government will pretend it didn't happen, and they'll lie and make a hell of a lot of people angry."

It was hardly surprising that the Government's pride and sense of infallibility expanded what should only have been an ugly incident into a crisis that rocked the country. An American intelligence officer was with Bui Van Luong, the Minister of the Interior, when he was sent by Diem to Hué in order to give the President a personal report on the situation. The facts soon became apparent, and the American suggested that the remedy was simple: reparations of about five hundred thousand piasters (about seven thousand dollars), and an immediate public statement admitting that the Government troops were at fault. The minister reportedly answered, "The money is all right, but we can't issue the statement. We can't admit that we did it." Because Bui Van Luong was so afraid to tell Diem the truth, he returned to Saigon and told Diem that the Government version of the incident was correct—that the Vietcong had engineered the incident. Once again the carefully rigged system of the Palace had done its job; Diem, completely separated from reality, was permitted to think what he wanted to think.

Thus began the Buddhist crisis. It was to last for four months, and it was finally to create the atmosphere in which the Government fell. In the beginning it was primarily religious, with limited objectives; in the end it was primarily a political movement clearly trying to bring down the Government, to which all dissident elements in the country had rallied. It was to encompass all the problems of the Government: its inability to rule its own people; the failure of the American mission to influence Diem; the growing power of the Nhus; and the Government's totally unrealistic assessment of the population. Observing the Government during those four months was like watching a government trying to commit suicide.

In dealing with the Buddhist crisis, the Government was limited by its previous attitudes and by its estrangement from the masses. The kind of simple gestures which would have settled the crisis immediately—such as a propitiatory appearance by Diem at a pagoda, which would have generated some badly needed popularity—were alien to its character. Moreover, almost as soon as the crisis reached its peak, in the fourth week, such a gambit became impossible, for by that time it would have been interpreted not as a sign of generosity—for this was a government which had never operated generously before and had never shown itself willing to compromise—but as a sign of weakness.

In the Buddhist crisis the Government was not dealing with Americans who would naïvely accept its words and signed pieces of paper at face value, but with its own shrewd people, who knew more about the Government than *it* knew about *them,* who could predict Government reactions and who could behave on the assumption that these reactions would certainly be clumsy.

The religious division between Catholics and Buddhists had begun at the time of the partition of the country in 1954. At that time about seven hundred thousand Catholic refugees, many led by their priests, fled from the North to South Vietnam because they feared reprisals and persecution at the hands of the Communists. A lonely, undesirable minority as far as most Southerners were concerned, they found a friend in Diem, became his most enthusiastic supporters and established their own communities. Diem, suspicious of Buddhists and of Southerners, felt that he could trust the newcomers; after all, they were refugees and Catholics, and they had no one to turn to but him. Catholic priests naturally encouraged the relationship and thus became a vital part of the Government; Diem in turn used his religion to prop up his weak administration. Favoritism and abuses inevitably resulted; members of the faith became village leaders, and soon most district and province chiefs were Catholics—often in a province whose population was completely Buddhist. So many members of the trusted secret police apparatus were also of the Church that in central Vietnam the hated local security men were first and foremost thought of as Catholics, not as Government officials.

Anxious and desperate to support Diem, the Americans encouraged some of these practices. As early as 1955, Graham Greene wrote in a newspaper article, "Mr. Diem's general piety has been exploited by his American advisers until the Church is in danger of sharing the unpopularity of the U.S.A. . . . Diem's ministers are not all Catholics, but Diem, justifiably suspicious of many of his supporters, has confined the actual Government to himself and members of his family. Diem may well leave his tolerant country a legacy of anti-Catholicism." Catholics benefited from the relief and aid programs, received priority to build schools and permission to cut and sell lumber from carefully protected national reserves, and were granted special commercial-trade benefits. Because priests interceded for them, in the Government's land-development schemes Catholics often were given the best lands, and during the building of the strategic hamlets they were often exempted from the physical labor performed by Buddhists. In 1957 and 1958, when the Government opened land-development centers in the central highlands, the province chiefs in the central coastal region forced Buddhists to move to them, but Catholics were often exempted. In some areas there was mass conversion of villages to avoid this uprooting. In addition, young Buddhist priests were harassed and often forbidden by the authorities to travel in the interior, and there were persistent reports that several of them had been murdered. (After the November 1, 1963, coup, the Buddhist inhabitants of many of these land-development areas returned to their former villages, and one of General Khanh's* first orders after taking power in 1964 granted them permission to do so.)

Yet official religious discrimination was the exception. What the situation boiled down to was that an authoritarian Government, which was more mandarin than Catholic, nonetheless seemed to the Buddhists to be *Catholic*-authoritarian, particularly because in the central coastal region young priests were taking advantage of the prevailing sentiment in Saigon and indulging in the kind of abuses that Diem himself would never have countenanced.

Thus, the religious dispute was as much a product of the regime's shakiness as a cause, and its explosiveness could be traced to the fact that the Americans had backed a man whose minority religion was regarded by many Vietnamese as the religion of the West and of colonialism. The Buddhists resented the fact that they were second-class citizens in a country where their religion had once flowered and dominated. They felt that since foreign powers had come to play a major role in Vietnam, they had been neglected; this had been true under the French, and now the Buddhists never saw the American ambassador or a reporter, and they never won fellowships to the United States.

These grievances had been smoldering when the incident took place in Hué. The Buddhists considered theirs the majority religion, and it was true that the Catholics held power and office far out of proportion to their number but that was partly because of necessity. In general they were wealthier, better educated and better trained because of their advantages under the French, and they had been quicker in spotting the nature and the threat of Communism in Vietnam—for obvious reasons they had more motivation to oppose it. Lastly, in any society, and particularly in a new one, education and wealth give the privileged a head start, so naturally, the elite do their best to perpetuate the status quo.

During the latter years of Diem's regime, however, Buddhism began to attract many Vietnamese who were opposed to the Ngos. There was no political opposition party, and the family controlled virtually every organization in the country. In these circumstances Buddhism had an attraction because it was *not* Catholic, *not* under the auspices of the Ngo family— and because it was traditionally Vietnamese. Almost as soon as the incident in Hué took place, before a protest movement was even under way, a Vietnamese professor told Sheehan: "You Americans look around and see that the Vietnamese are orderly and quiet, and you think everything is all right here. But this is not so. We Vietnamese have been living under oppression for centuries. When the time is right, the people express themselves in one way or another. Today they dare not make outright political protests, so they express their feeling through religion."

*General Nguyen Khanh, a Buddhist, was the leader of a group of younger officers who took control of the South Vietnamese government on January 29, 1964, in a bloodless coup against the older officers who had staged the original coup against Diem. He proved no better at establishing political stability, however, and was himself overthrown in February 1965.

Early in May a group of Buddhist elders went to see Diem. They were representative of the older and more moderate Buddhist leadership, and they wanted to discuss the Hué incident and several other, long-standing grievances, such as the right to fly the flag. Diem met with them for several hours, then authorized his spokesman to issue a statement to the reporters that he had told the Buddhists they were "damn fools" to be concerned about religious freedom; the constitution of the country guaranteed it, and *he* was the constitution. After the meeting the Buddhists had a statement of their own; they said quietly that the President had been very nice, but that they were not satisfied with his answers.

To most reporters and observers, that seemed the end of that: the Buddhists would return to their pagodas in anger, another element of the restless population would be outraged by the Government, the American mission would say that Diem had treated the Buddhists with firmness, thus gaining their respect, and business would continue as usual.

We were wrong. The first thing we learned about the Buddhist leaders was that they were remarkably tough. On occasion they were passive and unworldly, at other times they were overly suspicious or too calculating for their own good, but always they were resolute and committed. There was no bluff to them; they had considerable popular support and their followers would do almost anything they wanted; and they never indulged in empty threats.

At the time of that first meeting the Government held that the Buddhist protest was to be taken not as a legitimate grievance of the population worthy of investigation, but as an affront to the President. The Government line of reasoning was very simple: protesting the lack of religious freedom was an insult to Diem because he ruled the country and he was against such discrimination. In effect, the Buddhists were saying that he was unjust, but this was not so. Besides, he was very well informed about what had happened in Hué and how the population felt. Why, his own Minister of the Interior had confirmed that the Communists had thrown a grenade, and his officials here in Saigon knew that the people were with him, and that the trouble was being caused by some radical priests whom the population would know better than to follow.

But this new challenge posed complicated problems that Diem was ill prepared to meet. He could not satisfy them with empty promises—as he could the Americans; or play one faction against another—as he could with the Army; or cut off any funds, since such a threat meant nothing to the Buddhists. He could not imprison them as he would a group of political leaders; to arrest priests was more difficult, more dangerous and would have vast international implications—quite apart from the fact that trying to check aroused Buddhists is like trying to stop quicksilver. The Buddhists also turned out to have an extremely effective intelligence system, for there were many of them in clerical and menial jobs throughout the key areas of the Administration who provided the latest information on what the Government was doing and thinking.

Diem continued to be ill informed. Midway through the Buddhist crisis he summoned Lieutenant Colonel Pham Ngoc Tao, an extremely bright officer who had once served as province chief in Kien Hoa. He was a former Vietminh leader and his brother was Hanoi's ambassador to East Germany. Because of Palace intrigues, Tao had been transferred to a relatively unimportant job inspecting strategic hamlets, but this duty took him regularly into the countryside. He and Diem retained a mutual personal affection for each other—though it later turned out that at that very moment he was one of the chief plotters in the young officers' coup because he felt that the Government was completely out of control.

After greeting Tao, Diem immediately asked him what the people in the countryside were thinking. Fully aware of the populace's discontent and realizing what Diem's reaction would be, Tao quickly changed the subject. The two men chatted for a few minutes and then Diem repeated the question. Again Colonel Tao evaded answering.

But Diem would not be put off. "What do the people think?" he said.

"Well, Mr. President," Colonel Tao said as diplomatically as he could, "the people are not very happy."

At which Diem charged out of his chair in a rage and said angrily, "It is all Communist propaganda."

I returned from vacation on May 28; by then any normal government would have settled the Buddhist incident, but in Vietnam it was just beginning. In the early afternoon of my first day back several hundred monks suddenly materialized in front of the old opera house—which was where the National Assembly convened—to draw attention to the start of a two-day hunger strike. The monks showed considerable organizational ability; obviously they were going to be formidable foes. Closely watched at their pagodas by secret police, they had quietly slipped into four buses (with drawn shades) in different parts of town, had circled separately all over the city and had disembarked in the central square at exactly 2 P.M., to begin their protest. They stayed there for three hours and then marched back to their pagodas at 5 P.M., just as many Vietnamese were returning from work. This demonstration made a profound impression: people were startled and moved, for no open protest against the Government had been held in Saigon for many years.

Thus were we reporters initiated into a new world, that of Vietnamese Buddhism, a world in sharp contrast to the Vietnam we knew. We spent endless hours waiting at pagodas and sparring verbally with agile Vietnamese spokesmen; we drank innumerable cups of tea served with the penetrating odor of rotting cabbage wafting in the background (even today when I am offered tea, I automatically sniff for the smell of boiling cabbage). Unlike the Vietnamese we knew best—the lean, rugged Army officers whose lined faces were eloquent evidence that they had survived two decades of warfare, or the sharp-faced Vietnamese newsmen who had lived by their wits and survived intrigue—the Buddhist monks looked like people who had been sheltered from the world. Their faces were smooth and unlined, almost a little sickly, and their hands were soft. Unlike many educated Vietnamese, they had had little contact with the Western world. Only one of them had been to the United States, for a year of study at Yale; because of this, he had once met Ambassador Nolting and was known among his peers as "the American Buddhist." If a priest spoke French or English, he automatically became a spokesman.

At times the Buddhist monks were incredibly naïve about the outside world, but they were also cynical and quick to suspect the worst of everyone. Once I asked Duc Nghiep, one of their spokesmen, his opinion of Madame Nhu. "She is the Vietnamese Lady Macbeth," he answered. "She and her husband want to kill the King of England." A little later he said that many of the Buddhists wanted to burn themselves to death to protest the lack of religious freedom. I asked him why he didn't set fire to himself. "Every priest has his job to do," he answered seriously. "Some priests burn themselves; my job is to talk to you."

If an American reporter wrote a story that displeased the Buddhists they were not only apt to hold press conferences denouncing him, but they were sure that he must have been bought by the Ngo family. They did not understand the function of a free press, but they quickly sensed that it could be used and that it gave them some protection. Early in the crisis reporters received an anonymous tip that Buddhists distributing literature had been arrested by the police. When newsmen arrived on the scene they found only a few monks. Where were the police, the reporters asked. "Oh, we told them that we had called the foreign press, and so they let us go," one of the monks said. Thereafter a deputation of us called on one of the Buddhist leaders to explain that reporters were not policemen or bodyguards.

On another occasion during the middle of the crisis we were all gathered at the Xa Loi pagoda because we'd heard that something was going to happen. Duc Nghiep walked up to us and suggested that we go home. "There will be no human sacrifice today, gentlemen," he said. Half an hour after we had departed, the Buddhists charged out of Xa Loi and held a large demonstration in front of the residence of Ambassador Nolting. Later one of the reporters asked Duc Nghiep why he had sent us away. "Ah," said the Buddhist, "because when you left, the secret police left too, and when they were gone we could leave the pagoda and demonstrate."

Diem regarded the Buddhists with a certain amount of tolerance—though he felt more at ease with Catholics around him—probably because he did not consider Buddhism a truly serious religion. But in this struggle he was a victim of his own vanity—and very much a prisoner of his family. Archbishop Thuc and the Nhus all urged a hard line against the Buddhists; since the crisis had emanated from his own area, Thuc felt that concessions to the monks would be a slap at him. The Nhus opposed conciliation simply on principle and were openly contemptuous of Buddhists—Mrs. Nhu going so far as to state publicly that they were Communist-dominated. She also felt that culturally they were beneath the Ngo family and Catholics in general. "It is embarrassing to see people so uncultured claiming to be leaders," she told me. In another and quite revealing interview with Charley Mohr, she said that there were few devout Buddhists, and that worried Buddhist leaders were using the crisis to try to convert people to Buddhism, "otherwise they fear that eighty percent of the country would become Catholic."

Of all the members of the family, only Ngo Dinh Can, ruler of Hué, was reported to be urging a conciliatory approach. Considered by many people to be the most practical of all the brothers and the most Vietnamese (he was very limited in foreign languages and never saw Western visitors), he was rumored to keep a very accurate intelligence service on what the population in his province were doing and thinking, and he knew enough to be worried about the growing strength of the Buddhists.

The country was ripe for a group which would stand up to the family. As the protest continued, it seemed to be gaining strength and enthusiasm and a wider base of support. On June 4 I wrote that what had started as a religious protest had become "predominantly political," and that the Buddhists were providing "a spearhead for other discontented elements." By June 11 I was reporting that the dispute "had become a full-scale political protest," and by July 2 I was writing that "Diem and his family are now engaged in an all-out fight for political survival . . . Before, there was no organized dissent. Now a small patch of yellow cloth, normally a sign of Buddhist loyalty, is worn widely and defiantly as a badge of political opposition . . . The younger priests now give the impression of trying to keep the dispute simmering so that eventually someone else will capitalize on the feeling of protest . . ."

At the beginning of the crisis the priests had seemed frightened and a little unsure of themselves, but then they grew more confident; they were well aware that at least two groups were plotting coups. By the end of June the family was tightening its security measures, and the tension was building in Saigon.

Throughout all of this the American embassy was the unhappy partner of the Government. Day after day, as the Buddhist protests increased and received world-wide publicity, the Americans became more embarrassed. The image—largely created by the Americans—of Diem leading a widespread, solid national movement toward certain victory was being shattered, and so was the idea that the Americans could influence the Ngo family. Every day the embassy urged a quick settlement; every day it received a chilly response. "The longer this goes on, the more Diem turns toward the bosom of his family," one foreign service officer told me. The Americans were also angered by Madame Nhu's anti-Buddhist statements, and they urged Diem to control her. "The Americans want this to go away. They want to make everyone happy," Madame Nhu later told me. "Trueheart [William Trueheart, the deputy chief of mission in charge of the embassy during Nolting's absence on home leave] told the President that if I was not silenced they would have to withdraw support. The Americans were trying to blackmail me.''

In this crisis, with our international prestige linked to Vietnam, all the weaknesses of the American tactics toward Diem became evident. Basically Nolting's idea had been the "money in the bank" policy—that is, he would go along with Diem as often as possible in order to gain the President's confidence, in the hope that when the embassy wanted to make a stand on a matter truly important to American interests it would have "credit in the bank." The policy backfired, however; Diem trusted Nolting personally, but there would be no credit for the ambassador to draw on. A particularly humiliating example was when Jim Robinson of NBC was expelled for calling the family a "clique"; Nolting spent more than three hours arguing the expulsion unsuccessfully with Diem. Later, American policy opposed Diem's decision to break off relations with Laos, but Nolting could not change the ruler's mind. Finally, the embassy was never able to persuade Diem to make the kind of concessions to Prince Sihanouk, the Cambodian leader, that the United States felt were desirable for peaceful relations between the two countries.

At times Nolting would gain minor victories, but despite his good will and good intentions the relationship between the two men was undermined by the fundamental differences between their two governments. The psychology and outlook of the Ngo family were so completely alien to those of Washington that the alliance was almost doomed from the start. At best the two administrations could have had a paper agreement; in theory they might agree; but in practice they were talking about different problems, different beliefs, different worlds, and—despite their mutual fear of Communism—different enemies. The Vietnamese were not really interested in what the Americans thought about the Buddhist crisis; they knew that their ally was nervous about the international implications of that struggle and that the Americans' chief concern was the war, not the survival of the family and its conception of domestic balance. The Ngos felt that their basic duty was to stay in power; they did not want American advice in any area—particularly in what they considered a domestic problem. The Americans, on the other hand, disapproved of the Government's position in the Buddhist crisis, and saw it as an opportunity to reunite the people and instill a sense of national purpose. They received assurances from Diem that he was working toward a conciliation, but looked in vain for such a gesture.

During these weeks, when the Americans were obviously trapped by their own policy, reporters talking to embassy officials were surprised by how poorly, particularly in the beginning, the mission was informed about developments in the Government and among the Buddhists. At the same time, because American policy heretofore had deliberately included inordinate praise of the family, Washington was also circumscribed. It could put little effective pressure on Diem behind the scenes; yet any public statement dissociating the United States even slightly was extremely awkward, because it would contrast so sharply with previous statements and would have a profound effect on Vietnamese domestic politics. The turmoil in Saigon during those days was such that any whisper of withdrawal of American support for Diem might easily have touched off a coup. Thus, the American officials had little room to maneuver in, and while they coaxed the family they watched American prestige being dragged down with it.

But even as the Americans were attempting to persuade Diem to make a move of conciliation toward the Buddhists, the Nhus were countering with pressures of their own. On June 8, Madame Nhu issued a strong statement in direct contradiction to the stated Government policy of reconciliation. Madame said that the Buddhists had been infiltrated by Communists and that they were being duped, and she threatened strong Government action against them. Once again this was an example of the power and shrewdness of the Nhus; they often announced policy without consulting Diem, knowing that he would never contradict them publicly or rebuke them privately. They also realized that if they seized the initiative he would eventually come around to their position.

"If that's policy, it's a disaster," said one American embassy official after her speech. But to the Buddhists it *was* policy, for they had to live in the country and were subject to the whims and beliefs of the family. Since Madame Nhu's remarks helped to convince the Buddhists that they would be captives of the Nhus, the price of reconciliation went up immediately.

While the Buddhist movement had been gathering momentum, its leaders had talked to reporters about the possibility of such dramatic protests as a monk burning himself to death; none of us, however, took such threats seriously. On the morning of June 11, I was sleeping late when I got a panicky call from Nguyen Ngoc Rao, the Vietnamese reporter for UPI. His voice was almost out of control; all I could understand was that I should get to the corner of Le Van Duyet and Phan Dinh Phung streets as quickly as possible. I grabbed Ray Herndon of UPI, who was staying at the house, and we dashed for the corner six blocks away. As we arrived we saw a crowd of chanting Buddhists in their orange robes. Just another demonstration, I thought; we had become so used to these by then that I silently cursed Rao for waking me up. But at that moment I looked into the center of the circle and saw a man burning himself to death.

I was to see that sight again, but once was enough. Flames were coming from a human being; his body was slowly withering and shriveling up, his head blackening and charring. In the air was the smell of burning flesh; human beings burn surprisingly quickly. Behind me I could hear the sobbing of the Vietnamese who were now gathering. I was too shocked to cry, too confused to take notes or ask questions, too bewildered even to think.

Later we learned that the man was a priest named Thich Quang Duc

Thich Quang Duc, a 73-year-old Buddhist monk, sits motionless in the middle of a busy Saigon intersection while flames engulf him on June 11, 1963. (AP/Wide World Photos)

who had come to the square as part of a Buddhist procession, had been doused with gasoline by two other priests, had then assumed the cross-legged "lotus" position and had set a match to himself. As he burned he never moved a muscle, never uttered a sound, his outward composure in sharp contrast to the wailing people around him. I had never felt such conflicting emotions: one part of me wanted to extinguish the fire, another warned that I had no right to interfere, another told me that it was too late, another asked whether I was a reporter or a human being. All around this scene of medieval horror were the signs of modern times: a young Buddhist priest with a microphone saying calmly over and over again in Vietnamese and English, "A Buddhist priest burns himself to death. A Buddhist priest becomes a martyr." Pictures were being taken of the immolation; Malcolm Browne and Bill Ha Van Tran had been tipped off earlier, and both had taken dramatic photos of the burning.

To Madame Nhu this event was simply a barbecue and an affront, but to thousands of Vietnamese it was an emotional and momentous occasion. The Buddhist leaders played this reaction skillfully; they took Quang Duc's heart to the pagoda and placed it in a jar, claiming that since the heart did not burn, Quang Duc had left this world unsatisfied. This simply added to the legend; Quang Duc had become a martyr for the people in many parts of Vietnam.

The Government, now very much on the defensive, began to circulate rumors: that Quang Duc's fellow priests had set him on fire, and that he had been unable to feel any pain because he had been heavily dosed with morphine. These reports simply made the population angrier; no Vietnamese and few Americans believed them.

For whether the Government liked it or not, the Quang Duc suicide had electrified the population, though the dramatic effect was somewhat mitigated later when other Buddhists rushed to burn themselves to death too. Whatever complaint an individual Vietnamese harbored against the Government, he was sure—however irrationally—that Quang Duc had killed himself for *his* particular grievance.

The United States was staggered by the suicide and by the world's reaction to it, and Washington redoubled its efforts for a settlement. It quietly warned the Ngo family that the United States might have to dissociate itself from the Government unless it made peace with the Buddhists. Under this unwanted pressure from the Americans, the Government finally met with the Buddhists, and on June 16 the two sides produced a joint communiqué. It was a curious mixture of the views of both sides, but on the most crucial of the five Buddhist demands—the admission of responsibility for the Hué incident—the announcement simply stated that an all-government commission would investigate the circumstances of the deaths. The communiqué was signed by President Diem; at the bottom he added a special notation saying that he had believed in these points all along—thus saving face by implying that he was conceding nothing.

The joint communiqué pleased neither side; it simply hardened the disagreement and changed the complexion of the protest. For it was only a piece of paper; it had no more meaning than the good will of both parties, and simply the act of signing angered the Nhus and disturbed the younger Buddhist priests.

The communiqué was signed early in the morning, and according to a reliable Palace source the Ngo family was having chicken soup for lunch when Madame Nhu read it. She berated Diem for cowardice and called him a jellyfish for even negotiating. "You defeated the Binh Xuyen, you defeated the Hoa Hao [two sects], you defeated the paratroopers, and now you have lost to a few miserable unarmed bonzes," she said. "You are a coward."

Diem allegedly answered, "You do not understand this affair. It has international implications. We had to settle it."

At this point, it is said, Madame Nhu picked up the tureen of soup and threw it across the table. "And so, there was no chicken soup for lunch," said my Palace informant.

Among the Buddhists the reaction toward the document was one of deep suspicion. On the morning the communiqué was issued, several reporters drove to the Xa Loi pagoda to talk with Duc Nghiep. "When I tell some of the other priests what has been signed they will be very angry," he confided.

Suspicions increased in the following days. Not only were there no gestures of reconciliation; just the opposite began to take place. First Nhu issued a secret memorandum to his Cong Hoa Youth movement, calling the Buddhists rebels and Communist-infiltrated, and suggesting that the group urge the Government not to accept the joint communiqué. (The Government almost never made a step without this kind of elaborate sham of popular backing. Although Diem was the head of the Government and had signed the communiqué, Nhu was playing his usual game of telling one of his groups to demand what he had intended all along. He would then tell Diem that the people wanted the Government to turn against the Buddhists, and the family could proceed to do as it wished— in response, of course, to popular demand.)

The attacks on the Buddhists in the English-language newspaper, which was the mouthpiece of the Nhus, worried the Buddhists. Moreover, reporters and diplomatic officials were informed by their Palace sources that the communiqué was not to be interpreted as a sign of weakness; the Government simply intended to wait until the fuss died down and would then arrest some of the Buddhist leaders. Through their own intelligence sources the Buddhists began to glean quite detailed accounts of the Government's plans.

At this time there was a marked change in the Buddhist leadership. Until then the leaders had been the older monks more conscious of tradition, generally more conservative and not as interested in politics as the younger priests. Young Buddhists had been a force in the dispute but the older men had been able to control them up to the signing of the communiqué. Now, however, in late June, the younger leaders, realizing that they were in the movement too deeply for an easy retreat, knowing that they were marked men—and not unhappy about the fact, for they wanted the Government to fall and they wanted to be political—took over. It was easy enough for them to do so; the older Buddhists had been undercut by the Government's behavior since the signing of the communiqué, and their role in Buddhist councils had been weakened.

The young priests represented a new force in Vietnamese politics. Generally in their thirties and early forties, they were men who were clearly affected by living in a nation which had undergone thirty years of political revolution and war. They had grown up in a country in which the mandarin way of doing things had almost always failed, and they had noted the appeal to the population of the Vietminh's dramatic techniques. They were highly skilled in politics, and they had a keen insight about the psychology of their people. Foreigners were always awed at the way the priests could move their people, whether joking with them or inciting them; their mass meetings, in which they encouraged the Buddhist population to participate, resembled the civil rights rallies in Southern Negro churches. They were articulate, brilliant men; the Vietnamese Buddhist movement was clearly one of the few in the country where men of true talent, instead of second-raters, had risen to the top. They could discuss the populace, the war, the family and American foreign policy skillfully and with originality.

Once I told one of the most brilliant of these priests that a friend of mine sympathized fully with their cause, but that he felt they were bad Buddhists. Good Buddhists, my friend had said, were interested in another time and place, not in worldly events. Duc Nghiep looked at me and snapped, "Tell your friend that on his way to the next world a Buddhist priest has responsibilities in this one." He explained further: it was wrong that President Diem had lost the confidence of his people and that his soldiers were like mercenaries who fought with their bodies but not with their souls. Then he looked sad (the Buddhists were always very good at looking sad), and said, "I am a refugee from the North. I know the Vietminh, and I know what they do to religion. Ho Chi Minh is my real enemy, but he is more clever than Ngo Dinh Diem. When Ho Chi Minh stands in front of me he is always shaking my hand and smiling, and when he stabs me it is from behind. But this government is clumsy, and it is trying to stab me from the front. It is all very sad."

President Diem was sixty-two years old, a Catholic, a product of a different generation and of a respectable conservative order; his Buddhist opponents were different in every sense. I believe that the Buddhist crisis was a conflict of generations; it was also a protest against an authoritarian regime, a conflict of two religions, a conflict between the haves and have-nots, but more than anything else it seemed to me a conflict between twentieth-century Asians and the generation which had preceded them. One generation was stiff and righteous in its attempts to cope with new forces by relying on tradition; the other was young and facile, acutely attuned to the rising expectations and aspirations of a repressed population. The young Buddhists resembled the men coming to power everywhere throughout the underdeveloped world, leaders who despite great political and economic problems were able to hold power because of their ability to sense their people's wants.

In the weeks that followed, these leaders skillfully played on the Government's weaknesses. Gradually they turned to provoking it. "We shall throw them the banana peel for them to fall on," one priest told a group of Buddhist youth. They seized the initiative; the Government reacted to *them*, rather than the reverse. Often the Government broke up their demonstrations with violence and bloodshed, and as Bull Connor* and his police dogs in Birmingham were to etch indelibly the civil rights movement in the minds of millions of Americans, so the Buddhists used the Government's repeated clumsiness to commit their people further to their cause and to strengthen the movement. "There is blood on the

---

*Eugene "Bull" Connor, the police commissioner of Birmingham, Alabama, during the 1960s, became a symbol of white Southern racism and brutality when he turned police dogs on civil rights demonstrators in the spring of 1963.

orange robes," a spokesman would say at a demonstration, and the emotional response was always astonishing.

In response, the Government had no policy and no initiative; Diem was too proud. In any case, it was too late to make the kind of gestures which earlier would have ended the conflict; on the other hand, he had promised the Americans that he would not do what he and the Nhus wanted to do —crush the Buddhists.

By late June the Ngo family knew it was in a fight for survival, and that coups were no longer merely being discussed but were actually developing. Stricter security precautions were taken; streets around the Palace were blocked off, security policemen with radiophones were stationed at key spots, all unusual movements were watched and the various secret police agencies were on constant alert. Certain units whose loyalty was considered questionable, such as the air-borne, were ordered on operations designed primarily to keep them out of Saigon. Diem suddenly promoted a large number of young officers, but for some reason he promoted staff officers rather than field commanders. Early in July, Nguyen Ngoc Tho, the Vice-President, announced that a preliminary investigation of the Hué incident confirmed the Government account that the Vietcong were responsible for the deaths. Buddhist leaders in Hué retorted that there had been no investigation—or at least, no Buddhists had been interviewed. Saigon hummed with rumors of intrigue. Watching this slow process of disintegration, it was inconceivable to us reporters that it could be settled without bloodshed.

In mid-July, Ambassador Nolting rushed back from his vacation to try and settle the Buddhist crisis once and for all; reportedly he had been instructed by President Kennedy to "go back there and see if you can't get that guy to play ball." At the airport he made a brief statement which reaffirmed the American belief in religious freedom and failed to mention Diem by name. Later that day Nolting met with reporters at his office. He said he had returned to try to convince Diem to "change his image, both here and overseas." (I remembered the words because it seemed so characteristic of American policy to be worried about images at this moment.) I asked Nolting if he didn't think that in trying to get Diem to change his image the ambassador would be in conflict with Mr. and Mrs. Nhu. The ambassador thought for a moment, and then said no, he didn't.

Nolting's return had little effect; neither side could turn back. Gradually the crisis began to spill into the countryside, and the Americans became even more alarmed. Buddhists demonstrating in Saigon in mid-July were badly roughed up and their pagodas were closed. In an audience with Diem, Nolting urged him to announce a dramatic new policy; the Americans were hoping desperately for that new image. Finally, on July 19, Diem spoke on the radio for about two minutes, and in a cold, brief statement granted one minor concession about the flying of flags. He had little else to say except that the population should respect him, that he would be fair, and that he was forming a special Government committee to investigate Buddhist complaints. But even as he spoke the pagodas were still sealed off with barbed wire.

Of course Diem's broadcast did not have the desired effect on the population or on the Buddhists in particular. In this situation Nolting was almost powerless. He had committed himself totally to Diem; his whole policy was based on his personal relationship with the President and on his ability to influence him. The policy had failed, not because of the ambassador's lack of dedication or skill as a diplomat, but simply because his faith was never reciprocated; it was accepted, but never returned. Now it was rumored that Washington suspected that the policy had failed in other areas, too, and that Nolting would be replaced by a new ambassador. Friends of Nolting's felt he had been badly treated; for months he had not been told whether his tour would be extended. On his departure for home leave at the beginning of the Buddhist crisis, he had told reporters that he was coming back, although at the time Saigon was rife with informed reports that he was through—that he would return only to pick up his suitcases. Eventually it turned out that Nolting apparently was given almost no advance notice of Henry Cabot Lodge's appointment.

At this moment Nolting, cornered, was to involve himself in Vietnamese politics one more time. In late July the most important aspect of the Buddhist crisis was not whether the "good" Buddhists or the "wicked" Government were at fault; the real question—and everyone in Saigon and Washington knew it—was whether the Government was competent to handle the discord, or whether its clumsiness and short-sightedness would allow the Buddhists to become a major and unpredictable force in Vietnamese politics.

It was at this point that Nolting stepped in gratuitously. He said in an interview that he had never seen any evidence of religious persecution in Vietnam; taking matters a step further, he added that he was tired of everyone's tendency to take "his eye off the ball" by spending too much time and energy on the Buddhist question. The crisis was a side issue, the ambassador said; the important thing was to win the war.

Wittingly or unwittingly, with this statement Nolting placed the United States squarely behind Diem in the crisis. The Nhu forces were delighted with the interview: the *Times of Vietnam*, the English-language daily which faithfully reflected the views of Mr. and Mrs. Nhu, headlined the story and labeled Nolting "the first American ambassador to Vietnam really worthy of being addressed by his title." Ambassador Lodge, the paper added, "has mighty big shoes to fill."

Rarely had I seen my Vietnamese friends so angry. They were almost irrational about Nolting, not because he had claimed not to have seen any evidence of discrimination, but because the whole interview seemed to them to symbolize the United States' disregard for their country and problems. "It is always the same with you goddamn Americans," one Vietnamese told me. "During the French Indochina war you told us that if we fought the Communists for the French, you would see that we got independence very soon. Now you tell us to fight the Communists for Diem, and that when there is peace you will get us a good government. We are no longer interested in your goddamn advice."

The Buddhists were no longer interested in Nolting. Duc Nghiep said, "It is only the last present of Mr. Nolting to Mr. Diem. I do not think Mr. Cabolodge [rhymes with camouflage] will be President Diem's cup of tea."

Apparently Nolting realized belatedly what a tempest he had created with his inadvertent and revealing slip. Two days later a CBS television team who had come to his office for an interview watched in amazement as Nolting told an aide to replace the portrait of Jefferson on the wall behind his desk with one of Washington, who, he said, was "less controversial."

Before Nolting departed, Nhu told him that he wanted to name a strategic hamlet after the ambassador at a public ceremony. Since this was obviously a scheme to associate the Americans even more fully with the Nhus in the public mind, Nolting tried to get out of it gracefully by pleading a heavy schedule. But the Nhus were very determined people; Nhu told Nolting to pick any day that would be convenient for him, and the ambassador, trapped, had to give in.

The day was a disaster. A helicopter had killed a little girl in the village the day before while preparations for the ceremonies were being made, and a truck in the caravan ran over another child on the day of the event. The villagers were all carrying small American flags, but their enthusiasm was as ersatz as the occasion itself; they looked pathetically confused and frightened, and with good reason—naming the hamlet after an American ambassador would make it a prime target for the Vietcong.

The reporters who covered the ceremony all noted in their stories that Nolting had done his best to avoid the whole business. Angrily Nolting called up John Mecklin, his public affairs officer, demanded to know how we had gotten that information, and then accused Mecklin of leaking the story. Mecklin replied that no leak was involved, that the story was true, that any reporter with a modicum of intuition would have suspected it and then confirmed it easily, and that the best thing the reporters could have done for Nolting was to publicize his distaste for the affair. Everyone in Saigon, Mecklin said, knew that the ceremony was a fraud; how could anyone take seriously the story that the villagers were supposed to have competed for the honor of having their hamlet named after Nolting by writing the best essay about what the ambassador had done for their country?

Later Nolting called Mecklin back and apologized.

On August 5 the burnings started again, apparently without the knowledge of the Buddhist leadership in Saigon. On that day a monk burned himself to death in Phan Thiet, a small seaport north of the capital. The Government carried off the body.

The suicide in Phan Thiet brought forth more bitter comments from Madame Nhu; she said that she hoped there would be more burnings and that she would clap her hands if there were; the Buddhists should be beaten ten times harder for their behavior, she added. Her comments only provoked further horror. On Monday, August 15, another Buddhist burned himself to death in Hué; the Government troops, using bayonets and swinging steel helmets like billy clubs, snatched the body from the other priests. This in turn bred more death; three days later a Buddhist nun burned herself to death in the seacoast town of Ninh Hoa, allegedly to protest the Government's seizing the body of the Hué priest.

On that very day, Nolting left Vietnam. In the past, airport departures or arrivals had reflected the mood of the mission and of "the team." Such scenes had usually resembled one of Saigon's private parties; senior officers were very much in evidence, reporters were isolated and junior officers avoided being seen with them. But on this day there was a curious change. There was so much bitterness in the American embassy, so many civilians were so fed up with our policy and its equivocations, and so tired of the family's arrogance that we correspondents were now sought out, even welcomed. For the first time officials talked openly with us; no longer were we the enemy, no longer were they worried about being seen with us.

Nolting seemed lonely. In a prepared statement he talked of the mutual bonds of "humility and tolerance, respect for others and a deep sense of social justice" which united the Vietnamese—born of different religions, he emphasized—and the Americans. He added that during his time in Vietnam, progress had been made in education, agriculture and commerce, and in "the inculcation of democratic principles."

Early the next morning a fifty-year-old Buddhist priest burned himself to death. A few days later, Nhu raided the pagodas.

Chapter 9

The Raid on the Pagodas

Within weeks of my arrival in Saigon in 1962 I had lunch with John Richardson, the chief of the CIA in Vietnam. He was a good man, honest and dedicated, and in his personal philosophy he leaned toward the viewpoint of the American right—though this was not by any means reflected in his operatives. Our talk was pleasant that day, but peculiarly involved in a long, abstract discussion on the nature of counterinsurgency. I was never quite sure that I understood Richardson correctly, for our terms and points of reference were so different.

One part of that first conversation I remember distinctly: our discussion of the Nhus. Nhu, Richardson said, was a great nationalist. When I mentioned some of Nhu's anti-American remarks and the resentment many anti-Communists felt toward him, Richardson said that the anti-Americanism was simply a product of Nhu's nationalism. He was a proud Asian, but he was also for us; more important, he was the one man who understood the strategic hamlet program. As for Mrs. Nhu, she too was a nationalist, according to Richardson—perhaps a bit extreme occasionally, and sometimes a little emotional, but that was typical of women who entered politics—look at Mrs. Roosevelt.

I was new in Saigon at the time, but I was not that new. On the way back to town our host, one of the embassy officials, suggested that I write a story about what he termed the change in Nhu: "The new Nhu." I said that I would wait.

What happened in the following months convinced me that Nhu was anything but a nationalist: he seemed to me to be a born intriguer, suspicious of his ally, taking great delight in dividing his people and in controlling the population—altogether a brilliant but warped man.

The disparity between Richardson's and my views evolved in part from the different nature of our jobs. The CIA was not simply a group of sophisticated young Americans who were predicting events in a somewhat predictable nation. Had this been its role it would have accomplished it handily—but it would also have exposed the weakness of our policy. The fact was, the CIA was not in Saigon just to analyze and evaluate, it was a participant in some of our programs, trying to make them work in order to turn our overall policy into a success. I am not familiar with the full extent of the CIA's responsibilities in Vietnam, but I do know that it was directly involved in the montagnard* arming and training program, as well as in the operation of the strategic hamlet program in some areas. Also, part of Richardson's assignment was "to get close to Nhu." Since Nhu was the key man in the Ngo family, and therefore of the Government, it followed that in Vietnam part of the CIA's role was to influence the Government in the direction we wanted it to take.

In Richardson's eyes Nhu was the most influential man in the country (which perhaps he was), not the most hated man (which he certainly was). In staying close to Nhu, Richardson had to pay the price of taking Nhu's words for an event, even of seeing the situation through his eyes. Consequently, it would have placed his position with Nhu in jeopardy if his agents were working the other side of the street and gleaning intelligence —as they should have been—from anti-Nhu sources. Furthermore, since Nhu and his wife were hated and feared in Vietnam, the fact that our intelligence chief was close to Nhu placed a considerable damper on the gathering of intelligence. One of the most frequent criticisms about the CIA by responsible Vietnamese—indeed about the entire American mission—was that information given Americans about the Ngos went right back to the Palace, apparently in an attempt to buy confidence from the suspicious family.

Thus, with the onset of the American buildup the CIA was operating under considerable pressure in Saigon. As the situation there became more tense, many wary Vietnamese would tell reporters or young political officers what they were hesitant to take to higher embassy officials or the CIA. This was the penalty suffered by an agency whose top members were part of the team.

As the Buddhist crisis developed, the tension and uncertainty in Saigon continued to build. Amid all the rumors it became obvious that two main coups were in the works. It pointed up the degree of the Government's alienation that both revolts were headed by men who until recently had been among the last of Diem's loyal followers. One coup was the senior officers' plot, headed by Duong Van Minh, Le Van Kim and Tran Van Don; the other was the junior officers' coup, and during early August this seemed the more likely one to materialize. Eventually, under somewhat different circumstances, the latter did take place as the Nguyen Khanh coup replacing the older officers' junta, but at the time many of us thought it would take place immediately because its planning was extremely advanced and its leaders impressed us as being bolder than the generals. However, the generals had a habit of ordering key battalions out of town every time the young Turks were ready to strike.

One day in August an important Vietnamese whom I trusted said he

*The montagnard tribes who inhabited the central highlands of South Vietnam were isolated from the rest of the country by geography, culture, and language. Because their territory was of considerable strategic importance, the CIA attempted to enlist them in the war against the Vietcong.

wanted me to have lunch with him and one of his friends. After lunch we repaired to the friend's house in Cholon, the Chinese section of Saigon, where I was told that my two companions were part of the young officers' group which was planning a coup. I was surprised to be given this information, but even more surprised when they told me that they wanted me to cover the story from the inside. They could guarantee nothing if things went sour. Certainly, if the coup failed I would have to leave the country, and there might be even more unpleasant results.

I left them to consider the proposal for a while, talked with Sheehan, decided that journalistically it was worth the risk for such a story, and agreed. Burt Glinn, a photographer then in Saigon for the *Saturday Evening Post,* was also told of the plan, and he too was ready to try his luck. The leaders of the coup gave us a military radio and we were assigned a band and call numbers. We were to be "kidnaped" by the coup plotters and taken to their headquarters; they thought that this would give us a measure of protection if the coup backfired. After that, there was nothing to do but sit back and wait nervously. On several occasions during the next few weeks we were alerted, but each time the generals, now preparing their own coup, switched battalions on the plotters.

But during this same period CIA agents were telling me that their superiors in Vietnam were still so optimistic that they were not taking the turmoil and unrest very seriously. Yet it was well known that the Nhus were angry over what they felt was Diem's weak handling of the Buddhists, and there were reliable reports that Nhu was planning a coup of his own, which would begin with an attack on the Buddhists and would end by making him the strongest man in the country. Finally this became more than a rumor; details of the plan began to filter down. Hearing these, Nick Turner of Reuters went to see Nhu. "I hear you are planning a coup and that you will raze Xa Loi," Nick said. (Only a Reuters man can make a statement like that and get away with it.)

Nhu smiled. At first he denied it; then he began to talk. He said that if the Buddhist question were not solved, it would soon lead to a coup which would be anti-American, anti-Buddhist and anti-weak Government. If such a coup took place, say, at midnight, Xa Loi would be razed by 2 A.M. (Actually Nhu's timing was slightly off; the raid on Xa Loi began at 12:30 A.M. and ended at 2:30 A.M.) There was only one man capable of leading such a coup: Nhu himself. After Turner filed his remarkable story, he was called to the American embassy and asked if he believed Nhu was serious; he answered that he was 99 percent certain.

By this time Nhu had brought his personal military arm, the special forces under Colonel Le Quang Tung, into the city. Tung's troops were an American brainchild. Selected for their physique, specially trained, specially well paid, they were conceived by the American military as an elite force to be employed in counterguerrilla warfare. But the Ngo family had seen fit to make them the political and protective private army of the family, and they had done very little guerrilla fighting. Two battalions of these troops had quietly been brought into Saigon in July, making a total of four in the city.

On August 17 I cabled my office and suggested to my editors that they use every single word coming out of Saigon. Something was on the way, I said, and it was not just Henry Cabot Lodge.

The Buddhists themselves appeared to be at least as much aware of all developments, and their protest seemed to have a mounting intensity. On Sunday, August 18, they put on one of their most impressive demonstrations. Fifteen thousand enthusiastic people, many of them young, flocked to the Xa Loi pagoda. Nguyen Ngoc Rao, the UPI reporter, said that it was the only emotional crowd he could recall since the early days of Diem. The streets were jammed, and when it began to rain the people refused to go home.

It was also a joyous, boisterous crowd. Filming the proceedings on top of the pagoda were two ABC-TV reporters, one of whom was Charles P. Arnot. Suddenly a priest gestured toward the two reporters and spoke a few words; a tremendous roar of laughter went up from the mob. "Thich Quang Do has just told the Buddhists that the foreign correspondents have pledged to go on a day-long hunger strike," Rao whispered to me. Then Quang Do asked the correspondents to address the crowd. Arnot replied that he would be delighted to, but that he would have to cable New York for permission.

The mood of the demonstration was buoyant, but if the priests had said the word, fifteen thousand Buddhists would have marched on Gia Long Palace immediately. However, Lodge was due in a week, and the Buddhists were clearly holding their fire for his arrival. As I wrote two days later—on the eve of what was to be the pagoda crackdown—the Buddhists were playing "a fast and dangerous game."

On Monday, August 19, a Vietnamese friend called; he was much more cautious than usual, and we made an appointment to walk together along the river front. There he told me that Nhu planned to raid the pagodas and that Colonel Tung's troops would be used. That same day we learned that Nhu had held a meeting of the generals and had chastised them for not taking sufficient precautions against a coup. He told them that one was likely to take place, and that if it did, the family planned to evacuate to a hiding place outside the city while the generals surrounded the capital and razed it with artillery instead of fighting at close quarters. If there was a coup, Nhu said, it would be inspired by the intellectuals and would have Western support. (Incidentally, this was the second time that Nhu had talked to the generals about the possibility of a coup; on the first occasion he said that he had heard rumors of one, and that perhaps some of them knew about it. If so, he suggested that they stay and talk with him after the meeting. None stayed.)

That night I filed complete details, including verbatim dialogue, about Nhu's second meeting with the generals, which had taken place only thirty-six hours earlier. I asked a Vietnamese friend what Nhu's reaction would be to the story.

"It will make him glad," the Vietnamese said.

"Why?"

"Because it will make him think that he can't trust the generals," the Vietnamese said. I still did not understand.

"He already distrusts the generals, and this will convince him that he is right and that he is brilliant," the Vietnamese answered.

On the surface, Saigon went its charming, attractive, corrupt way; the security precautions remained tight, the girls remained pretty, and a reporter could write whatever kind of mood piece he wanted ("In this tense city . . ." "In this happy city where tension lurks beneath the tranquil surface . . ." "The tense surface of Saigon today belies . . ."). By this time Sheehan, Perry, Turner, Rao, An and myself had created a small but first-rate intelligence network. Each of us had a different specialty and area: An, for instance, had the best military contacts in the country, since he had served in the Army with many of the majors and lieutenant colonels as a young officer; Rao, by courage and endless hard work, had built a network within Diem's secret police force—such a good network, in fact, that after the coup he was ineffective as a reporter for several weeks because all of his sources were in hiding. We had long suspected that a showdown was coming, and each of us had carefully been cultivating sources so that we would be ready for it. Now, that Monday, a long afternoon of checking on the part of all of us indicated that something was imminent—Rao, for instance, had found that the secret and combat police were on some sort of alert—but we failed to find out exactly what it was. We were all exhausted; for the past five days Sheehan, Turner and I had taken turns staying up all night in order to warn the others in case something broke. Tired and irritable, that evening we decided that the strike would have to come to us.

But on Tuesday afternoon, August 20, I had a drink with Dang Duc Khoi, Diem's information officer who had long since become disenchanted with the President and tired of all the intrigue. "On that matter you inquired about yesterday [the raid on the pagodas]," he said, "I think it will come tonight or tomorrow." I checked another source and received confirmation, then returned to the office and filed a story which said that despite all of the American and Vietnamese officials' talk about the dispute having ended, nothing had been settled, that the Government and the Buddhists were further apart than ever, that the Buddhists were not eager for a settlement, that the Government's initiative had been reduced to deciding whether or not it should keep the bodies of burned monks, that Nhu was restless—and that a showdown was near.

We prepared for a long wait; not sure whether the climax would come that night, the next day or at all, we decided to carry on as if the situation were normal. Several of us were eating when Mert Perry arrived in a cab. An anonymous Buddhist had just called our office and warned that the crackdown was coming that night. The Buddhists, it turned out later, were tipped off by two sources. First, the Buddhist wives of some of the combat police had called and said that their husbands were going to arrest the Buddhist leaders that night; second, people living in areas around the pagodas had warned that secret policemen had been moving into the neighborhood all day. This was an excellent example of the advantage of having the population on your side in a political war.

The group split up and we each started checking different areas. Mert and I toured the pagodas. They were all tightly locked; they were expecting the raid, and the streets around them were deserted and quiet. At the An Quang pagoda the young priests were overjoyed to see us; they must have thought that our presence meant protection. At Xa Loi everything was calm, and some of the leaders were asleep. When we woke them they told us that they knew about the raid, and then went back to bed. Mert and I hurried out; we suspected that the attack was near, and we didn't want to be caught in it.

Mert returned to the office and I to the house, but I had no sooner settled down than Sheehan raced up the driveway in a cab, shouting that he had just seen three trucks filled with troops roar past the house headed in the direction of the An Quang pagoda. I leaped into his cab and we headed for Xa Loi, which was four blocks in the other direction. On the way we passed the Third District police station; in the lot by the headquarters were hundreds of troops in full battle gear and about twenty trucks, some of which were already setting out in the direction of Xa Loi.

We arrived at the pagoda as convoys converged from every direction; it was like being caught in the middle of a vast military operation. Though two hundred troops could have accomplished the mission, several thousand seemed to have been assigned. We were caught in a sea of soldiers; a block and a half from the pagoda there was a traffic jam of troop trucks, and we jumped out of the cab.

What followed was a horror spectacle. Had Nhu wanted to arrest the Buddhist leaders it could have been accomplished efficiently in a few moments, but these troops were enacting a passion play of revenge and terror. Hundreds of them charged inside, and the night was filled with a discordant jumble of the screams of the Buddhists, the shouts and cries of the attackers, the shattering of glass, the cracking of pistols and occasional explosions—all this punctuated by the sound of the gong on top of the pagoda being struck wildly back and forth, clanging desperately in the dark. Around me Vietnamese officers barked orders; unit after unit moved up and charged into the pagoda as if they were sure that the Buddhists had a battalion inside and reinforcements were needed.

There was one particularly chilling sight. A squad of Colonel Tung's special forces, identifiable by their berets and their size, trotted forward in a V-form riot formation, each carrying submachine guns at high port. As they pranced into the pagoda, looking something like a smart football team coming up to the line of scrimmage, the mark of American instruction was all over them, and the endless clanging of that gong seemed to me to signal the end of a foreign policy.

At that moment, similar units were breaking into pagodas in Hué, smashing the giant statue of Buddha and killing, according to the American consul, thirty priests and students. But as I stood listening to the screams in Saigon and watching Buddhists being carried out, it was impossible for me to tell how many were killed and injured; later I learned that several monks were listed as missing and that about thirty were injured or wounded, but the true toll was never known.

The orgy lasted for about two hours because many Buddhists had barricaded themselves inside various rooms of the pagoda and the troops had to take doors off hinges to reach their victims. Though the Buddhists were certainly not cooperating in their arrest, I was puzzled that some of the leaders had not fled to a hiding place, once they knew that the strike was coming. After the coup I asked Thich Quang Do about this, and he answered, "We had done nothing wrong; therefore we could not flee. If we had, it would have been an admission that we were guilty." But my own impression was that the Buddhists were ready to have some martyrs and also that they might have miscalculated the extent of the crackdown; that night raids were conducted not only in Hué and Saigon, but in every major city in the central coastal region; thousands of priests were picked up. There was another possibility: an expectation on the part of the leadership that at the last minute there would be a countercoup by the generals or junior officers.

At this point my problems changed: I had the story, but wasn't sure how to get it out. I slipped away and returned to Sheehan's office. It was two-thirty in the morning, which meant that it was two-thirty in the afternoon in New York. Neil and I compared notes; his vantage point had been better and he had more details than I did. Then we began to try to file. Neil managed to reach the U.S. Army's communications system and was able to talk a specialist there into sending out about a hundred and fifty words—complete with pistol shots and screams—that gave him a world beat. Then we went to the embassy to see what we could find out from them, and whether they would file our stories for us.

There was nothing to learn there, for to our astonishment the embassy had been caught completely unaware by the raids. Another good story, I thought. One of the top officials asked, "Why didn't you tell us?" It seemed incredible that all those people who had been tipping us off for the last thirty-six hours had either not called the embassy—or that if they had, the report had not reached the top officials who were still being assured by the Ngos that there would be no raids. But what happened in the next few days was even more astounding: the raids having taken place, the embassy was unable to learn what had happened or who had been responsible.

Through one more private channel Sheehan and I sent out brief additional reports of three hundred words on what was at least a fifteen-hundred-word story. While this was enough to satisfy my editors in New

York, I felt terribly frustrated; there was so much more to report. Even in that first story, however, I had noted that the raids bore the stamp of Ngo Dinh Nhu; I felt that I had never made a safer assumption.

Sheehan and I toured the city. We saw the tanks and troops, but of course we could not tell who was ordering their movements. When we returned to the office a couple of hours later, there were new developments: martial law had been proclaimed, as well as curfew, the Army had allegedly taken over all civilian functions, and strict censorship was enforced. We found out later that way back in July the generals had decided that one way to get troops into the city for their own coup was to impose a state of martial law; they figured that after Diem had declared it, the troops which would be moved into the city to enforce it could stage their revolt. But when this idea was suggested to the brothers, Nhu, who had been planning the pagoda crackdown, saw it as a perfect cover for his own plot. Adopting the generals' plan in part, he raided the pagodas, using only his own special troops; the Army had taken the initial blame, and the generals had been beaten to the punch.

Plastered to store fronts in Saigon was a long and involved handbill, supposedly written by the Army, which announced that its day of nationalism had finally come. Though the tone of this broadside sounded like something that Nhu, not the Army, had written, everyone's confusion at this point was understandable. The city was filled with troops, and the declaration of martial law and the alleged role of the Army were matters we hadn't counted on and which had to be explained. In our stories written on August 21 we reported the martial law, but added that the exact role of the Army was unclear and that Nhu had obviously played a strong part in what had taken place.

At noon on August 21, under the most difficult conditions—after almost no sleep, with tension everywhere, great fear on the part of our best Vietnamese sources, the curfew which made travel at night impossible, and no communications lines—we went to work to track down the real story.

It was a time of rumors, and thus a time not to be too hasty at the typewriter. In such circumstances a prominent person who has not been seen is often alleged to be either in power or dead, and a reporter can dig up anything he wants to hear. Information is everywhere; it is the evaluation both of that intelligence and of the people who give it which becomes all-important. In trying to determine what had happened and who was in power, our appraisal of the facts as we knew them went something like this:

1. The strike had all the characteristics of the one proposed by Nhu and repeated to us by knowledgeable friends. In addition, the Buddhist sources had confirmed that virtually the same plan was to be executed at that particular moment. Moreover, on the night of the raids I had identified Tung's special forces and two of Nhu's top aides directing

actions at Xa Loi. Lastly, one of our Vietnamese friends had talked to an air-borne soldier who was very angry because many of Tung's troops were wearing air-borne uniforms that night. The implications of this disguise were obvious.

2. It seemed very unlikely to us that the Army would have staged a coup with a blood bath. Though there might be some officers who were annoyed with the Buddhists, one of the first things the Army would seek if it came to power was a rapprochement with the Buddhists.

3. The Ngo family distrusted, feared and felt contempt for the Army, and the purpose of much of its intrigue was to divide it. Yet according to the announcement, the Army and the Ngo family were now sharing power. It was not like the Ngo family to share power with anyone, or any institution—least of all the Army.

4. One correspondent had an interview with Madame Nhu on the day after the pagoda raids. She was in a state of euphoria, chattering like a schoolgirl after a prom. She told the reporter that the Government had crushed the Communist-Buddhists, and referred to this as "the happiest day in my life since we crushed the Binh Xuyen* in 1955." In many ways Madame Nhu was the most forthright member of the family, and she could not possibly have been overjoyed at the idea of the family turning over part of its power to the military. Since for a long time she had been the most active proponent of a strong policy against the Buddhists, it seemed probable that she was celebrating the Ngo family's victory.

5. There were constant humiliations of American officials on the day after the raids. Telephone lines to the houses of the top officials were cut, and the car of the head of the USOM, Joe Brant, was stopped and searched at the entrance on his way to and from work. Other Americans were kept waiting interminably for appointments with Government officials and in securing permits to drive after curfew hours. If the Army had really been in charge, it would immediately have moved to reassure the Americans that it wanted them there and that it needed their support.

All of these factors were in my mind when I started my leg work; it would take very hard evidence indeed to convince me that the pagoda raids had been the Army's show. On the morning of August 22 everything pointed in the other direction.

One of the first conversations I had that morning was with John Richardson, who had asked to see me. In the first hours after the pagoda raids there was already a rumor spreading around among responsible Vietnamese that the CIA had known of the crackdown, indeed had given its approval, and that the event had been specifically timed to occur between American ambassadors so that the United States would not be embarrassed by the affair. In Vietnamese minds this was a logical extension of

---

*The Binh Xuyen was a group of gangsters, with its own private army, that challenged Diem's power at the start of his rule in 1955. Diem's bold and successful drive to eject the Binh Xuyen from Saigon impressed high officials in Washington and cemented the American commitment to his government.

Richardson's close relationship with Nhu and the CIA's with Colonel Tung. It was inconceivable to the Vietnamese that the CIA had not known of the raid, and they were therefore sure that the CIA had sponsored it indirectly or at the very least permitted it. The Vietnamese were ready and anxious to believe the very worst about the Americans at that time.

That morning Richardson was a tired and shaken man. He refuted the rumor immediately. "It's not true," he said. "We just didn't know. We just didn't *know,* I can assure you."

After I left Richardson's office, I continued to check details. Soon a pattern began to develop. Shortly I met an American intelligence friend and asked him who was responsible.

"Nhu and Colonel Tung," he said, and then listed the units which had been involved. "It didn't have a damn thing to do with the Army," he said.

"Why didn't you know?" I asked.

"We should have known," he said. "We had every damn warning you can get. We kept telling *them*"—meaning his CIA superiors—"that Tung had his special forces in town and that something like this might happen. We could have been spared this. We could have headed it off."

Like every other American at this moment he was bitter and angry. The violence of the pagoda raids had come as a shock to almost all the Westerners in Vietnam, and now, as people had time to think, the implications of the event were becoming clear. It meant the death of a policy; it was the end of trying to fool ourselves about our conciliatory effect on Diem, for now the Government would be even more under the influence of the Nhus. Further, since American equipment and American-trained troops had been used, the population would have even less confidence in the United States.

Finally, the violation of sacred promises was a direct slap at the Americans, and since this humiliation had come just as a new American ambassador was on his way, it limited his actions by presenting him with a *fait accompli.* (On the night of August 22, General Ton That Dinh, the one general who had been in on the planning of the strike, told a friend of mine, "I, Dinh, am a great national hero. I have defeated the American Cabot Lodge. He was on his way here to pull a coup d'état, but I, Dinh, the hero, have foiled him.")

However, gathering news and writing it was by then a secondary problem. All normal means of communication were now useless because of the heavy-handed censorship of the regime, and no serious reporter wanted his name to appear over a story which had been strained through censorship. So that day we began to use pigeons: civilians or military personnel flying to other Asian cities who could carry our copy out and then relay it to our home offices. From then on, this meant late-morning deadlines in order to catch the plane, which in turn meant that we had to be at work by 7 A.M., rushing to see sources, often allowing not more than thirty minutes for the actual writing of a story, and then racing to the airport to smuggle out the copy with the passenger.

On August 22 we worked all day to put together a full picture of what had happened. Back at the office Sheehan and I swapped notes and then began writing. It seemed obvious that Nhu had used the Army as a front for his strike, in order to hide his own hand and to give the impression that the raid enjoyed far broader backing than it did—that this was an action of national unity. The story caused the *Times* some confusion because it conflicted directly with what the State Department was telling Washington reporters. The *Times* editors fretted for a while and then ran the two stories side by side on the front page under a headline reading: "Two Versions of the Crisis in Vietnam; One Lays Plot to Nhu, Other to Army." The paper introduced the two pieces with a statement which said:

> The confused situation in South Vietnam was reflected yesterday in conflicting versions of the role played by the Army high command in the Saigon regime's attacks this week against the Buddhists. A dispatch from Saigon quoted reliable sources there as having said that the drive had been planned and executed in its initial stage without the knowledge of the Army. But information received in Washington pictured South Vietnam's Army commanders as having put pressure on President Ngo Dinh Diem to persuade him to act.

My story began: "Highly reliable sources here said today that the decision to attack Buddhist pagodas in South Vietnam was planned and executed by Nhu," that the Army had not seized power and in fact knew nothing about it until the raids were well under way. It said that the troops involved were under the command of Colonel Tung, and that Nhu had acted to teach the Buddhists and the Americans a lesson, and to present Lodge with a *fait accompli.*

Our Washington story showed that Nhu had succeeded in confusing the issue by his use of the Army, for it stated that it was the generals who had pressured Diem into acting.

Later Sheehan and I tried as best we could to reconstruct what had happened in the embassy after the raid.

In general the inclination—indeed, the policy—had been to believe what the Ngo family said. With Nolting gone, Richardson was probably the most influential American in the mission; Diem would not see Trueheart, but Nhu would talk to Richardson. Undoubtedly Nhu fed Richardson his version of the pagoda raids—that the generals had forced the hand of the brothers. The Vietnamese generals had almost no confidence in General Harkins; evidently they were not able to state their case strongly enough to the American military mission and had to turn to lower-ranking CIA agents.

Richardson had always seen events as Nhu wanted him to; like Harkins, the CIA chief felt that our policy was working and the war being won. While high American officials were very unhappy about the pagoda raids, they realized—consciously or subconsciously—that a rejection of Nhu's version meant a complete reevaluation of our stand. Since these American officials were very much a part of that policy and had publicly committed their careers to it, they were in no hurry to write it off. Moreover, Richardson did not have the private sources which would refute Nhu's story, for to have listened to such voices earlier would have been to doubt the effectiveness of the policy. And so Saigon misinformed Washington. It was the last stammer of the old guard.

Meanwhile we reporters continued to file stories in a vacuum; we didn't know what was getting out, what was being printed or what play it was getting if a story was used. Then, four days later, Lee Griggs returned from Manila with a folder filled with messages. My pieces were getting into the paper, it turned out, and there were some complimentary notes, including a particularly nice cable from James Reston:* KEEP GOING BECAUSE WE'RE ONLY GETTING PROPAGANDA THIS END. I also received my first inkling that Washington had been wrong on what had happened: YOUR STORY ON NHU TWINED WITH SZULCS WASHINGTON SAYS GENERALS FORCED NHU TO SILENCE BUDDHISTS. Finally, there was a cable from our foreign desk: STATE DEPARTMENT NOW COMING AROUND TO YOUR VIEW WHAT HAPPENED AND WHO DID IT AT PAGODAS STOP CHEERS AND MORE CHEERS.

Sitting in the office, I clutched the cables and yelled for Sheehan. Hearing the commotion, Mert Perry came downstairs and read the message; together the three of us laughed and laughed. Mert said that it appeared that Washington had finally got the little picture, and went upstairs to get beer for us. Charley Mohr said, "You guys are the first reporters I've ever known who scooped the State Department by four days."

Holding up the cables proudly, I said to Charley, "Well, that's the end of the press controversy out here. We've finally broken through. Now they'll understand."

I was wrong; the stakes were simply bigger from then on, and the press controversy had just begun.

---

*James Reston, a well-known columnist for the *New York Times,* was head of the newspaper's Washington bureau in the 1960s, while Tad Szulc was a *Times* correspondent covering the State Department.

Chapter 10

A Slow Change
in American Policy

Henry Cabot Lodge did not really switch policies when he arrived in Vietnam, but a new policy needed to be evolved. The old policy lay shattered in the Xa Loi pagoda, in the broken promises handed Nolting by Diem, and in the phony version of the raids given the embassy by Nhu. The old policy had not ended at the behest of the Americans; it had been violated so outrageously by the Ngo family that one Western ambassador referred to the pagoda crackdown as "the end of the gallant American effort here."

Only a handful of the most faithful remained loyal to the Ngo family; in Washington the Vietnamese ambassador—Madame Nhu's father—and all but one member of his staff resigned, and her mother, the Vietnamese observer at the UN, also resigned.

The Army, embittered because it had been slandered by being blamed for the raids, was more confused and divided than ever. The brothers offered cash bonuses to some generals as a means to appease them and to cause further dissension; nominally the cash was "to be divided among the troops for their valor," but no one was naïve enough to believe that it would ever reach even a general's chief of staff.

Government workers felt dejected, and American hamlet officials noted that they were having a harder time than ever getting Vietnamese civil servants to go out in the field. The populace itself was angry, not just at the family, but at the United States. In Vietnam, as elsewhere, the tendency is always to blame someone else, and the majority believed that since the special forces troops had been paid for and trained by the United States, the Americans must have been in on the planning.

Saigon had become a city of fear. Nhu's Cong Hoa Youth, who were nothing but armed civil servants, marched through the city's slum areas warning the people that if they participated in any anti-Government activity they would be arrested. Many Vietnamese officials took to sleeping in different houses every night and communicating with one another only by courier. Americans with close Vietnamese friends were unable to see them; many high civilian Vietnamese were arrested; a few fled the country. Some key military men were placed under full-time surveillance by the Government, and the Marine commander, warned that he would be imprisoned if he stayed in Saigon, promptly took his troops out on a series of operations to avoid this.

The Americans in Saigon were confused and unsure of the next step. For despite all the warning signs, the American mission had little in the way of contingency plans; they had really believed their own words about there being no alternative to the Ngo family.

A couple of days later a statement broadcast over the Voice of America, a carefully calculated reference to the fact that the United States now absolved the generals from the pagoda raids and blamed them on Nhu, was perhaps a subtle hint that Washington was no longer fully committed to the Ngos. But the mission had few strong contacts with the Vietnamese Army at this point, and it was certainly not trusted by the dissident elements of the military. The generals were uncertain about American intentions, for no groundwork had been laid. The ordinary Vietnamese were no surer of what the United States planned to do; the last American face they had seen was that of an embarrassed Ambassador Nolting having a hamlet named after him, and the last public comment had been that of General Harkins saying that the strategic hamlet program was working and that victory was near. Thus, the Voice of America broadcast reached unreceptive ears.

In the middle of all this confusion, the Nhus were happy and confident. Diem was little heard from or seen, and the Nhus dominated the Government. Cong Hoa officials told reporters that there were plans for a huge mass meeting at which Nhu would be urged to take power. Eventually this was postponed because of the frigid American reaction to the idea; at that point the Americans were exerting considerable pressure on the Nhus to leave the Government. But Nhu and his agents continued to be active. More arrests followed—of professors, lawyers, civil servants, and some key young officers who were reportedly imprisoned primarily as a warning to their superiors. Nhu seemed to be completely carried away with himself. A few days after the raids he sent out a directive to all civil servants demanding that they confess their thoughts during the Buddhist crisis and the martial-law period.

"You are asked to confess sincerely and with a sense of responsibility and honor," the directive said. Typical questions were: "What ideas did you have when 'the Buddhist affair' flared up in Hué until the joint communiqué was signed (ideas about the acts of the Government and those of the Buddhist extremists)?" Then followed an extraordinary sentence: "This part of the directive will be devoted to self-confession about your behavior without time limits. The self-confessor will comment on his behavior since his acts were related to [*sic*] the following items: Your sense of responsibility and your way of serving. Your bad habits. You are requested to outline a method to eliminate your listed drawbacks." Lastly, each civil servant was directed to sign with the following notation: "I certify that this self-confession is sincere."

In an interview with a Canadian reporter, Nhu stated that it was "extremely unpleasant, a real martyrship for me to engage in politics," but that his country's needs demanded it. He also said that even if the Americans cut off aid to Vietnam, the war would be won because of the strategic hamlet program and because of the hamlet cadres "who are loyal to me."

Nhu and Diem had always triumphed in the past because they were almost the only men in Saigon, Asian or Western, who knew exactly what they wanted. Other Vietnamese had been divided, irresolute or naïve; as for the Americans, potentially they could have wielded a great deal of influence, but since they did not have to live under the Government they were supporting, they had used this power without much discipline, almost idly, and had not taken the day-to-day political developments as seriously as their position and responsibilities called for. Now Nhu, who was sure that he was winning the war, thanks to the twisted reports of his hand-picked men, really believed that he had triumphed over his two other enemies as well—the United States and the Buddhists.

In all of Saigon there was only one loud voice of protest: in the days after the pagoda raids, the Buddhists' place as demonstrators was taken by the students. Saigon's students, traditionally uninterested in politics, living in comfort far removed from the grimness of the guerrilla war, became the new protesters against the Government by going on strike at the schools and inviting mass arrests. First it was the university students, and thousands of them were arrested; when they were gone, their places were taken by the high school students, and thousands of them were arrested. For a week the Saigon streets were filled with students being carted off to indoctrination centers.

The Government reacted in the only way it knew how—by beating some of the leaders and arresting most of the followers. Of course the regime charged that the students had been infiltrated by Communists, and a press conference was held in which two alleged Communist teenagers confessed that they had corrupted an entire high school. But if they were Communist-influenced, these students came from the most unlikely backgrounds: at the universities they came from Saigon's best homes, and most of the rebellious high schools were in neighborhoods composed primarily of Catholic refugees from North Vietnam, Army officers and upper-echelon civil servants. Again and again we reporters saw high Army officers trying to negotiate the release of a son from a compound, and most of the students also had brothers or friends who were Army officers. The Government was handling the situation as it had handled other protests, but each time it was cornered, the wall behind it was closer.

This was the situation into which our new ambassador was thrust. As any housewife with a television set knows, Lodge is a handsome man, the image of the perfect American ambassador. He is not unaware of this. His back-

Henry Cabot Lodge presents his credentials as the new American ambassador to South Vietnam on August 26, 1963. (UPI/Bettmann Newsphotos)

ground is patrician, and he is always conscious of his reputation and his dignity; but while he can be extremely charming, he can also be quite rude. He is a total politician in the best sense; that is, he is attuned to the needs, ambitions and motivations of others. Yet his background, coolness and reserve mark him as essentially different from other, more genial and back-slapping politicians. Some of this reserve is inherent—the product of his breeding, education and prestige, but I suspect that some of it is deliberate —Lodge's way of emphasizing his variance from the norm. Because of this distant attitude he does not have the best reputation among Republican politicians, and he was not beloved by the press corps at the UN.

In Vietnam all this was different. Lodge became known as a difficult, demanding man to work for, but he had the respect of his subordinates and of the reporters. He turned out to be a shrewd, tough operator, very much a match for the Ngo family. He was absolutely single-minded, he worked hard and did his homework, and he had no illusions about the task facing the United States. He quickly analyzed the situation in Saigon, and today in Washington he is considered to have been the best ambassador we have ever had there. Above all, he wanted to know what was going on in the country, even when it looked like bad news. He also played his hand very close to the vest. "He doesn't trust anyone," one aide told me, "and because of that he's never had any confidences broken." Sheehan, who comes from Massachusetts, said, "Lodge is what my Irish mother would call a crafty Yankee."

The pagoda crackdown, which in a sense was a slap in the face to Lodge, had taken place while he was en route to Saigon. But I don't believe that it affected his attitude toward the family; it became evident that even before he left Washington he had learned enough to believe that the family was incapable of ruling the country and of prosecuting a difficult war. Shortly after he had taken up his new post, Lodge had lunch with a journalist and questioned him closely for more than an hour on the family and on the war. The reporter gave him a pessimistic report, and then asked, "And what's your impression, Mr. Ambassador?"

"About the same as yours," Lodge answered coolly.

Though Lodge did not believe the war was going well, or even being fought very hard, the fact that Harkins was an old family friend from Boston days placed him in a difficult position, since Harkins would never admit that things were not running smoothly. However, this did not deter Lodge from speaking his mind on several occasions. Once after spending several hours with Diem, he told his embassy aides that the man couldn't possibly rule the country; the President couldn't even speak coherently. While Lodge had ticked off American grievances and recommendations, his host had stared at the ceiling, and when the ambassador was finished the President poured out a babble of words about something totally unrelated. Lodge was told that this always took place whenever the Americans asked for anything.

Lodge soon found out that the feeling among the different sections of the mission about the need for a radical change in policy far exceeded that of the Washington people concerned with the area. Without experiencing the situation first-hand, the State Department could not perceive the sense of crisis and bitterness and frustration which existed in the mission. On his arrival Lodge had found a virtually mutinous embassy on his hands; the Americans had had enough of the Ngo family, of our acceptance of Ngo dictums and of official pretenses covering up failures of policy. At a meeting with AID officials Lodge was stunned by their vehemence. William Flippen, for six years a key official in Saigon, deputy chief of the AID mission and one of the ranking members of the American staff, delivered a bitter attack on our previous policy. Flippen added that the American military had been consistently wrong in its reports and interpretations ever since he arrived in Vietnam, and stated flatly that the war was being lost. The chief of the strategic hamlet program, Rufus Phillips, told Lodge that the program was in serious trouble and that the war was going particularly badly in the Delta. One after another, Americans spoke of the deterioration in their areas of responsibility.

At the USIS the new ambassador received a similarly cold analysis of the Government and the attitude of the population from some of the service's most knowledgeable field workers. "Maybe USOM can sell its pig program in the countryside," one USIS officer said, "but we can't sell this Government to the people, and we only bring ourselves down to its level when we try."

In the CIA most of the young agents were also brutally frank about the Government's unpopularity and its inability to fight a war. There was only one man—Richardson—who did not agree with these assessments; the CIA chief was too much a part of the old policy to change his opinion at this date. Reportedly Richardson believed that it was unrealistic to switch governments now and that at least Nhu had shown that he was smarter than the generals.

What we saw in Saigon was some evidence of the alignments which at this time were taking place in Washington. There, too, the military stuck to its previous position, but some civilians had expressed doubts even before the Buddhist crisis: "That's a very fragile situation out there—it could go either way," one notoriously optimistic—in public—high official had told Sheehan privately in April 1963. The religious controversy and the Government's inability to cope with it strengthened the doubts of these civilians: how could a regime unable to settle the Buddhist crisis be effective in administering the hamlet program and in fighting the war?

Thus, by the summer of 1963 some high State Department people had already become receptive to the idea of change. This included men like Averell Harriman, the Undersecretary of State, and Roger Hilsman, the Assistant Secretary of State for Far Eastern Affairs. Curiously, the Secretary of State himself, Dean Rusk, never chose to play a major part in this continuing foreign-policy crisis; the foremost civilian role was McNamara's.

According to some of his advisers, President Kennedy had ambivalent feelings. Privately he did not believe the glowing reports handed in by the military; he was angered and irritated by the Ngo family—particularly by Madame Nhu—and yet he was reluctant to act. But the crackdown on the pagodas enraged the President personally. He and other Washington officials considered it not only the end of a policy, but a betrayal by an ally as well. And as the Buddhist crisis continued, it inevitably undercut those spokesmen who had praised Diem's political acumen. Thereafter, according to friends, Kennedy began to think that change was inevitable. "His position became one of hoping to bring others—particularly McNamara and the military—along with him, and to do it as subtly as he could," one White House aide said.

Immediately after the strike on the pagodas, Washington received information from some Vietnamese generals that Nhu was reportedly dealing with Hanoi; if this were true, the generals said, they must act, and they wanted to know the position of the United States. It was a very blunt question.

At virtually the same time the Americans accepted Nhu's version of the raids and blamed them on the generals. When this news went out over the Voice of America, reports reached Washington of complaints from the generals that the United States was unfairly blackening the name of the Vietnamese Army, and that the Americans should issue a correction. Also, Admiral Felt in Honolulu allegedly told the State Department that a revised statement was desirable. As a result, on August 24 a cable was sent to Saigon for Lodge's approval. It said in effect that State was planning a press briefing to say that the pagoda strike had been carried out by Nhu and his special forces. In the same cable the State Department reportedly also instructed Lodge to tell the generals that their question about action in the event of Nhu dealing with Hanoi was of course hypothetical, but that the United States was always interested in supporting anti-Communist governments.

This message received broad support: by Roswell Gilpatric, the Undersecretary of Defense, by Richard Helms, the deputy at CIA (since it was a Saturday, many of the top men were not in their offices), by Rusk and George Ball at the State Department and by the President at the White House. When Mike Forrestal, head of the Vietnam Task Force who was drafting the cable, called General Krulak at the Pentagon about Taylor's position, Krulak verbally gave Taylor's approval. (All of this is significant, because a month later, when the military hardened on its basic position —that the status quo was the best platform from which to wage the war —an attempt was made to show that Hilsman and the State Department had gone ahead without Defense Department approval.) By 4 P.M. the next day Lodge had responded affirmatively to the cable, and State Department reporters were given the new and accurate version of the pagoda raids.

But the second half of the cable produced no dramatic changes in Saigon. The generals, divided and frightened, were still unsure of the American position, and for the moment Nhu was very much in charge of the city.

Thus, in early September, when there was no real change in the internal situation in Vietnam, the White House began an agonizing reappraisal of our policy. The President was receiving a barrage of reports: journalistic ones, traditionally pessimistic; from Lodge and the State Department, now suddenly pessimistic; from Nolting, now back in Washington after being replaced—cold-shouldered, bitter and angry but as optimistic as ever, siding with the rosy Defense Department view; and finally, there were the military reports quoting endless statistics on how well the war was going.

In these circumstances the President once more was deceived by the American military. In order to weigh as best he could the conflicting reports he was receiving, he sent, in early September, two men to Vietnam. Joe Mendenhall, the former Number Two man in the American embassy in Saigon and now a member of the State Department's policy staff, was to report back to Kennedy on the civilian situation; the military reporter was once again General Krulak, a two-star Marine general who was rumored to be the next commandant of the Corps.

The two men spent less than a week in Saigon. As they were leaving,

Mendenhall told one American civilian, "Well, I know how bad it is, but I think I'm going to have trouble with Krulak."

He had more than trouble. When the two gave their reports before a group of top policy makers, including the President, Mendenhall expressed his deep pessimism. Krulak, however, was glowingly optimistic and talked about the growth of the strategic hamlet program and the number of operations Government troops were conducting. When both had finished, President Kennedy turned to them and said, "Are you gentlemen sure you visited the same country?"

Fortunately, at this time the President received one more key report on the deterioration in the Delta, and it was from an impeccable source: Rufus Phillips, the young civilian in charge of the strategic hamlet program. A 1951 graduate of Yale, Phillips had served as a young Army officer in Vietnam, where, in 1956, he had met Colonel Lansdale during the latter's years as adviser to Diem. Phillips had become a protégé of Lansdale's; like the colonel, he believed that there was a good chance of making Vietnam a stable country. In 1962, when the American buildup took place, Lansdale was unable to return to Vietnam. The reasons why are not clear; some say that he was too pessimistic, some that he had created too many enemies within the military establishment. Still, young Phillips was chosen to head the hamlet program.

When I first met him, Phillips was very much a member of the team; he was optimistic, and he generated idealism to his civilian staff working as advisers in each province. He and I differed sharply on the effectiveness of that effort, but I always enjoyed talking to him; he struck me as having the greatest knowledge of Vietnam of all the high officials of the civilian mission, and he discussed the country and the war in more than clichés and with great feeling. By July 1963 his own associates in the Delta, including Ralph Harwood, his deputy in the Delta, were warning Saigon that the program was not working and that in many of the lowland areas the Vietcong were taking over virtually unchallenged. By August the reports were increasingly ominous, and when Phillips went down to the Delta, took a look and decided that the situation was indeed grim, he did what most of his colleagues in the upper reaches of the mission would not do: he admitted that he had been wrong and that the program was failing. It was to be an act of considerable personal courage.

In early September Phillips returned to Washington and warned the President about the hamlet program in the Delta; he said that Nhu had tricked the Americans, that in two key provinces, Dinh Tuong and Long An, it was largely a paper program and that the Vietcong were making great headway. Phillips was immediately and bitterly challenged by Krulak, who doubted his veracity and his competence, but the expert testimony of the young civilian undoubtedly convinced the President of what he already suspected—that the military was reporting the war inaccurately.

I heard about Phillips' dissent and visit to Washington in an unusual way. I was talking to a friend of mine at the USIS when his wife, who had just had lunch with the wife of one of the generals, came in. She told us that her friend had said that her husband was "going to get that ———— Rufus Phillips if it was the last thing he did." From that it was easy to piece the story together.

Back in Saigon we watched the rapid development of a split between the civilian and military missions. Reporters found that at MACV they were still treated coldly, whereas they were not only treated well at the embassy, but from time to time were even tipped off by its officials about Government defeats.

A similar division was taking place in Washington. Finally, in late September, President Kennedy decided to send his two top Pentagon officials, Secretary McNamara and General Taylor, to Saigon for one more special report on the country. Though Kennedy aides were later to explain that this was part of the President's attempt to coax the military, it looked like a whitewash to outsiders. Why send the two top Defense Department officials if not to back up the military, who were already reporting so optimistically?

The visit looked even more like a whitewash when, on September 25, after less than twenty-four hours in the country and after the first meetings with American officials, Arthur Sylvester, the assistant secretary for public affairs, told us at a briefing that the war was "getting better and better, rather than worse and worse." Indeed, he added, the Government was "rapidly approaching" the point militarily where the "goals set will be reached relatively shortly."

There must have been a reaction to this blatant news management in both Saigon and Washington, because two days later Sylvester noted that his first briefing might have "tended to throw things out of focus"; in fact, he admitted it was possible that his remarks "were tending to suggest I was trying to plaster things over with a pretty brush."

Behind all this double talk an absorbing behind-the-scenes struggle was taking place between Harkins and Lodge, each of whom was trying to press his views on the two visitors. Lodge was ready for his first move even before the jet bringing the Washington officials had landed. As the two men were descending the ramp, Lodge assigned two of his aides to block Harkins so that the ambassador would be the first to greet the Secretary. Harkins was caught in a trap as the crowd surged forward, and we could hear him shouting plaintively from behind a group of photographers, "Please, gentlemen, please let me through to greet the Secretary."

Harkins had one advantage: the trip was under the auspices of MACV, and therefore he could arrange the schedule of what the two visitors would see. On the other hand, the Secretary was staying with Lodge, and the ambassador had the opportunity to work on McNamara each morning at breakfast and each night when the daily inspections were over. Lodge deliberately gave Harkins a head start; for the first three days the Secretary and his party flew to various corps areas where the military was in charge. With little variation he was given the standard briefings and statistics—except in the Delta, where the Americans were considerably more cautious.

But midway through their stay Lodge began his campaign; he disagreed forcefully with the conclusions of the military and he expressed strong doubts about the progress of the war. Key civilian personnel working in the Delta in different capacities were quietly brought up to Saigon to meet the Secretary.

This conflict was something new for McNamara. He had been to Saigon before, and he had met frequently in Honolulu with the Saigon team. Each time he had been given the team report: MACV would say that the war was being won; the embassy would say that the war was being won and that Diem was coming around; the CIA would say that things were going well and that the montagnards were coming around. Then, if it was a Saigon visit, McNamara would go to the Palace and be told in a five-hour monologue that the war was being won and that the Americans finally understood its nature. Lastly, he would visit a couple of specially selected sites where the news was good. Duly impressed with the effectiveness of the programs and the team, he would leave Saigon a less wise man than when he arrived.

In my opinion McNamara may well be this country's most distinguished civil servant of the last decade. Brilliant and tireless, he rides herd over the vast and tangled responsibilities of the Pentagon, where he must involve himself daily with awesome problems that are almost beyond human comprehension. He is the final civilian control over a center of power whose strength is expanding at the same rate that the complexity of its weaponry is increasing. Yet one of McNamara's most fervent admirers among the Pentagon "whiz kids," the group of bright young civilians that McNamara has gathered around him, notes that his chief is interested in everything "but men and ideas." Unfortunately, the war in Vietnam was little else. In addition, I don't think McNamara's political ear is tuned to the quiet voices, and I don't think he fully realized why he was getting such unanimity—American and Vietnamese—of official opinion. He had spent a lifetime looking for facts and figures and depending on them—in the past they had not let him down.

Sheehan recalls that in May 1962 he went on a visit to the first of a series of the hamlets which were later to prove such a flop. McNamara, Harkins, General Lyman Lemnitzer, Nolting and then Brigadier General Nguyen Khanh, McNamara's escort officer, were touring an area that had been under Vietcong control. To Sheehan the population seemed very unfriendly; all the people stayed indoors except for one old man who strolled out to look at the foreigners. After talking with the old man, McNamara inspected the nearly completed fortifications around the hamlet as Nolting explained their purpose. They watched a group of obviously hostile peasants digging a moat under Government supervision. The peasants kept their backs to the Americans, but "I had the feeling that they would have enjoyed cutting our throats and burying us in that ditch," Sheehan said. McNamara, who asked a barrage of questions, wanted to know where the peasants would hide when the Vietcong attacked. There was a long pause while the generals tried to think of a plausible answer; the Vietnamese had privately told American reporters that there were few young men in the hamlet because most of them were out fighting with the Vietcong, and that a number of the remaining families in the hamlet were sympathetic to the guerrillas. Finally General Khanh told McNamara that the people could take refuge in the blockhouses with the Civil Guard troops. But this did not satisfy the Secretary of Defense, so Khanh invented the story that if the hamlet was attacked the peasants would lie down on the floor in their huts to avoid the gunfire.

Apparently such weird explanations and lame answers had satisfied McNamara in the past. Now, even as late as September 1963, he showed his insensitivity to the situation on a tour of the country by asking all his questions in the presence of General Harkins, thus talking only to largely inhibited officers.

In the Pentagon much of McNamara's success has been the result of selecting a group of bright civilians who examined military goals and priorities and gave him objective viewpoints and alternatives. In Vietnam this technique could not be applied; McNamara had no civilian eyes with him and he was entirely dependent on the Harkins line. If he'd had a civilian "whiz kid" in Saigon reporting directly to him, things might have been different; perhaps McNamara trusted the advice he was getting and felt that the war was a place for military expertise only, or perhaps the military would have resented the presence of a civilian reporting back to their chief. In any case, when Lodge disagreed flatly with Harkins, McNamara for the first time ran into real dissent from sources that he respected.

The tip-off on the struggle between Harkins and Lodge came the next to the last day of the trip, when McNamara canceled a final military tour of the countryside, sent Taylor off by himself, and stayed behind for more talks with civilians. The next day, when McNamara and Taylor left, the word was out; for the first time the Secretary had not only been thoroughly briefed on the political chaos in the country, but had been given a dark picture of the progress of the war. Lodge was satisfied that he had broken through (a high officer in the embassy who did not like Lodge personally called it "a goddamn *tour de force*").

When McNamara returned to Washington he reportedly told Kennedy that the military had been wrong, that the war was not going well and that the official version of military events was inaccurate. Out of this came a curious statement which expressed concern about the political situation, urged the Vietnamese to continue the fight and further said that the Americans hoped to bring home most of their advisers by 1965. Lodge was surprised by the statement, but in Saigon it was written off as election-year rhetoric. What was important was that behind the scenes Lodge's view-point had prevailed. The Kennedy Administration no longer believed the war was being won, and the United States intended slowly to reverse its total commitment to Diem. Ironically—and not entirely by chance—the key men in this movement to disengage ourselves gradually from a government which so loudly proclaimed its anti-Communist stand were two Republicans, Lodge and McNamara. Taylor never changed his position, but President Kennedy, aided by Lodge, had been largely successful in bringing McNamara around to his own opinion.

At the time of the McNamara-Taylor visit, the Government had been tidying up loose ends in an attempt to placate the Americans in Saigon; such surface gestures had always satisfied them in the past. The curfew, still in force, was gradually pushed back, and finally martial law itself, which had never been anything but Nhu's way of harassing his opponents, was rescinded. President Diem issued a statement saying that the Buddhist problem had been solved; the Vietnam press announced that Foreign Minister Vu Van Mau, who had been arrested on his way out of the country, had not been arrested at all but simply unavoidably detained; Ambassador Tran Van Chuong in Washington had not resigned, as everyone (including him) had thought: he had been discharged and it was only because of an unfortunate delay in communications from Saigon that the news did not reach him in time.

But Lodge was not interested in such gestures. Step by step he and Washington had been moving to demonstrate to the Vietnamese population that we no longer considered the Ngo family indispensable to the war, and that our future support would be given to the country and to the people, not to the Ngo family. Ever since his arrival Lodge had shown this in a number of small ways which differed sharply from the actions of his predecessor. On the night the pagodas were sacked, two young Buddhists had taken refuge in the USOM building next door to Xa Loi. Twice the Government asked that they be returned, and twice Lodge refused; in fact, on one of his first public trips in Saigon he paid a call on the two Buddhists. When Thich Tri Quang, the enigmatic leader of the Buddhist movement, received asylum at the U.S. embassy, Lodge not only refused to return him to the Government, but in an attempt to counter some of the hostility toward the United States, which had been engendered by the pagoda raids, let it be known that we were "delighted" to be his hosts—thus producing the curious situation of two supposed allies fighting a war against Communism and bickering over the harboring of a "Communist agent" by one of them.

When Madame Nhu on a trip in Europe criticized American junior officers for acting like "little soldiers of fortune," Lodge deliberately and publicly took exception to her words as "shocking and cruel." This was the first public statement Lodge made after his arrival in Saigon, and it was received with relief by almost every American there, who had heard Madame attack everything from our soldiers to our Bill of Rights. Lodge's defense of our soldiers was certainly understandable, but it was also the first step in the United States' long-awaited confrontation with Diem.

Besides being blunt in public, Lodge talked scornfully about the family in private, knowing full well that in a city where there were no secrets, his words would soon be all over town. Also, certain U.S. aid was being withheld; lastly, Richardson, Nhu's greatest American ally, had been sent home.

Perhaps another ambassador might not have been so determined to get his way in this unpleasant situation, but Lodge was no ordinary ambassador. He carried unusual credentials, and he had arrived at the very time when it was fortunate to have as mission chief a man of reputation who was not a career officer worried so much about his next assignment as the job at hand. Lodge could talk directly to the White House whenever he wanted, and his requests merited special attention. As an American of national reputation, and as a former Republican nominee for Vice-President, his presence gave a handsome bipartisan veneer to our troubled policy in Vietnam. Moreover, if he were not treated with respect, he might resign in a huff and give the Republicans a major campaign issue. Needless to say, he received every consideration from Washington.

There was another reason why Lodge's personal credentials were a particular advantage in this unusual situation. A career diplomat might have regarded the inevitable decision about the Ngo family with some fear and trepidation; there were still shadows from the McCarthy era. A career man might have been in more of a quandary about the choice to be made; perhaps the status quo might have seemed more desirable than a potential future attack for being too liberal.

But Lodge's reputation in this regard was impeccable, and in him the Kennedy Administration had not only a man willing to take a risk, but an ideal political buffer for the possible consequences of this new policy. Aside from bearing a great Republican name, hadn't no less an authority than Richard Nixon once said that he had stood up to the Russians more than any other American? No one in the mainstream of American politics was likely to charge Lodge with being soft on Communists.

The new policy being fashioned by Lodge and by Washington was to support the war effort fully but to disengage the United States from anything that could be interpreted as a personal commitment to the family. "Anything that helps the war we support; everything that hurts the war we oppose" was the phrase used. Thus were we moving steadily toward creating an atmosphere in which a coup d'état could take place, for the all-out support which had previously been thrown to the Ngo family was now directed exclusively to the anti-Communist war effort.

In starting afresh, Washington and Lodge were on shaky ground, for they could expect potentially vast repercussions in American domestic politics; in the middle of a war they were facing the unknown in preference to a government which had publicly proclaimed that it was anti-Communist. The Ngo brothers had always played this card well in the past, but now the feeling was growing in Saigon and Washington that the

United States could no longer afford to be blackmailed into endless support of a government simply because it was anti-Communist.

At this time a key Vietnamese in Saigon was Colonel Le Quang Tung, the head of the special forces. The Americans had been backing him as part of our policy, but to both the Army and the population he was a symbol of the Ngo regime. As long as the United States continued to support the Nhu-Tung private little army, any policy demanding change would be ineffective.

Sheehan and I had come on this controversy in early September. That was a fascinating time for a reporter in Vietnam, because everyone was talking. The departure of Nolting, the arrival of Lodge, the failure of our past policy and the disgust of most Americans for it had opened many mouths. My office, knowing that I was exhausted after covering the crisis for more than four months, offered me a long break in Tokyo, but I turned it down; there were many subsurface stories, and it was no time to pull a man out who had been building up his sources. My visa had little enough time to go, and I had better stay in Saigon as long as I could.

During this period Sheehan and I were following up on a hunch, and in talking to a friend I casually asked about Colonel Tung's relations with the U.S. mission; I knew that we had been financing Tung in the past, but I did not know the details. Our friend smiled and said, "Well, they almost cut the little bastard off the other day." Since he was an old friend and since it was the time of the great thaw, he began to talk.

It turned out that one of the central debates within the American mission was: what to do about Tung. To Americans he was the most obvious symbol of the treachery of that night; but more than that, to the Vietnamese military he was a symbol of the family's political control of the Army. The Americans were arguing among themselves that the Vietnamese officers would never believe that there was any change of heart on the part of the United States as long as Tung was financed.

Our basic information, coming from several sources close to the CIA, was that the agency had originally organized and paid for Tung's operation to the tune of a quarter of a million dollars a month, and that it was still paying this sum. Sheehan and I checked hard, had this figure confirmed to us, and used it in our story. But more than a year later, another CIA friend claimed that by the time the pagoda crackdown took place, the agency no longer financed all of Tung's operation. By then, he said, the CIA paid for only a part of Tung's force, and most of the money now came from regular Military Assistance Program funds. As proof of this, our informant claimed that a few weeks after Washington finally decided to cut Tung off, the news was broken to him, not by a CIA man, but by Major General Stilwell of MACV.

After gathering the information, there was still a question of whether or not to file such a story; this is always a difficult decision, and in this case publication of these facts would certainly affect long-range plans. A considerable public and editorial outcry was going on in the United States about the pagoda sacking, and the State Department had publicly condemned the treatment of the Buddhists; yet the story would publicize the fact that the United States was still deeply involved with those responsible—Nhu and Tung.

But the role of Tung illuminated the basic problem of the American-Ngo relationship. We had initiated certain programs designed to win the war, but they were quickly twisted by the family into a means to bolster their personal power and safeguard their survival. Therefore I decided that I had a legitimate story.

Sheehan and I did two more days of leg work. Neil was convinced that Nhu was not unhappy about our earlier stories of how he had handled the pagoda raids. One of our Palace sources told us that "Nhu will like your pieces because they will show how he has outsmarted the Americans. He will be torn between not wanting to upset the Americans, because he wants more aid, and of wanting everyone in Washington to know how clever he is." But Sheehan felt certain that now Nhu and Tung would be enraged by publication of this story because we were shaking the money tree, and therefore, to protect our sources and ourselves as much as possible, we slipped our dispatches out of the country with a friend en route to the Philippines, and instructed our employers not to use our by-lines. The *Times* ran the story with a Manila dateline, with an adjoining story from Washington, written by Reston, to give the Administration's reaction —which was that it would neither confirm nor deny the stories but that it was extremely angry about them. Washington claimed that the special forces units were fighting the guerrillas, a point I had disputed strongly. The whole argument of my story was that the men who knew Tung best felt that his six battalions were almost never used against the Vietcong— that they were, in fact, a private security force.

In late October the Administration quietly made a new decision about Colonel Tung. No longer would there be "business as usual." On October 19 he was notified that his troops would only receive pay if they were used against the Vietcong, and then only if they notified their American advisers about every movement.

"The cut," I wrote that day, "will probably have more psychological and political than economic impact. Observers here believed that the cutback was bound to increase the growing tension between the United States and the ruling Ngo family, who are currently cooperating in an uneasy alliance against Communist guerrillas."

Colonel Tung was very angry when told of the new plan. When Sheehan called him up and tried to get an interview, the colonel said, "I am a soldier and I do not interfere with politics," and hung up. But immediately our phone began to buzz so loudly that we couldn't use it for two days.

Chapter 11

The Saigon Press Controversy

In the middle of all this I had gotten a letter from a friend in New York in early September, enclosing a column about me from the New York *Journal-American.* Among other things it said that I was soft on Communism and that I was paving the way for a bearded Vietnamese Fidel Castro. When I showed it to a friend at the embassy, he said, "Well, I think you have to expect this sort of thing. There may be more."

There was more. A few days later Joseph Alsop, after a brief visit to Vietnam, wrote a column which attacked a group of "young crusaders" of the press corps in Vietnam who were responsible for the peculiar state of psychosis which existed among the inhabitants of Gia Long Palace. Suddenly reporters who had covered the complex evolution of the Buddhist crisis for four long months, who had realized that the monks were an emerging political force long before the American embassy did, found themselves charged by one visiting reporter with not having understood the movement's political implications; reporters who had been covering the disintegration in the Delta for more than a year and a half and had gone on more than thirty missions there were surprised to see themselves accused by Mr. Alsop of not having visited what he quaintly referred to as "the front." Though at this time Lodge was slowly changing the policy to an anti-Diem stance, Alsop withheld any criticism of the more prestigious Lodge. However, being criticized by Alsop is no small honor in our profession, and we felt that our stock was rising. The so-called "press controversy" of Vietnam had begun.

Indeed, suddenly there was no shortage of criticism. One source of this was the Kennedy Administration, which, when finally forced to make decisions on Vietnam, was so entangled in conflicting currents within its own establishment that it was difficult for it to change its position. The Administration was being pressured by mounting forces in the United States and in Vietnam, and yet it was understandably hesitant about making changes in the middle of a war. In a speech to the nation the President told Diem, in effect, to make reforms—or else we could continue supporting him anyway. ("He has tried to change Diem on television and so far he has failed," James Reston wrote about Kennedy.)

Washington simply did not want to read much of the reporting from Vietnam because it made the situation sound like a major foreign policy failure, and each day there was more evidence that the Americans were being led around by the nose by the Ngo family. In addition, the Administration was angered by its own ineptitude, first, in letting the pagoda crackdown take place; second, in not having diagnosed it correctly; and third, by not having an answer when it finally did learn what had happened. In some ways Vietnam was second only to the Bay of Pigs as an Administration failure. But there was a major difference: the Bay of Pigs debacle had taken place only ninety miles from home; the bungling was obvious even to the most myopic, and it could not be hidden or, in the Washington phrase, "papered over." But Vietnam was twelve thousand miles away; the situation there was infinitely more complicated, and it required sophistication and interest for the public to follow it. Therefore it was relatively easy for Administration spokesmen to make a series of glib statements about Vietnam, and to attack a handful of young newspapermen without established reputations.

So the Vietnamese press corps came under fire. White House reporters were constantly told by Pierre Salinger* and other members of the White House staff that the Vietnamese reporting was inaccurate and the work of young, emotional correspondents; White House assistants, more interested in the President's political standing at home than the status of the guerrilla war, would explain knowingly that reporters in Vietnam never went out on operations. In the higher reaches of the Pentagon, where the realities of the war rarely penetrated, the criticism was particularly vehement. Defense Department reporters were told by General Victor Krulak, the Pentagon's specialist on counterinsurgency, that he simply couldn't understand what was going on in Vietnam: experienced reporters like Richard Tregaskis and Maggie Higgins had found that the war was being won, but a bunch of young cubs who kept writing about the political side were defeatists.

On October 22 Arthur Ochs Sulzberger, the new publisher of the *Times*, went to the White House to pay a courtesy call on the President of the United States. Except for Vietnam, the Administration was riding high. Kennedy was sure that Goldwater would be his opponent in the next year's presidential election and that the Democrats would win easily. Almost the first question from President Kennedy was, "What do you think of your young man in Saigon?" Mr. Sulzberger answered that he thought I was doing fine. The President suggested to the publisher that perhaps I was too close to the story, and too involved—which is the most insidious kind of comment one can make about a reporter. No, said Sulzberger, he did not think that I was too involved. The President then asked if the publisher had been thinking of transferring me to another area. No, said the publisher, the *Times* was quite satisfied with my present assignment. (As a matter of fact, at that particular point I was supposed to go on

*Pierre Salinger served as White House press secretary in the Kennedy Administration.

a breather for a two-week rest, but to its everlasting credit the *Times* immediately canceled the holiday lest it appear to have acquiesced to this pressure.)

Other attacks on us came from varying sources. In the Hearst chain Frank Conniff singled me out in a long article. However, Conniff was by far our most honorable critic; he later came to Vietnam, sensed the military cover-up and wrote quite fairly about us in subsequent columns. The most curious attack of all was that of *Time,* which criticized two of its own reporters in the process.

There had been a long, simmering dispute between *Time* reporters in Vietnam and their editors in New York—a far sharper division than the usual one between field and office. (*Time* employs immensely talented people and puts out a very professional magazine, but I have always observed that *Time* reporters have to do an undue amount of apologizing to news sources about the final product.) These *Time* reporters felt strongly that the magazine was giving too optimistic a view of a war that they saw was barely being fought and in which the enemy was becoming stronger all the time. Not surprisingly, as *Time*'s method of reporting the war paralleled the Pentagon's, so its published accounts paralleled the Pentagon's optimistic version—a case of the chiefs telling the Indians what the Indians had seen.

Periodically Charley Mohr, *Time*'s chief correspondent in Southeast Asia, would return to New York for conferences during which he would argue for tougher coverage on Vietnam. Instead his editors, who had lunched with Secretary McNamara and other Pentagon officials, and had seen the most secret of charts and the most secret of arrows and been given what the Pentagon called "the big picture," would explain patiently to Mohr that he understood only a portion of the big picture. And *Time*'s coverage—paralleling the official version—would continue.

Part of the reason for this, I think, was the particular way in which *Time*'s executives view the magazine: to a large degree they see it not just as a magazine of reporting, but as an instrument of policy making. Thus, what *Time*'s editors *want* to happen is as important as what is happening. In Vietnam, where U.S. prestige was staked against a Communist enemy, and the government was Christian and anti-Communist, *Time* had a strong commitment to Diem.

The squabble between the *Time* editors and reporters had started in 1962, but in April 1963, after Dick Clurman, *Time*'s chief of correspondents and one of the foremost defenders of working reporters among the magazine's executives, had visited Saigon, there was a slight improvement. Clurman had met some of the other reporters, had talked with their sources, and had heard Diem and Nhu complain about what was wrong with American advice while at the same time Nolting was telling him there was no disagreement on the advice.

Mohr and Mert Perry felt somewhat encouraged, and during most of the Buddhist crisis they were relatively pleased with the stories that appeared in the magazine. But their journalistic optimism ended in August 1963, with the cover story on Madame Nhu. Mohr, whose file for the story is one of the most brilliant I've ever read, drew rave notices and enthusiastic cables from his home office for his leg work and writing. But he was deeply disappointed with the final results; he felt that it was too flattering and that it overemphasized the personable aspect of Madame (ironically, his lead had begun: "Vietnam is a graveyard of lost hopes, destroyed vanity, glib promises, and good intentions . . .") and played down her destructive influence on the country. Charley and his editors exchanged brief and uncomplimentary letters, and then he went back to work.

Several days later, in mid-August, Mohr was asked for a piece on the Saigon press corps. He filed a long and detailed one, flattering to the reporters, and analyzed the reasons for the controversy. It never appeared in print, but Mohr was extremely busy during those hectic weeks and had little time to think of anything except the story at hand. Although nominally based in Hong Kong, he was spending all his time in Saigon; he saw his wife Norma only when she flew in from Hong Kong to smuggle out copy.

Mohr is a reporter's reporter. At that time he was thirty-four years old, a man of immense vitality and enthusiasm who was in love with his work and who brought a sense of excitement to everything he did. He was one of *Time*'s stars: White House correspondent at twenty-seven, then chief of the New Delhi bureau, then head of the coveted Southeast Asia bureau. He was a particular favorite of Henry Luce's,* who, on introducing him to a gathering of top business executives, had referred to him as "a reporter—and how!" In the course of collecting material for the Madame Nhu story he had charmed the First Lady; she had granted twelve hours of interviews and at one point had said, "I am telling you things I have never told anyone else in my life." A few days before the *Time* story came out, I asked Madame about the forthcoming piece. "I feel like I am sitting on—how do you say it—a volcano," she answered, "but whatever it says, I have decided that the fault will not be that of Mr. Mohr, but of the rewriting man."

Mohr had spent most of 1963 in Vietnam, but he also had a full-time colleague based there. Mert Perry is what in the trade is called a "stringer," which means that he files for a publication and that his copy is often used, but that he does not enjoy staff status. Yet Perry was in every sense a *Time* reporter. He had been sent to Saigon by UPI but had resigned to take the *Time* job, which paid far more money. Trained as a wire-service man, Perry gave *Time* extraordinary coverage. By August 1963 he had been in Vietnam for nearly two years; he knew the Delta well and had been on countless operations in the field, and he had seen adviser after adviser try to grapple with the same problems. Of all the correspon-

*Henry Luce was the founder and publisher of a magazine empire that included *Time*, *Life*, and *Fortune*.

dents in Vietnam he was probably the best liked by American officers, and his apartment served as a meeting place for them when they came in from the field—in no small part because his wife Darlene was a very good cook.

In early September, when Washington was still searching for answers, Mohr was asked by his editors to do an exhaustive roundup on the state of the war in Vietnam, including a realistic view of the situation in the Delta. Both Mohr and Perry did a vast amount of leg work for this assignment; they filed twenty-five pages of copy in three days.

Mohr's story, the toughest written to that date by a resident correspondent, began, "The war in Vietnam is being lost." Charley went on to say that not everyone in Vietnam "would be willing to go so far at this point. But those men who know Vietnam best and have given the best of their energies and a portion of their souls to this program are suddenly becoming passionate on this subject." Washington, Mohr noted, had asked all its Saigon officials for detailed reports on what was happening, and had given these officials a chance ". . . to bare their souls. Much of what they write may be diluted by the time it reaches Washington. However, these men realize that they are in the middle of a first-class major foreign policy crisis and that history will be a harsh judge. 'I am laying it on the line,' said one. 'Now is the time for the truth. There are no qualifications in what I write.' Another said: 'I am going on the record in black and white. The war will be lost in a year, but I gave myself some leeway and said three years.' Another said that his program in the countryside is 'dead.' One source said that American military reporting in the country 'has been wrong and false —lies, really. We are now paying the price.' "

This was strong stuff at a time when Washington was trying to make up its mind what to do. The story left no doubt that the American mission had come to the end of one road, and that our past policy had failed. Unfortunately, this was not what the editors of *Time* wanted to hear; in New York, Mohr's file was put aside, and Greg Dunne, a young contributing editor, was told to write an optimistic piece. Dunne refused and announced that he would write no more stories about Vietnam, but others stepped in. Eventually a story was printed which bore no relation to Mohr and Perry's file; among other things, it said that "Government troops are fighting better than ever."

But this type of optimism was so markedly different from most of the other dispatches that Americans were reading or hearing from the *Times*, the AP, UPI, *Newsweek,* CBS and NBC that an explanation was called for. Otto Fuerbringer, managing editor of *Time,* decided to produce his own interpretation. He summoned a writer to his office, and with what Stanley Karnow, a former *Time* employee, called in the January 1964 issue of *Nieman Reports,* "nothing but his own preconceptions to guide him, dictated the gist of an article for his magazine's 'Press' section." Karnow, Mohr's predecessor as *Time* bureau chief in Southeast Asia, who had quit to work for the *Saturday Evening Post* for just such reasons as this, called the piece "a devastating compendium of bitter innuendoes and clever generalities, all blatantly impeaching American correspondents in Vietnam for distorting the news." The war, the *Time* article hinted, was going better than a small journalistically incestuous group of reporters was saying; these correspondents were nothing but a group of malcontents who sat around the eighth floor of the Caravelle Hotel interviewing each other and never ventured into the countryside.

The printed piece was truly staggering, for it was an indictment not only of us, but of two of *Time*'s own reporters as well. It read as if written by a high Pentagon PIO, and it set off a minor furor in the newspaper world.

In New York, Clurman tried desperately to block publication of the article. Within *Time*'s hierarchy Clurman could not stop the piece on his own; the only man who could overrule Fuerbringer was Henry Luce. But Luce was in Atlanta at a football game, and though he sensed disaster, Clurman could not reach him in time. The article was printed.

In an attempt to keep Mohr, a favorite correspondent, Clurman then made a last-ditch effort. He cabled Charley in Saigon, warning him about the story and asking him to meet Clurman in Paris before resigning. But of course when Mohr received the cable—which was the first indication he had of what was afoot—he immediately began thinking about another job. Appalled by the article when he finally saw it, he flew to Paris, where he told Clurman that there was only one thing which could prevent his resignation: equal space in *Time*, under his own by-line, to refute the Fuerbringer attack. Clurman, who knew how important saving face is to Westerners, believed that this would be impossible, but he flew back to New York to talk to his chief.

Luce, who was surprised and embarrassed about the mounting uproar over the "Press" item, was in a tight spot. A refutation of the piece would humiliate his strongest editor, Fuerbringer, a man considered by many of his colleagues to be the architect of *Time*'s dazzling finished product; on the other hand, by doing nothing he would lose a justifiably angry and talented reporter. So he ordered Clurman to go to Saigon to write a *second* "Press" story on the reporters. Mohr, who had handed in his resignation, accompanied Clurman around the city as a sort of *eminence grise*, a façade that cracked whenever Clurman interviewed reporters about their copy and their ideas—at which point Mohr would explode, charging that Clurman, not the reporters, should be on the defensive and answering the questions.

After spending many hours with all of us going over our copy, Clurman became convinced that the "Press" story had been outrageous—but he also realized that a second piece was pointless. Nevertheless, orders were handed down that it be written. Once again there was a struggle between Clurman and Fuerbringer over the tone of the article; at one point Fuerbringer apparently led, then Clurman staged a comeback, but the final version was heavily "Fuerbringerized." Though the piece came as close as *Time* ever ventures in admitting that a mistake had been made, it still claimed that the war was going better than the press corps reported, and it was still an attack on our judgment.

While in Saigon, Clurman had written an article for *Life* on the state of the war; on his return he found it so altered by editors that he insisted on having his by-line removed. Both Mohr and Perry had resigned. Since Mohr was a well-known reporter, he had received offers from the *Wall Street Journal, Newsweek* and the *New York Times;* he accepted the *Times* job, returned home, was assigned to cover Barry Goldwater in the '64 campaign, and is now the *New York Times'* White House correspondent. It was more difficult for Perry to resign because he was not so well known as Mohr, but eventually he joined the staff of the Chicago *Daily News.*

The upshot of all the fuss was that *Time's* reputation with working newspapermen suffered considerably. There was also a certain malicious delight within the profession that Mohr and Perry had caught Fuerbringer red-handed; *Newsweek* and other publications ran pieces about the controversy with great relish.

For all the uproar generated by this teapot tempest, remarkably little light was shed on the roots of the journalistic problems in Vietnam. The traditional right of American journalists to report what they see was at stake here, even though the situation was a particularly sensitive one: ambiguous involvement in a wretched war with a ruthless enemy. Be-

David Halberstam and friends in a light moment during the Saigon press controversy assume the pose of "See no evil, hear no evil, speak no evil." Halberstam is in the center, Mert Perry of *Time* Magazine is on the left, and Ray Herndon of UPI is on the right.

cause the news was bad, there were many people who for varying reasons did not want it exposed. Yet an American reporter must believe, if he believes nothing else, that the United States has never survived in times of crisis by playing ostrich. Too much policy and too deep a commitment had already been made in Vietnam on the basis of too little factual information.

Therefore when the Pulitzer Prize for foreign reporting was awarded to Mal Browne and to me in the spring of 1964, it had a very special meaning for me; the Supreme Court within our own profession had upheld the right of a reporter to follow his conscience even in a delicate situation such as this. I think the reason that men such as James Reston went to bat for the Vietnam reporters before the Pulitzer committee was because this principle is so fundamental to journalism.

Much of the criticism of the Saigon press corps had been insidious; for instance, the critics singled out a few of us who were young, and failed to mention older, more established reporters such as Jim Robinson of NBC, Peter Kalischer and Bernie Kalb of CBS, Stan Karnow of the *Saturday Evening Post* and Pepper Martin of *U.S. News & World Report.* Probably most malicious of all was the insinuation that those few Americans who knew the country better than others, who had friends there and who cared the most about the war, were deliberately or capriciously writing pessimistic stories.

Ironically, the real weaknesses of the Saigon press corps were almost never cited by our critics. What was particularly shocking was that such a major American commitment—this country's only war—was covered by so few reporters. For most of my tour—until late 1963—I was the only full-time staff correspondent of an American daily newspaper. I believe that the Washington *Post,* the New York *Herald Tribune,* the Baltimore *Sun* and other papers which have great influence in the United States failed to meet their obligations during those months in 1962 and early 1963. If some of us had more journalistic power than was merited, it had been granted us purely by default.

In retrospect, there is one thing that was constantly overlooked in the press controversy: the stanch backing I received from the *Times* and the support Browne and Sheehan received from their offices during those weeks. It was not the kind of imbroglio that any publisher seeks; news executives rightfully believe that reporters should not be seen and that they are most effective when most anonymous. Yet the *Times* stood up quietly to great pressure and treated me very well. Once in the middle of it all, when they queried me on a Maggie Higgins story about how well the war was going in the Delta, I fired off an angry and thoughtless cable threatening to resign. But I was always supported by the great strength of the paper which backed a young reporter despite unrelenting and insidious pressure. It was a hard way to learn how a great newspaper operates under fire, but it was a very good lesson.

Chapter 12

The Final Days of Ngo Dinh Diem

In September and October of 1963 the entire fabric of Vietnam began to come apart. The Communists kept making major advances in the Mekong Delta. In Saigon the Government had turned on its two major sources of support, the Americans and the Army, and had deliberately provoked them. President Kennedy tried first to push for what Washington naïvely called reforms—which in effect meant ousting the Nhus—but this simply provoked fresh outbursts from the Government. The Nhus were not about to oust themselves from the Government.

The *Times of Vietnam* accused the United States of trying to buy coups d'état, specifying that John McCone, head of the CIA, and William Colby, his chief for Southeast Asia, were responsible. The paper quoted a Vietnamese general as saying that though he had rejected the offers of interventionists, "you should have seen what the foreign adventurers offered me." A West-German reporter for the magazine *Der Spiegel*, who was in Madame Nhu's office when she was correcting page proofs of one of the paper's stories about an alleged CIA plot, was stunned to hear her say over the phone, "Yes, but I want you to put Colonel Richardson's name in the story too."

Nhu held a press conference during which he made a prolonged attack on the Americans, accusing the United States "of having caused the process of disintegration in Vietnam."

In Central Vietnam, citizens who were caught listening to the Voice of America were arrested. Some Americans, particularly those in the USIS, were threatened; after Nhu carefully leaked reports that he planned to raid and bomb the USIS, Marine guards were put on duty there around the clock and vital papers were removed.

In mid-October *Newsweek* asked Ambassador Lodge to pose for a special cover photo; the picture was to be taken on a main Saigon street. The magazine wanted a student in the shot, and so the photographer stopped a fifteen-year-old girl and asked her to stand next to the ambassador. The picture was duly taken, Lodge departed, and the girl was immediately arrested by the secret police.

At this time Nhu let it be openly known that he had entered into exploratory negotiations with Hanoi; he was doing this through a French diplomat in North Vietnam who had come to Saigon on a visit and had been introduced to Nhu by a Polish member of the International Control Conference. Just why he was playing this game is hard to determine; in part he may have been hoping to blackmail the Americans and make them uneasy, but he probably also considered the strategic hamlet program so successful that he could win the war without the Americans—and of course, he was fascinated by the idea of dealing with the Communists.

Next, Nhu summoned a group of American reporters to tell them that the Vietnamese had "lost faith in America." He charged that the CIA had tried to instigate two coups against him; interrogation of the Buddhists proved that CIA agents were repeatedly urging the monks to stage a revolt. "It is incomprehensible to me that the CIA, which had backed a winning program, should reverse itself. I do not believe the leaders of the CIA really concurred in this," Nhu said.

In this increasingly tense atmosphere there were three major plots: the planned but hitherto unmaterialized coups of the junior officers and of the generals, and a fake coup to be staged by Nhu. Nothing can better stress the basic frustrations of American policy in Vietnam than the incredible amount of intrigue taking place in this country which was, after all, at war. The divisiveness at work in those days would have reduced the closest of relationships to enmity.

Nhu's plot, of which the CIA was well informed, and which was a tribute to his wild and imaginative mind, was scheduled to take place in early November. Nhu was aware of the officers' coups, and he was trying to move to head them off. "Coups," he had told an aide, "are like eggs, and they must be smashed before they are hatched."

Nhu's plan called for some special forces troops under Colonel Tung to stage a fake revolt in Saigon. Diem, Nhu and certain members of the household would then flee to a refuge prepared in advance at Cape Saint Jacques, the nearby seaside resort, where special communications facilities would have been installed. General Ton That Dinh, one of the trusted generals and a commander of loyal troops, would wait outside Saigon while hired gangsters would run riot in the city for several days, stealing and looting—particularly from Americans. In the confusion Colonel Tung's agents would then announce the formation of a revolutionary government which would include—without their consent—such prominent anti-Diem politicians as former Ambassador Chuong. Thereafter the revolutionary government's radio would attack the Americans, declare that it wanted to end the war against the Communists and indicate that it was sympathetic to a neutralist settlement. After several days of this, Dinh's loyal troops would march into the city and quickly crush the so-called revolt. This false coup would scare the Americans, would prove to them that the only alternative to the Ngo brothers was neutralism, and would demonstrate that the Army still supported the family.

But almost as soon as Nhu began preparing the headquarters at Cape Saint Jacques, the instigators of the two other coups heard of his plans.

The junior officers, who had been plotting for more than a year under various leaders and with different military units, had nearly tried a coup in July, only to have two key battalions ordered out of town at the last moment. This group included men like Lieutenant Colonel Pham Ngoc Tao, in the past one of Diem's brightest and most loyal officers—a man who represented the younger generation and who wanted to wage the war in an entirely new way. Other officers came from some of the elite air-borne and Marine units; there was also Colonel Do Mau, the chief of military security whom Nhu had so mistrusted when he was personally loyal that in desperation he had finally become dissident, and Colonel Tran Thien Khiem, the chief of staff of the Joint General Staff who had saved Diem from the paratroopers in 1960 and had turned on the Government in the spring of 1963.

The junior officers' group had been organized by Dr. Tran Kim Tuyen, the brilliant little man who headed Diem's secret police apparatus until he had a falling out with Madame Nhu in 1961. Tuyen, who had an organization reaching into many units of the Army, was able to gather together a select number of combat units for a coup. But in the middle of the Buddhist crisis Diem suddenly appointed him envoy to the United Arab Republic in order to get him out of the country; the brothers were reportedly loath to arrest the doctor, in the belief that he probably had too much incriminating information on Palace activities. When Tuyen left the country in September, the group was taken over by Colonel Mau, who in turn had a large number of security contacts of his own.

The generals' coup was also headed by men who had long remained close to Diem, who had helped him stave off earlier coups, and whose national loyalties were above suspicion. One of the leaders was General Duong Van Minh—"Big Minh" to Americans and Vietnamese because of his size—the closest approximation to a national hero in the South because he had personally led troops against the Binh Xuyen gangster sect in 1955. Minh had used his great prestige in Diem's first year to rally many other Army officers to the President, but later, because Nhu considered him a possible threat, he had been stripped of his troops and given the meaningless title of military adviser. General Tran Van Don, another highly respected officer, who had been given the nominal title of Chief of the Army and who had no troops directly under him, was also mistrusted by the regime. General Le Van Kim, considered by many Americans to be the most intelligent of the generals, had been under suspicion since the 1960 paratrooper coup—not because of any participation in it, but simply because Diem felt that he had not rallied to his side quickly enough. (Such was the Ngos' paranoia that one officer who had risked his life to save Diem that night by slipping through rebel lines was thereafter under great suspicion because the brothers felt he had moved *too* easily through the enemy units.)

These three generals had started preparing their coup in June by quietly mustering support. They enjoyed vast prestige within the Vietnamese Army; in fact, they had everything they needed for a coup except troops.

In late October tension rose as all three plots grew to fruition. Reportedly the generals tried and failed to coordinate their coup with that of the junior officers. The latter had set October 24 as their target date, but the generals, who feared that the rival group lacked sufficient troops and who wanted to control the situation themselves, foiled the young Turks once again by simply sending a key regiment out of town for the day.

I remember October 24 very distinctly because I had been tipped off about the impending coup. It was supposed to take place at 1 P.M., right in the middle of the siesta, when Saigon would be caught completely off guard. I had lunch with Jerry King, the *Times* man from Kuala Lumpur who had been sent to Vietnam to stand by in case I was expelled from the country, Ray Herndon of UPI, and Dick Holbrooke, a young man attached to USOM who had once worked for the *Times* as a copy boy. We were sitting in a Chinese restaurant two blocks from the Palace, and every five minutes during the meal one of us would get up and make a quick tour of the block. But nothing happened—which was just as well; when the real coup came a week later, that particular restaurant was badly shot up in the first hour of fighting.

In the Vietnamese Army, titles were next to meaningless. The delicate balance of the Ngo rule rested mainly on two men—the commanders of the Third and Fourth Corps*—who had been promoted for their loyalty to Diem, not because of merit. The Fourth Corps included the Seventh Division, which was stationed at My Tho, a quick trip down a main highway; the Third Corps had jurisdiction over the troops in and around Saigon, and its headquarters was in the city. The generals commanding these two outfits, Huynh Van Cao of the Fourth Corps, and Ton That Dinh of the Third, were the two Army officers Diem trusted implicitly. Both were of course from the central coastal region, members of the Can Lao Party, and Catholics (Dinh was a convert). Neither was considered competent by his colleagues—militarily Cao was thought to be a catastrophe—but they provided insurance to the family that the troops close to Saigon would not turn against them, and if other units rebelled they could bail Diem out. They also served as a deterrent to coups; thinking about Dinh's and Cao's troops, would-be plotters were easily discouraged.

The three leaders of the generals' coup, Minh, Kim and Don, counted on Dinh as a key to their success. With Dinh on their side, a coup would be assured; without him, they might win out but it would probably be a

*South Vietnam was divided for military purposes into four large districts or corps, beginning with the first corps area in the North and progressing downward to the fourth corps, which encompassed the Mekong Delta in the south.

bloody and divisive affair. Dinh was Diem's favorite; he considered Dinh virtually an adopted son and had promoted him ahead of senior and more talented officers. Young, cunning, ambitious and vain, Dinh wore a paratrooper's beret at a jaunty angle; his jungle camouflage uniform was skintight, and wherever he went a huge, hulking Cambodian bodyguard who spoke neither French nor Vietnamese lurked menacingly in the background. The general delighted in having newspaper photographers around, and he was often accompanied by his personal Vietnamese cameraman so that there would be a complete record of the days and deeds of Ton That Dinh.

Dinh was the only general who had been given advance warning of the pagoda raids, and he had been told by the brothers that he was the great hero of this anti-American incident. Dinh, who readily believed them, thereafter became military governor of Saigon, and he threw his weight around by letting the other generals know that he might arrest them at any moment.

Dinh summoned a Vietnamese to dinner one night and told him that he—the guest—had been greatly honored. When the guest asked why, General Dinh answered, "Because you are having dinner with a great national hero." "That's nice," said the guest. "Where is he?" "It is me," answered General Dinh. "I have defeated the Americans and saved the country."

During the time when he was riding particularly high, Dinh held a press conference which turned into a farce. He immediately got in over his head by attacking a "certain foreign power"—obviously the United States—which he said had been plotting against his country. When Ray Herndon, who is a tough, brassy reporter, rose and asked what foreign power he was talking about, Dinh stalled. Herndon persisted; surely, he said, anyone who had as much information about the coup as General Dinh must know which country had attempted it. Again Dinh was evasive. "Well," said Herndon, "if you'd like to call your superiors to find out, we'll be delighted to wait." The Americans and the Vietnamese reporters in the audience roared with laughter.

Embarrassed, humiliated, having lost face, Dinh returned to his headquarters, and it was then that the three leaders of the generals' coup sensed that this was the best possible moment to play on his vanity. They were waiting for him at his quarters, and they immediately started telling him what a great hero he was and how the whole country looked up to him. Nhu didn't appreciate him fully, they said; how typical of Nhu! As a national hero he had made a good beginning with his military conduct after the pagoda raids, but now political moves must follow: the people were tired of the listless, ineffectual Cabinet of Ngo Dinh Diem. The country needed active young men in politics, and the Army particularly needed him in the Government to boost its sagging morale. (An indication of the effectiveness of this appeal to Dinh's enormous ego is that the first time Herndon saw him after the November coup, Dinh grabbed his hand and said, "Ah, you are my great friend. You are the one who started it all, who drove me into making the coup. You are the hero of the revolution." Whereupon the general sat down and gave Ray an exclusive interview—whose main theme seemed to be that Dinh was "the master of the coup d'état.")

The plotters suggested that Dinh talk to Diem and exert his great influence to place the military in the Cabinet. Dinh should become Minister of the Interior, Big Minh should become Minister of Defense, and Tran Van Minh—"Little Minh"—would make a good Minister of Education who would keep the students in line. The three leaders also proposed officers for other posts.

The generals were sure that these suggestions would enrage the brothers and that they would turn on Dinh. The scheme worked perfectly. In due course Dinh went to see Diem and proposed a new role for the military and particularly for himself. He, Dinh, the hero of the Republic, was needed by the people as Minister of the Interior. Diem, who was extremely touchy about his police apparatus and the role of the military, was stunned; the last thing he wanted was to have Army officers in the Cabinet. After giving Dinh an angry lecture and a blunt rejection, he told him to go to the mountain resort of Dalat and rest for a while; in effect, Dinh was temporarily relieved. "Stay out of politics and leave them to me," Diem told the general.

Dinh returned to the three generals doubly humiliated; not only had he failed to bring them into the Government, as he had boasted he could, but in addition he had been sent to Dalat and told that he wasn't needed. The generals were very sympathetic. Dinh was being badly treated by the brothers, they said; it was all Nhu's fault. So began the process of winning Dinh's participation in the plot. They bribed a fortune-teller to tell Dinh that she foresaw a long life of politics for him, and they constantly played on his vanity by reminding him of the country's need for him. Diem and Nhu made the plotters' job easier; frightened by Dinh's request, they had the general watched by security officers. In Saigon's cocoon of intrigue, Dinh immediately discovered this fact, and it simply accelerated his drift toward disloyalty.

The generals had slowly brought into their plot other officers of different background and temperament, and after Dinh's return from Dalat, the generals, moving very cautiously and concealing from him how advanced their plans were—for they did not trust Dinh, not even after he had committed himself to them—began to urge him to stage a coup. By this time they had spent several weeks softening him up, and they felt that he was so bitter against the family that it was safe to tip their hand. They were right; when the generals approached him, Dinh was already drawing up plans for a coup of his own.

The next problem to be faced was that of moving soldiers into the city without alerting Diem and Nhu. This was difficult, because the brothers had developed elaborate means of keeping watch on all troop movements (for instance, Captain Ba of a key armored unit at My Tho had to call the Palace every hour on the hour to report his whereabouts). One early plan

called for the generals to feed Diem exaggerated reports of a major Vietcong buildup in D-Zone, just north of Saigon. For some reason Diem had
always had a particular fascination for D-Zone operations, and it was
hoped that this would allow the generals to move large numbers of troops
to a point accessible to the city which would serve as a staging area. With
this idea in mind, the leaders set about recruiting units for the coup.

Dinh and his Third Corps troops were of prime importance, but almost
equally crucial was the role of the Seventh Division under General Cao's
command. Three days before the coup Dinh sent his deputy, Colonel
Nguyen Huu Co, to My Tho to talk with some officers whom the plotters
thought they might enlist in their cause. The excuse for Co's visit was that
under a forthcoming change of corps boundaries, the Seventh Division
would be under Dinh's control. In conversations with the deputy division
commander, two regimental commanders, the armored-unit commander
and the My Tho province chief, Co told them that it was the duty of the
Army to overthrow the Ngos because the family had alienated the population and could not govern. To protect his chief as long as possible, he said
that every general but Dinh was participating in the coup, and that Dinh
was expected to join it in the near future.

The entire incident was reported to Diem by the My Tho province
chief the next day. At this point, according to Palace sources, Diem and
Nhu no longer entirely trusted Dinh, but felt that he could still be used
against the other generals because, according to their information, he had
not yet fully committed himself. So the brothers summoned Dinh, and
Diem read him the account of Co's conversation with the My Tho officials.
At this point Dinh put on an emotional show. He is an explosive man, he
can be a very good actor, and on this occasion he pulled out all stops.
Weeping, he put his head in his hands and wailed, "This is my fault.
Because you have suspected me, I have not really worked for the last
fifteen days. I have stayed home because I was sad. But I am not against
you—I was sad because I thought you no longer trusted me. So Co has
profited from my absence to make trouble." Dinh then calmed down and
suggested that Co be arrested and shot, but Nhu opposed this. He wanted
the deputy arrested and interrogated to get the names of the other plotters.

Taking advantage of his audience with the brothers, Dinh continued
to play the hurt child; he said that some of Nhu's security men were
handing in false reports about him. Nhu answered that they had not
distrusted Dinh; they felt that he was the most trustworthy man in the
country, but they had been preoccupied with other matters. Indeed, said
Nhu, because of Dinh's heroic performance during the Buddhist crisis,
they were thinking of promoting him to major general. They had not quite
gotten around to it yet, but now of course he, Nhu, would take care of it
immediately.

At this, Dinh, knowing how Nhu's mind worked, suggested that they
plan a countercoup. Whether Dinh, aware of the loyalty of the My Tho

province chief, deliberately sent Co down there as bait to leak the plans for the coup to Diem and Nhu, or whether his proposal for a countercoup was an improvisation on the spot to extricate himself from a sticky situation is not known. No matter, he suggested a massive show of force: troops and tanks moved into Saigon to crush the plotters. The idea of a coup within a coup had great appeal to Nhu; the ordinary way of stopping a revolt was much too simple for him. He quickly agreed, and told Dinh to "get together with the other two members of the Can Lao Party," Lieutenant Colonel Nguyen Ngoc Khoi, commander of the Presidential Guard, and Colonel Tung. Diem okayed the plan. "You have full authority to get what you need," he said.

The next day, in a meeting with Tung and Khoi, Dinh told them that a major show of force was necessary and that they must have tanks because "armor is dangerous." Tung and Khoi, who were considered by other Vietnamese officers to be parlor soldiers without combat records, quickly agreed to let Dinh bring in his tanks. But Dinh was worried about the four battalions of special forces troops which Colonel Tung had previously brought into the city at Nhu's order; they would make such a formidable force if added to the Presidential Guard that other units might waver. So he told Tung and Khoi that if all the reserve forces were brought into Saigon, the Americans would be angry and claim that the Vietnamese were not prosecuting the war. "We must fool the Americans," he said to Tung. "You must send your four special forces battalions out of Saigon and tell the Americans that they have been ordered into combat. That will deceive them."

The following day, the one before the coup, Tung moved his four units out of the city after getting the approval of the brothers. Dinh then drew up plans to move large forces into the city, and Diem approved this too, thus legalizing what Nhu called "Operation Bravo Two" ("Bravo One" was Nhu's original fake-coup plan). And so it came about that Ngo Dinh Diem, who had spent so many hours trying to prevent revolts and who had gone to such elaborate lengths to stop this one, made possible the coup that ended his reign.

The three generals, who had been kept fully informed of Dinh's plans, now notified the Americans that they were planning a coup. Reportedly they did not deal with the American military, whom they still distrusted, but with Lodge's office. They did not ask for any assistance, but they said that the coup would be pro-American, and asked the mission not to thwart it. In turn, the embassy did not offer any aid, but it did make arrangements to stay in full communication with the rebels.

Sheehan and I knew that a coup was in the making. While one of our sources was reluctant to talk at any length, he seemed convinced that this time the rebellion would really take place. At this time, in late October, Sheehan's Tokyo office insisted that he take a two-week rest. Sheehan protested vigorously and warned that a coup was coming, but Tokyo ordered him out anyway. However, before he left we worked out a code; in case I learned more details and a definite date, I was to send him a message in Tokyo asking him to buy me a doll. When Sheehan arrived in Tokyo he posted signs all over the UPI cable room giving his hotel number and asking to be called immediately if any cable mentioning a doll arrived for him.

Early on the morning of October 31 a Vietnamese messenger came to the office and asked for Sheehan or me. When I identified myself he turned to one of our assistants and said something in Vietnamese; after being assured that I was indeed Halberstam, the visitor handed me a scrap of paper saying, "Buy me a bottle of whiskey at the PX." This was the agreed-upon signal from one of our sources that the coup was on its way. Immediately I cabled Sheehan to buy me the doll; in Tokyo the clerk at the desk looked at it, casually put it aside, and never called Sheehan.

Earlier I had sent a message to my office indicating that things were growing tense again and expressing the hope that they would run all possible copy from Saigon. Now Ray Herndon and I made some plans for emergency filing, and then went back to work. We learned that the coup was to take place at 1:30 P.M. the next day, Friday, November 1.

Both the CIA and the embassy were sure that there would be a coup; the military, under General Harkins, did not believe it, although a large number of junior officers had warned that a buildup was taking place. On the morning of November 1 the mission sent a coded cable to Washington saying that the coup would come at noon, or rather that State and CIA predicted it would come, but that MACV did not concur. Later in the afternoon, after the fighting had broken out, an officer at MACV called the embassy and asked that the MACV statement of dissent be stricken. Ironically, the issue of *Pacific Stars and Stripes* which arrived in Saigon that night featured a long interview with General Charles Timmes, the chief of the Military Assistance and Advisory Group, in which Timmes claimed that the Vietnamese troops were "loyal to their government." In the post-coup embarrassment, Timmes claimed that he had been misquoted, that he had said that the troops were loyal "to their *country*" (a point never in doubt), and the offending *Stripes* reporter, Marine Sergeant Steve Stibbens, was quickly bundled off to Tokyo for a rest.

Admiral Harry Felt, the commander of the U.S. Forces in the Pacific, had been in Saigon for a couple of days and happened to be leaving at noon on the first. At 10 A.M. Lodge accompanied Felt on a courtesy call to Diem. It must have been an unusually tense encounter: Lodge knew that a coup was on its way, while Diem believed that his brother's countercoup was coming. The three men discussed rumors of a revolt, but the meeting was noncommittal.

By midmorning certain troop units were already entering the city. The commander of the Vietnamese Navy, Captain Ho Tan Quyen, was taken out of town and asked to join the revolt; when he refused he was shot in the back of the head. But at noon Tan Son Nhut airport was simply the scene of another VIP departure. In his press conference Admiral Felt praised the nation's leadership and said that the war effort was going well despite the growing Vietcong fire power—about which there was some concern. Someone asked where the arms were coming from, and after an embarrassed silence Admiral Felt smiled and said that perhaps General Don knew. Tran Van Don said that weapons were indeed a major problem, and then he too laughed and said that he did not know where they were coming from either.

As the press conference dragged on, I watched General Don closely because I knew that he was supposed to be one of the leaders of the coup. He was clearly impatient and kept glancing anxiously at his watch. (A week later during an interview I told him that when I had seen him worrying about the time, I'd had to restrain the impulse to ask more questions to prolong the press conference. He did not seem amused.)

When Herndon and I left, we drove back to the city by way of Dinh's Third Corps headquarters, for we had received a tip that it was swarming with tanks. Our information was correct; there were troops all over the place, and about fifteen tanks, some of them being fueled.

We felt more convinced than ever that a coup would take place, but for the moment there was nothing to do but return to town and go about our business. It was nearly 12:30; if a coup occurred we might not eat again for a day, so we had lunch with Mert Perry and Murray Gart of *Time*. It was a pleasant, sunny day, and the streets were empty in the center of Saigon, as they always were during the siesta.

As we finished lunch and started to leave, the proprietor of the restaurant came running up and said that troops were moving along the waterfront. Just then there was a quick burst of fire from that direction; we ran over toward the noise and saw troops taking up positions throughout the city.

We split up. Ray and I went back to the office, where we found Le Phuoc Ly, one of Sheehan's photographers; he had been working around his house when a convoy of troops had driven down the road from Bien Hoa. They had waved to him, and one of the soldiers who knew him had invited Ly to join them. "Come along, we are making the coup," the soldier said.

The rebels had done well. They had managed to move nearly forty armored vehicles into Saigon and to shift two air-borne battalions, whose inclinations they doubted, to D-Zone for the day. They had the troops, the communications and the orders.

Security officials, worried by all the troop movements, had called the Palace, but they had been assured by Nhu that it was all part of a Palace coup. However, at 1:30 two battalions of elite Marines sped into the city and quickly captured the radio station and the police station—but not before the commander of the central police telephoned Nhu, told him the Marines were there and that they were not friendly. For the first time Diem and Nhu were a little worried, and they told a Palace aide to call

General Dinh's headquarters. One of Dinh's aides took the call, and though Dinh was there, said that his chief was at General Staff headquarters. Diem demanded that Dinh be told to send troops immediately to the police station.

In the meanwhile, the generals were engineering one more vital part of the coup. Every Friday a luncheon to discuss varied military problems was held by the General Staff. On this occasion Lieutenant Colonel Khoi, head of the Presidential Guard; Colonel Le Quang Tung and his brother and right arm, Major Le Quang Trieu; the garrison commander of Saigon, Nguyen Van La; and Colonel Cao Van Vien, the air-borne commander, had been invited by General Don on the pretense of discussing changes in the boundaries of corps areas.

At 1:30, when all were assembled in the dining room, General Don announced that a coup was taking place, and pointedly invited the guests to join. Everyone accepted willingly save Colonel Tung and his brother. At this moment fighting was going on nearby between some of the coup troops and a few of Colonel Tung's soldiers still left in the city. The generals forced the colonel to telephone his officers and order them to surrender; then Tung, the symbol of the family to the other generals and one of the most hated men in the country, was taken outside and executed.

The coup continued to move with clockwork precision. Half an hour after his first call to Dinh, Diem tried to reach him again, this time making the call personally. Again he was informed that Dinh was not there, and the aide talking to the President heard Diem say to somebody beside him, "General Dinh must have been arrested by the other generals."

Rebel troops quickly surrounded the Presidential Guard barracks; cut off from the Palace, this small island of Diem supporters could not reach the President. Then the rebels brought up their tanks and blasted away at the barracks, but though the sound of battle was impressive, few men were killed. This strategy of the plotters was deliberate; their superior armor was used almost as psychological warfare, to discourage Vietnamese as much as possible from killing their countrymen.

At 3 P.M. Diem and Nhu began broadcasting from a Palace transmitter on the 49-meter band. The first broadcast called on corps and division commanders and province chiefs to protect the President of the Republic, and the announcer asked for acknowledgments. There were no acknowledgments. Instead, over Radio Saigon, now controlled by the rebels, came pledge after pledge of support from division and corps commanders and commanders of special units. The promises were made by the officers themselves; to anyone who knew them, their voices were identifiable. The lack of support for Diem was stunning; all the division commanders had turned on him, as had three of the four corps commanders. In the end there was only one officer in command of troops who remained loyal to the brothers—Huynh Van Cao.

During Friday afternoon the generals called Diem and Nhu several times, listing the units and commanders now allied against them, asking them to surrender and promising safe-conduct. But the brothers would not listen to these appeals; instead, they suggested that the generals come to the Palace "for consultations." Remembering that Diem had used these tactics to lull the paratroopers in 1960, the generals were not interested.

By late afternoon the desperate brothers were radioing the province chiefs to send the Civil Guard and irregular units to rescue them. In the last message from the Palace monitored by the rebels that night, Nhu called for the Cong Hoa Youth and the Paramilitary Girls to move into Saigon and save the family. But these personal units of Nhu's and Madame's never appeared; by early Saturday morning their few dedicated members were already hiding their uniforms or visiting relatives out of town.

About four o'clock on Friday, Diem telephoned Ambassador Lodge in his office to tell him that the Army was in rebellion. Lodge, who of course was fully aware of what was going on, reminded Diem that the rebels had offered him safe-conduct, and apparently suggested that the brothers surrender. He also offered Diem and Nhu asylum at the U.S. embassy, saying that he wanted to do everything he could to protect Diem. It is reported that Diem's only reply to this offer was, "I shall try to restore order."

Diem and Nhu still held out some hope that units of the Seventh Division might help them, but in any case, they had long been prepared for an emergency such as this. Under the Palace there was an air-conditioned bomb shelter with a complete communications apparatus. There were also three tunnels, each surfacing far from the Palace in different directions. When the battle for the Palace began early Saturday morning, the rebel troops and the Palace defenders did not know that they were fighting for an empty cage—the birds had flown. At about eight o'clock on Friday evening Diem and Nhu slipped out of the Palace through one of the tunnels, carrying with them a briefcase filled with American dollars. Waiting for them at the other end of the tunnel was a Red Cross car, which took them to the house of Ma Tuyen, a rich Chinese merchant in Cholon. A direct line had been installed between Ma Tuyen's house and the Palace for just such an emergency as this. Cholon is on the south side of Saigon; the brothers were still hoping that the Seventh Division would come to their rescue from that direction.

From Cholon the brothers continued to telephone the generals, not letting on, of course, that they were no longer at the Palace. Sometime after midnight Diem's military aide called Dinh's headquarters again, and this time Dinh came to the phone. He began to curse the brothers in the most insulting Vietnamese phrases. He told the aide, "You are finished. It is all over. I saved them on the twentieth of August, but now they are finished. Tell them to surrender." When they learned of Dinh's defection, the brothers must have realized that they were beaten, for Dinh's troops, added to the other units ranged against them, made their rescue impossible even if the Seventh Division had remained loyal.

Throughout Friday afternoon in Saigon we reporters were scrambling around, trying to determine which units were remaining loyal, which had defected, and what the strategies of each side were. It was quite a difficult job because both sides wore the same uniforms. We were also confused because by midafternoon there appeared to be a lull in the fighting, and it seemed possible that the rebels had lost their nerve. (Actually, they were simply moving more troops into the city and were giving the brothers time to surrender.)

At about five o'clock I hailed a taxi and took a tour through the city. The driver, probably guessing that I was a reporter, made a gesture of slashing his throat with his finger, broke into a wide grin and said, *"Tong Thong* [President Diem] *fini."* As we drove up one thoroughfare I saw columns and columns of air-borne troops marching alongside about twenty armored cars. Vo Huynh of NBC was with them, photographing the advance. I jumped out of the cab and asked him which side these troops were on. "Anti-Diem," he said. I already knew that the Marines were committed to the rebels; if the air-borne with this much armor, some of it from the Seventh Division, was part of the coup, the handwriting was on the wall. Using the facilities of the American military, I immediately sent out a few hundred words, but they never made the paper; the story was simply drowned by the vast amount of information being released in Washington. The story of the coup in the *Times* the next day was a Washington story.

The troops moving through Saigon made a striking sight. The population watched impassively; it had observed scenes like this before, and it did not believe any of it. The apathy was broken only by the children. In the center of Saigon one pro-Diem armored car was roaming the streets shooting at anything that moved, and sometimes the fire would be returned. As soon as any exchange ended, children would run out to the armored car and scoop up the brass from the used cartridges.

On Friday night we watched the shelling of the Presidential Guard barracks and other engagements in various parts of the city. Our sources confirmed that the Seventh Division was helping the rebels, and we wondered why there had not been any attack on the Palace. Finally one of our Vietnamese assistants learned from a friend at military headquarters that the assault on it would not come until sometime after three in the morning. I decided to go to bed and managed to sleep for about two hours, until the heavy firing around the Palace woke me up. I joined Herndon, and we took a circuitous route to the scene. As we watched, one tank after another moved in, and about two blocks from the building the Marines were advancing in columns in preparation for the attack. We stayed with them to observe the fire battle between the opposing armored forces—fought at such close range that a friend described it as "like watching two boxers in a closet." In short order the superior size and number of the rebel tanks proved to be overwhelming; several of the Palace tanks were knocked out, and an entire platoon of Diem's armor surrendered.

At about five o'clock Herndon and I moved up with the Marines to within a block of the Palace. It was still very dark, and the night was filled with the noise of heavy tank and antitank guns; the only light came from two burning tanks. Suddenly there was a tremendous explosion very close to us. I was terrified, for I suddenly remembered that one of our best sources had once told me that Nhu had lined the streets around the Palace with Claymoor mines, which were to be detonated electrically in case of a coup. I told Herndon about this, and after consultation we decided to cover the story from a little farther down the block.

At dawn on Saturday a white flag appeared at the Palace, and the firing halted momentarily. The Marines charged across the Palace lawn, with Herndon, myself, and Peter Kalischer of CBS right behind them. Suddenly a few defenders who evidently hadn't gotten the word kept firing; caught in the open, we hit the dirt until the last exchange ended. Then it was all over; the Government had fallen. The Marines charging through the Palace grabbed Madame Nhu's negligees and Nhu's whiskey; everything was there but the brothers.

It was a time of jubilation. In the streets around the building, Vietnamese students approached cautiously. When they saw that the Palace had surrendered they crowded around the tanks, hailing the soldiers, lifting them on their shoulders, handing them food and taking pictures of them. Young girls offered bouquets of flowers. The troops accepted what they were given, but they looked slightly confused; they had never been treated this way before by the population. One armored captain later told me he was staggered by the response; it was a nice feeling, he said, for in the past the people had always been afraid of the soldiers. Yet there was an air of restraint to the celebration that Saturday morning; it was as if the populace did not—could not—really believe that the Ngo family was no more.

At 8 A.M. the brothers were still alive, and they had been told that the rebels had taken the Palace. By then they must have known that there would be no help from My Tho. There are conflicting reports as to how the rebels discovered the brothers' hiding place. The one I'm inclined to believe is that a member of their own family, who had known of their advance plans and gone with them to Cholon, had betrayed them by getting word out to Colonel Do Mau. This seems to me the most likely version, because I know about some of the extreme precautions that were taken to conceal the identity of and to protect the alleged betrayer after Diem and Nhu had been eliminated. According to another account, one of the officers at the Palace told his captors about the hideout. A third rumor was that Diem himself, hearing of the capture of the Palace, telephoned the generals and offered to yield under certain conditions: that he be allowed to surrender honorably; that members of his family be allowed to leave the country; and that he be allowed to remain President for a brief interval in order to save face and retire gracefully. According to this version, the rebels agreed to the first two conditions and declined to accept the third, but Diem disclosed his whereabouts nonetheless.

However, the brothers' hiding place was discovered. Shortly after nine on Saturday morning the rebels sent three armored cars to a small Catholic church in Cholon near the merchant's house, where Diem and Nhu had just taken sanctuary. They were arrested and placed in the armored car at about nine-thirty. They left the church alive; they arrived dead at General Staff headquarters. Again there are divergent reports of what exactly happened. One story has it that Nhu antagonized one of his captors so much that the officer, who had had a friend killed by Nhu, lost his head and stabbed first Nhu and then Diem. According to another version, the officer in charge of the armored cars was General Mai Huu Xuan, a former high police official under the French who hated the brothers so much that he permitted the assassination.

My own feeling is that the brothers were killed because the generals did not trust either Diem or the Americans enough. They were afraid that the United States might propose that Diem be placed at the head of a coalition government, or that Diem might somehow stall them long enough for his American supporters to exert pressure for a place for him in a new government. (A high Vietnamese officer once told me that in a conversation just before the coup, a CIA man who was obviously trying to find out what the plotters were doing had said that if there was a coup, they should avoid killing Diem if possible. In recounting the incident to me, the officer was angry. "What the hell do the Americans want—for us to get rid of the Government and then be killed ourselves?" he said.)

Dinh did not know that the brothers were being assassinated, and apparently asked his fellow conspirators to spare their lives. When he was told over the telephone that they were both dead, he asked the speaker to repeat the news, and then slowly let his hands fall. One of his aides picked up the receiver, and the armored officer on the other end of the line went on to say that the brothers had committed suicide. Dinh's aide asked how this was possible. The officer said that the prisoners had grabbed a rifle from an enlisted man, and when Dinh's aide asked why only one man was guarding them, he was told that "someone was careless." Dinh wept at the news, but he was not so grief-stricken that it prevented him from dancing at a party that night.

The original death certificates contemptuously described Diem not as the head of state, but as "chief of province," one of the jobs he had held under the French as a young man, and Nhu as "chief of library service," one of his early posts. Reportedly they were buried in a small, quiet military ceremony outside of town on Saturday evening.

Chapter 13

What Should Be Done in Vietnam?

After the coup d'état I spent the next ten days in Saigon putting together an account of the fall of the Government and the changes taking place. Then friends in the Delta began to telephone and stop by the office, something they hadn't been able to do for a long time. They urged me to come down to My Tho on a visit, for they could talk openly again.

I spent most of the next month traveling through the Delta. It was a sentimental journey, for I knew that I was going home in mid-December, and that I was seeing for the last time the area I knew and liked the best, and where friends of mine had been killed. It was also a sad trip because of the contrast with the countryside I had first seen fourteen months before. Where there had been some hope and momentum then, now all I could see was decay and deterioration on our side, and an improvement in the Vietcong position. It was a bitter trip too, for the steep price necessary for victory a year before had more than doubled now; despite all the bloodshed and all the sacrifices, the winning of the war was further away than ever.

However, for once the job of a reporter in Vietnam was easy. The Vietnamese officers were talking candidly to the American advisers, and both were talking to the reporters. Those first few weeks after the coup were a time of great frankness and soul-searching, of mutual trust in many areas. In mid-November my old friend Colonel Pham Van Dong, who was now in command of the Seventh Division, invited me down to his headquarters. We had known each other well through the long and difficult months when he was held in great suspicion by Diem; in those days Sheehan and I had been forced to send messages to him through a third party. Widely admired by the Americans—one American colonel said he was the only Vietnamese he knew who was qualified to lead American troops—Dong was a North Vietnamese who was considered extremely tough; his appointment had given some of the advisers in the Seventh Division hope that the tide could still turn.

When I reached My Tho, some advisers took me by helicopter to western Dinh Tuong Province, where Dong was conducting an operation that day, just as he had every day the previous week, keeping his troops moving constantly in an attempt to seize the initiative from the enemy and to convince a population which had not seen the ARVN in eight months that the Government still existed. "We are trying to tell them about the coup d'état," the colonel said when I joined him, "but the Vietcong have gotten there first."

We sat around the command post and talked. The Americans were in a very good mood; for the first time in months they felt that they were chasing the enemy—and in an area where the Government had not been seen for a long time.

Colonel Dong called over the district chief who was in the command post, and introduced him as a former aide and old friend. "I think I trust this one," Dong said. Then he turned to the chief and asked him how many villages there were in his district.

The district chief said that there were twenty-four.

"How many do you control?" the colonel asked.

"Eight," the chief replied.

Then the colonel smiled and asked, "And how many did you report that you controlled?"

The chief looked slightly sheepish and then answered, "Twenty-four."

Then the Americans and Colonel Dong had a discussion about just how much of those two vital provinces, Long An and Dinh Tuong, the Government controlled. It was the kind of conversation almost unheard of in Vietnam, open and frank, with Americans arguing with a Vietnamese for being too optimistic. One of the officers pulled out a list of the hamlets in the two provinces. Of the two hundred and thirteen in Dinh Tuong and the two hundred and nineteen in Long An, Colonel Dong estimated that about 20 percent were politically and militarily controlled by the Government, but some of the Americans felt that 10 percent was more accurate.

Later I asked one of the senior advisers if the situation was really that bad. "Actually, I think it's worse," he said. "I don't think we've even begun to see the enemy's real capacity—I think they're playing cat and mouse with us. Many of these hamlets have never been hit by the VC, and the reason is that they don't have to hit them—they control them already."

The adviser went on to say that the strategic hamlets in the Delta had begun to serve as way-stations for the guerrillas. They would slip in at night, eat, and move on the next day. In some areas they made the peasants chop up the endless strands of barbed wire which had virtually become a symbol of Government failure; in others they made the people take the roofs off their huts as a sign of obedience. Slowly they were drawing closer to main district and provincial capitals, becoming bolder in their attacks. The noose was being tightened.

Until the coup, the mood in the Seventh Division had been one of pessimism. Yet Colonel Dong brought hope with him; the new junta had put its best man on the toughest assignment, and perhaps this was a harbinger of the future. Dong demonstrated what an advisory relationship could be; he asked the Americans to come to his briefings, he made it clear to his own officers that he liked the advisers and their advice, and whenever he telephoned one of his own officers he was punctilious about speaking to the man's American counterpart as well. The result was that the Vietnamese had to be candid with the Americans.

It was a time of brief optimism, however, for if there was any hope in November 1963, it was that something dramatic would happen—that there would be not just change, but virtual revolution—so that the downward spiral of nearly two decades could be reversed quickly. But the new junta was composed of men like Minh who were sympathetic to their American ally and to their own people, men willing to talk realistically about the problems around them. Essentially men of an older order who believed in the traditions by which they had risen to the top, they were anything but revolutionaries. Moreover, the system was so corroded and the Army so riddled with ineptitude that any reforms of Diem's successors were largely neutralized by the residue. It was a time for greatness and brilliance, and these qualities were not forthcoming.

In the Seventh Division, for instance, Colonel Dong maneuvered his troops brilliantly for three weeks—and at the end of November he was relieved. Just why I never learned; perhaps General Dinh was afraid of him, perhaps the other leaders, who were aware of his close relationship with junior officers, feared that he might lead a revolt, perhaps he had offended one of the generals, perhaps there was jealousy over the Americans' enthusiasm for him.

My long tour of the Delta had been depressing enough, but the removal of Dong hit me the hardest of all. It seemed that the old Vietnamese game was being played again, but it was much too late for that game. The times demanded talent, not pettiness. When I went out to Colonel Dong's house to see him, I learned that he had been posted to Formosa as a military attaché. It was an unhappy visit, for he was profoundly depressed about the state of the war.

No Westerner can return from Vietnam a proud or satisfied man. If he has any conscience at all he goes home with a profound sense of inadequacy, along with whatever scars and sympathies and experience he has acquired. The failure of the West in Indochina has been unnecessary, expensive and bloody; in Vietnam, Caucasians have staked their prestige and then showed only their worst and clumsiest side, as if anxious to confirm a Marxist caricature.

Whatever the capacity in which he has served, an American today comes back from Vietnam anguished, sad and more than a little bitter: bitter toward the Vietnamese (the easiest target), bitter toward his fellow Americans in Southeast Asia, and then, after exposure to his fellow countrymen in the United States, most of all bitter toward them. On his way through this affluent land (America in 1964 is overwhelming to anyone who has been to remote parts of the world for nearly three years), the returning traveler is asked or told:

"It sounds like a rat hole out there to me."

Or, "I hear they won't fight."

Or (from a bearded young integration worker in Mississippi), "I enjoyed your coverage of America's other colonial war."

Or, "Is there going to be a war out there?"

It is hard to reconcile the affluence of our society with the sights of Vietnam; the contrast is staggering. But what is more difficult to adjust to is America's indifference and ignorance, and so, many people coming back from Vietnam go through a period of bitterness during which they prefer the company of those who have been in Vietnam and know the country and care about it. When you meet these friends, now frustrated by a quieter, less committed life, everyone talks about going back to Vietnam. But very few do; it is hard to return, and there is not that much to go back to.

We live in a busy and complicated world; slowly other challenges and interests arise, and after a while you're able to forget something of what you have seen.

The months since I left Vietnam have not been happy ones for that country; neither have they been surprising. The later the date of an insurgency, the greater is the tide one has to turn, and the more limited is the capacity to turn it. The awaited miracle is still awaited. Vietnam does not lend itself to big miracles, only small ones: a badly hit helicopter making a safe landing, an ambushed Government force being rescued. Vietnam offers itself to whichever side pays a higher price, faces reality more readily, understands the nature of the conflict better and spends longer hours in the rice paddies and in teaching young peasant children how to read. But these are not miracles.

Over and over again I have been asked by people who have never been to Southeast Asia: Why don't they see it our way? Why don't they put aside their differences and fight in a common cause against a common enemy? But we have never been able to show the Vietnamese that the cause *is* common. We have never fully convinced them that *our* enemy is *their* enemy—in part because we have never understood their enemy.

As I write, there is political instability in Saigon. That is nothing new; there has been political instability there, accelerating and abating and accelerating again, since 1946, when the French Indochina war began. The only difference today is that in the past the unrest was below the surface; it could not readily be seen by the foreign eye. But it was real enough; it corroded the soul of a nation and it fomented a revolution that is still going on. But it took place in the hearts, and not until recently in the streets; and so, it was not the type of thing of which diplomacy is made.

After I had left Saigon, the generals' coup was overthrown at the end of January by the bloodless Nguyen Khanh coup. In effect this was a step forward in the political sophistication of the military. Khanh, ten years younger than the other generals, represented a new generation, and his goals were similar to those of the young officers whose coup the generals had thwarted. At this late date some younger ideas had come to the surface.

The generals, said Americans who were there at the time, seemed tired and lethargic, unable to respond to the urgency of the awesome challenges they had inherited. They had brought a certain amount of political stability to the country simply by overthrowing the detested Government, whereas Khanh brought youth and vigor. But in the fragile balance of post-Diem Vietnam, of newly won freedoms, of reluctance to return to the men and the ways of the past, Khanh's sudden power grab awakened old fears. The Buddhists and other new groups were eager to protect their new strength and influence. Lodge, who had understood the complexity of Vietnamese politics better than any American, was gone, and [Gen. Maxwell] Taylor had taken his place. Following the naval incident in the Tonkin Gulf, Khanh, encouraged by the Americans, moved to establish total power with a very strong central government. Riots started again in the streets; the result was not that Khanh became stronger, but that his government fell.

On August 7, 1964, Peter Grose, the acute *New York Times* reporter in Saigon, wrote:

> How did this disintegration come about? Observers on the scene think that in sum it was the result of an attempt to impose a neat, American-style solution on an Asian society in disarray. General Khanh's offensive went too far too fast, according to Vietnamese and foreign observers; it ignored the basic motives of self-interest that propel religious, political and social groups of this country. These observers felt that insofar as United States policy makers encouraged General Khanh in his bold moves to centralize power, they bear a major responsibility for the present situation. The risk they encouraged was not, in the view of these observers, well calculated.
>
> The opinion of these sources is that the Americans made the basic error of assuming that the primary interest of the Vietnamese people is the same as the primary interest of the American mission in Vietnam: defeat of the Vietcong insurgency.

Since the riots had succeeded in toppling Khanh's government, the Buddhists were stronger than ever. They enjoyed their new power and felt that they had a virtual veto over any government. Military rule soon ended and a caretaker civilian government was established under Tran Van Huong, a widely respected civil servant with a reputation for stubbornness and honesty. Again the Buddhists challenged Huong's right to run a government in which they were not the dominant factor; they also claimed that there were too many Diem holdovers—mostly civil servants —in his Administration. Huong replied that the Buddhist grievances against Diem had been justified, but that the ones against him were not and that his regime should be given time to prove itself. Once more there were riots in Saigon in late November 1964, but Huong stood firm. Though

Khanh, now commander of the Armed Forces, sulked in the wings, Huong was momentarily strengthened when other young officers rallied to his side.

During this period the Buddhists were making a strong bid for control. With the fall of the Diem government they had become the most powerful segment of the population. They were popular because they had largely been responsible for bringing down a hated government, and their leadership was skillful. But Diem had also been highly acclaimed in his early days, not because of his character or ability to govern, but because his first acts—the crushing of the gangster sects, for instance—had met popular response. How long the Buddhists' popularity would last if they went too far was a crucial question. Were they headed for political nihilism, and if so, would they be able to retain their following? Some Americans believed that one of their advantages was the war weariness felt by many Vietnamese.

In January they were able to provoke demonstrations which shook Huong's government, and General Khanh and the military returned to power in another bloodless coup. For the moment the Buddhists relaxed the tension, but their power seemed very real. The question then became whether Khanh and the young officers would be able to work out some sort of rapprochement with the Buddhists. If this was accomplished, it would bring Vietnam some needed political stability; if not, it appeared likely that some sort of final showdown between the Buddhists and the military would eventually take place.

What has been taking place in Vietnam in the last few months is what Ambassador Lodge has called the "process of political evolution." South Vietnam has never had a chance to evolve naturally; there have been no stable institutions or elections through which such a progression could take place. But the relatively crude political maneuvering that has been occurring recently, in which varying groups jockey for place, is the first glimmering of the democratic process. If the Vietnamese government and the Americans are lucky, there may be a vague grouping which will hold the disparate interest factions of the country in delicate balance: Buddhist, Catholic, young officers, old-guard traditionalists, Delta Vietnamese, central Vietnamese and refugees. But such beginnings are taking place at a very late and desperate date.

In the countryside the situation remains grim. Occasionally Government units have stood and fought with remarkable tenacity, and American officers report that they are enjoying increased success in getting a hearing for their ideas. But many of the techniques of the past remain: the large, fraudulent operations; the commitment of troops to indefensible points. Moreover, an insurgency is not like the war in Korea, where a force evicted from a position one day could return the next and recapture the territory. In the infinitely complex Vietnamese war, there are a large number of factors which tend to produce a spiral; this downward spiral produces its own momentum, and it is far easier for this movement to accelerate than it is to slow it down, much less reverse it.

And so, as this is written, it is very late in Vietnam. It was very late in 1951 when the French stayed on; it was later in 1954 when the war was finally over; it was later still in 1961 when Taylor made our last-gasp commitment; and it was even later in 1963 when that last gasp failed and Diem was overthrown. What is there to recommend at the end of that long road down which we have traveled for years and years when the policy was: *There is no place else to go*? How do you find somewhere else to go now?

The basic alternatives for Vietnam are the same now as they were in 1961; they are no different, no more palatable, no less of a nightmare.

First, there is a great deal of talk about the possibility of a neutral Vietnam. But under present conditions this is out of the question. There is not the remotest possibility of neutrality in the sense that Switzerland, Austria, India or even Laos are neutral—which is these countries' way of saying that they wish to be neither a battlefield nor a participant of either side in the Cold War. The first step toward a neutral Vietnam would undoubtedly be the withdrawal of all U.S. forces in the country and a cutback in American military aid; this would create a vacuum so that the Communists, the only truly organized force in the South, could subvert the country at their leisure—perhaps in six months, perhaps in two years. There would simply be no force to resist them, and if Hanoi offered us and the South Vietnamese a neutral solution, it would only mean a way of saving face for the United States.

What *about* withdrawal? Few Americans who have served in Vietnam can stomach this idea. It means that those Vietnamese who committed themselves fully to the United States will suffer the most under a Communist government, while we lucky few with blue passports retire unharmed; it means a drab, lifeless and controlled society for a people who deserve better. Withdrawal also means that the United States' prestige will be lowered throughout the world, and it means that the pressure of Communism on the rest of Southeast Asia will intensify. Lastly, withdrawal means that throughout the world the enemies of the West will be encouraged to try insurgencies like the one in Vietnam. Just as our commitment in Korea in 1950 has served to discourage overt Communist border crossings ever since, an anti-Communist victory in Vietnam would serve to discourage so-called wars of liberation.

The only other possibility—for blocking or bombing the so-called Ho Chi Minh trail would not effectively alter the balance of power in the South—is the one that every American President has shied away from for more than twelve years: the commitment of U.S. combat troops to South Vietnam. This most difficult of options would undoubtedly be even more frustrating than Korea; there we were fighting a uniformed, identifiable enemy which had crossed a border, in terrain which had a front. In Vietnam, however, Caucasians would be killing South Vietnamese on their own soil in a political war. If only 5 percent of the population in the South is committed to the Vietcong, the arrival of U.S. combat units would probably make enemies out of fence-sitters; certainly the guerrillas' cause would become a broader and more popular one. Whatever military gains were brought by U.S. troops might soon be countered by the political loss; the war would begin to parallel the French experience. It would be a war without fronts, fought against an elusive enemy, and extremely difficult for the American people to understand. The misconceptions, misinformation and lack of candor displayed by American officialdom in the past in Indochina does not give anyone confidence that our government would explain the conflict honestly to its own citizens.

So for the moment we are caught in the quagmire. Neutralization would only delay the inevitable momentarily, we would dishonor ourselves and our allies by pulling out, and, despite the fact that we are deeply involved in a very real war, we should think and prepare for a long, long time before going in with our own troops.

It is, of course, a Vietnamese war, though it is true that it could not continue for very long without the American military commitment. But neither could it go on if it did not have the support of a certain range of Vietnamese people. If and when it becomes a hopeless war and a hopeless cause, it will not be the Americans who know this first; it will be the Vietnamese, who have now lived without peace for over nineteen years. After three years, less than the equivalent of a combat battalion of Americans has died; Vietnamese by the hundreds and occasionally by the thousands die each month. If the war becomes intolerable, it will be the Vietnamese who will and must decide that almost anything—even being ruled by a Communist government in Hanoi—is better than endless bloodletting. What would trigger this decision no one knows: perhaps a neutralist coup by young officers willing to negotiate; perhaps the complete domination of the Delta by the Vietcong.

In the meantime we are committed to playing our part of the bargain as best we can, in a desperate hope that we have learned some of the lessons of Indochina in time to use them in Vietnam. Just conceivably, at this late date the dissenting forces in the country will band together when the imminent threat of a Communist take-over finally makes the enemy a common enemy; fear sometimes succeeds where all other motivations fail. If various political factions could unite, there might be a strong enough base for a viable military approach to a solution. But only an improvement in the military situation can make real negotiations possible.

But after nineteen years of Western mistakes, these hopes are very frail. Probably the lessons will not be learned in time for Vietnam. Perhaps at this moment we are gaining the knowledge necessary to deal with a situation in Thailand, or Angola, or a small republic in South America— some country where it is not yet too late, where now there is only a quiet crisis and still some flexibility. Perhaps we should be glad that so far Vietnam is the only country in which the West became the stubborn prisoner of its colonial past and a colonial war. We should remember that the French did not repeat their mistakes in French West Africa, that they did get out of Algeria just in time, and that the British dissolved their empire with remarkable skill.

Throughout the world the chickens are coming home to roost, and for better or for worse, the responsibility for their roosting rests with the United States. The presidency does not lend itself to the study of quiet crises: there are too many noisy ones at hand. Right now the President has a hundred Vietnams: there is Mississippi, the gold balance, Cuba, poverty, Britain and the Common Market, De Gaulle and the MLF, the Congo, the USSR—the list is endless. Mr. Johnson is a fire chief with too many blazes to put out, and too little time to worry about spots where at the moment there is only a little smoke—where the status quo is now tolerable to the United States but intolerable to the population of that country. In 1951— perhaps the year the war was really lost—who was listening to the quiet voices from Indochina?

Thus the problem is partly a matter of deciding what our global commitments and our priorities are. What is the range of our self-interest and security? Is every country not yet inside the Communist Bloc a part of the United States' responsibility? Is each country on the continent of South America worth fighting for, or do only some of them have the resources and strategic location that make them worth the challenge? In what case is there a common interest between the two countries to make a commitment plausible and potentially successful? Before we ever plant the flag again, we must make sure that grounds for mutual self-interest exist, that the situation has not deteriorated beyond control and, above all, that we are wanted.

Epilogue

Return to Vietnam

EDITOR'S NOTE: In late 1967, David Halberstam went back to South Vietnam to see if the massive American military effort then entering its third year had changed the country's prospects for survival. His conclusions appeared in "Return to Vietnam," which was first published in a somewhat longer version in the December 1967 issue of *Harper's Magazine.*

One of the great exports of South Vietnam has always been American optimism, but this time I thought when I returned that it would be at least tempered; there would be an end of illusion, a knowledge perhaps of just how dark the tunnel really is. But we flew into Tan Son Nhut and the scenes were familiar: the jetliner waiting too long on the tarmac, its air conditioning off, then the waiting room with the American AID men come out to welcome their new arrivals and steer them past all the waiting Vietnamese at immigration. Finally I got through customs and Mert Perry, an old friend, five years here and one of the very best reporters in town, met me and assured me I was wrong: the illusions still exist. When you pay $30 billion a year you buy at least a fair share of illusions.

I have never been a dove or a hawk—few reporters who have spent any length of time here are. When I was here in 1962 and 1963 I belonged to a group of reporters who thought the war was worth winning but who doubted the effectiveness of the fight against the enemy and sensed the seed of failure in our own efforts. That group was roundly attacked by American officialdom for being too pessimistic, but in retrospect I think the great sin was that we were not pessimistic enough.

More than three years later, I still think the enemy is a real one. I think the evidence is more complete than ever that Hanoi has controlled this war since 1957, but now I doubt our capacity to win. The important things in talking about Vietnam now are: Can the war be won? Do we have the resources to win, and can we really afford these resources? People here now are talking about reorganizing the Vietnamese Army, just as they did six years ago. But it is very late here, the fabric is strained at home now, and what guarantee is there that the Vietnamese Army can be reorganized, or that it will make any difference? Can you have a fine young army in a rotting society?

So is the war being won?

The answer is yes it is, and no it isn't. On those occasions when we can use our massive power, those rare instances when our main force units find

181

their main force units, our power is decisive, and there is more often than not a victory. Similarly in those areas which we choose to saturate with American troops, the Vietcong must move back, and in that specially protected, hothouse atmosphere a kind of pacification takes place. But the sense one finally gets is of the fragility of the situation rather than the permanence. It may be that to a particular American general, five months into his twelve months' tour, the progress of the war in his zone is a final and concrete entity, but to an experienced Indochina hand there is more hesitance. Progress at a given moment is a fleeting experience unless it is brought about by the deep-rooted desire of the Vietnamese peasants themselves. That is why I am so pessimistic, for the other war, the nation building, helping the Vietnamese to help themselves, has not changed.

There is no doubt that the arrival of half a million Americans here has brought considerable military progress to Vietnam. In 1965 the Arvin (Vietnamese Army) had been defeated and the country was the Vietcong's to take. The Americans instead came and have fought well. Even General Westmoreland's* critics—and their number is increasing—praise him for the way he imposed a growing American commitment on a very weak base, maneuvered his troops, and staved off defeat.

Nor is there any doubt of the massive power we have accumulated here. The mind boggles at the firepower an infantry company possesses. If anything we may have too much firepower, and with it there may be too much of a tendency not to come to grips with the more subtle problems of the war. The Vietcong and the regular North Vietnamese units have been hurt, and at times hurt badly, although it would be a great mistake to underestimate, as Westerners traditionally have, the enemy's resilience and durability, his ability to recover from his wounds, and his *passion* to keep coming.

The Americans here talk a good deal about rooting out the Vietcong infrastructure, the invisible shadow government which is the Communist key to local success. Yet it is frankly admitted that the infrastructure has barely been touched. Thus while the enemy has lost bodies, it has not lost its apparatus, which is a very important distinction. Hence the real power of the Vietcong has not been affected.

The escalation of the war has escalated the pressure the Vietcong are putting on the population. They no longer have the luxury of working side by side with the peasants in the field, nor do they have the Ngo Dinh Diem government to help them with their own recruiting as in the old days. The VC are inflicting higher taxes on the population, recruiting boys at younger and younger ages. A friend of mine who has always been a dissenter from official optimism feels that the most striking change in the last two years has been the weakening of the Vietcong. "In 1963 and 1964 they controlled fifty per cent of the population, and they did it while being

---

*General William Westmoreland, commander of American forces in Vietnam from 1965 to 1969, oversaw the U.S. military buildup of those years and initiated a policy of using American units to pursue the enemy actively.

liked," he said, "and now they are down to about twenty-five. The important thing, of course, is that the South Vietnamese government has not been able to move into the vacuum, there's been no real government pickup. But there's no doubt of the problems the VC face—a couple of years ago if I were a young Vietnamese boy I'd have gone with the VC, but now it's different. They're putting a lot of pressure on the population too. They've lost some of their mystique."

(It should be noted that this has been done at a very high price to the Vietnamese peasants. In the Delta, for instance, the Vietcong has been hurt, but not by an aggressive Vietnamese Army searching out and waiting at night for VC units, but rather by constant bombing and shelling of those villages not controlled by the government, so that finally life becomes unbearable. The people either drift out of the villages toward government-controlled areas, or sleep at night, not in their huts, but in the paddies themselves to escape the shelling. Thus they no longer welcome the Vietcong into their villages, and when they come into the government areas, they say, yes, we understand why you are shelling us, yes, we know it's the Vietcong's fault; but I have my doubts about what they really feel and what the final political outcome of this will be. In the past, methods such as this have come back to haunt us.)

The society is rotten, tired, and numb. It no longer cares. Twenty-one years of the war, of first the French and then Diem, have weakened the Vietnamese deeply. The sons are more corrupt than the fathers. The few patriots increasingly withdraw from the society and the struggle. The fine young men do not want to die in the U Minh forest; they want to drive their Hondas, get their draft deferments, and sit in the cafés. We are not building a nation.

Before I came back I was assured again and again by people who had been in Vietnam more recently that I would never recognize it, that it was not the same country. The American presence was so great. And yes, there is Cam Ranh Bay, and the endless Long Binh military complex outside Saigon, trucks, generators, barracks, helicopters as far as the eye can see. There is American television, and one sees American troops still in combat gear watching *Combat,* and a blonde weather girl pointing at the map of the U.S. and saying "Los Angeles is clear and sunny . . . ," and most Vietnamese seem to have Batman T-shirts for their kids. And there is a strip of bars in Bien Hoa so long that one American there calls it Tijuana East, with sign after sign offering CAR WASH. (The Vietnamese are ingenious that way. One friend of mine has a song which goes, "Baby, won't you wash my car.") All these are signs of Americanization, but what finally struck me was how little had really changed here.

For it is the essential problems of this society that have not changed. They are the same problems, virtually insoluble, caused by the same terrible historical truths. The government of Vietnam is largely meaningless to its citizens. The rare good province chief or district chief is talked about avidly in the American Mission. Yet it is a fact of life that most province and district chiefs are corrupt and incompetent. There is talk of improvement in the Vietnamese Army, yet it is widely known that the Arvin is still poorly led and barely motivated. Its officers represent a microcosm of existing privilege in Vietnam. It does not change, perhaps because it cannot change and let in new blood—but unless it does it is dooming itself to its own defeat.

The pacification program, known periodically as The Other War, heir apparent to a long line of programs tried, programs vaunted, programs praised, programs failed—*agrovilles,* strategic hamlets, spreading oil slicks, national priority areas—is a study in the past. At very best there is creeping pacification. Pacification, of course, is always difficult. The social and political problems which the Americans can avoid when they simply are fighting the war and killing VC suddenly reappear when we try to create something here.

The third day I was here I went to a briefing by a high pacification official. He began by saying that Quang Ngai province was going to be the success story of 1967, and to mark his words: *Quang Ngai.* Even as he was talking the Vietcong were walking into Quang Ngai and freeing twelve hundred prisoners from the jail there. He was saying *this* pacification program, his pacification program, was different from the other pacification programs, because this time we had the *resources.*

I thought to myself, My God man, didn't they tell you about the strategic hamlet program, how the province chiefs used to choke to death on resources, how they were afraid to stand out on the little airstrips for fear of being buried alive by resources tumbling out of the sky: barbed wire, bricks, pigs, rat killers, pig fatteners, mosquito killers, snow plows? In those days I talked with the British expert on Malaya, and he said there was one thing which bothered him about this war: too much in the way of resources, too many material goods. He had never seen so much gear in his life, stuff going to rust and rot, being black-marketed, creating all the wrong attitudes in the Vietnamese.

The day after the briefing I was with one of the rural pacification workers, a competent American professional who had spent four years here. He recounted his past year: more of the same Vietnamese apathy, American indifference to his pleas, faking of provincial operations, increased corruption by his Vietnamese counterpart, resources not reaching their destination, his counterpart's interest in his own building business.

The American had documented it all, handed in his report, and for a brief time the job of his Vietnamese counterpart was in the balance, and then he was given it back. "I'm going to stay in this country until I see that son of a bitch in jail." the American said. "Pacification," he said, "what the hell is pacification? You find it." Then he added: "We are losing. We are going to lose. We deserve to lose."

There is much subsurface criticism of Westmoreland here, particularly among experienced Americans, because they feel in large part he has abdicated his responsibilities with the Vietnamese. The job was just too tough, and so he preferred to work with the Americans, which was natural enough. Push an American button and an American jumps; push a Vietnamese button and then push it again. And then again.

Certainly Westmoreland accepts too much at face value what the Vietnamese say they are doing, and he is too eager to impress on reporters his own debatable view of the quality of Vietnamese troops. But at this late hour he cannot make the Vietnamese do what they really don't want to do. And so because the Americans were easier to work with and because the problems were so immediate—imminent defeat—he worked with the Americans and the situation of the Vietnamese military remained unchanged.

But the frustrations go so very deep. They are the product of the colonial era and the divisions brought about by the French-Indochina war, and to a much lesser degree the Diem era, both of which saw the destruction of anti-Communist nationalism. We are prisoners of that time now, more than we know. All of our failings, I think, are traced back to then. The enemy has had a revolution, and we, failing to have one, have tried to compensate for it piecemeal. But we have never really changed the order of the society. Rather, our presence, despite our words and our good intentions, has tended to confirm and strengthen the existing order.

The French-Indochina war divided this country in a more important way than the separation at the seventeenth parallel. In the process of driving the French out of Vietnam, the Vietminh—Communist led and Communist dominated—captured the nationalism of the country. They drove the white man out and they appealed to the highest aspirations of the best young Vietnamese of a whole generation. There was no other choice; it was French or Vietminh. If later some of these same Vietnamese became disillusioned because of the dominance of the Communists, the apparatus and the system survived.

The Communists had not only driven out the French, and developed a new and cunning type of warfare, they had also brought the best men in their ranks to the fore. They offered hopes to the peasants, they released something latent and very powerful in the country, and they broke down petty divisions until finally that which united them was stronger than that which divided them.

Equally important in these years was what happened on our side. Our Vietnamese, by and large, had fought under the French. The enemy had revolutionaries; we had functionaries with functionary mentalities. Our high officers were former French corporals.

Things which divided men below the seventeenth parallel were far more powerful than the things which united them. The nearest enemy was the real one; the Communists were an enemy, but they were distant, and there were the French and then the Americans to hold them off.

Under Diem and for a long time afterwards no book could be published here which told at all about any Vietnamese struggle against the French.

To this day, despite the talk of revolution, a Vietnamese who collaborated with the French can get a job with the Americans or his own government much more easily than anyone who had fought against the French but had become disillusioned. The Americans push hard for a Chieu Hoi center for defectors, but they admit privately it is almost impossible to integrate any ranking defector into the open society here on anything above a cab-driver level. The Army in the South, rather than having any national purpose, is riddled with intrigues and divisions.

I talked with a high-level defector, a major, and asked what he could do if given an Arvin battalion. "I could command a division in North Vietnam," he answered. "I have the ability to do that. But a platoon here, even a squad, I could not do that. What can you do? They have no purpose."

But if the troubles go back to the French, we can no longer blame them. When I was here in 1962 there was a tendency to blame everything on the French legacy of training, of tactics, of civil service. Now, however, we have been here long enough on our own. The French are a vanishing scapegoat.

One of the smartest Americans in the Embassy, spelling out the progress the Americans had made here since 1965—the dead VC, the improved security in certain areas—told me, "The VC are hurting and they're licking their wounds, real hurts and real wounds this time. This time we're really getting to them. The trouble is that every single thing that's taking place here is directly attributable to the presence of half a million Americans."

Was there anything local that was viable? I asked him.

"No," he said, "I don't think so. We can go into an area and improve the security. Pacify if you want to call it that. But then pull the American boots out of the area and it would go Red in a week."

Recently the American Mission, realizing that among the longest suffering people in this country were the Arvin veterans, decided to do something to improve their morale and at the same time perhaps to improve the society. The Mission decided to offer 120 four-year scholarships to colleges in the United States for deserving veterans, with a full English-language course thrown in. It was a widely praised idea in Mission circles, and no one really minded that it came from the Americans and not the Vietnamese. And the Vietnamese were enthusiastic.

The idea was taken to the Ministry of Education, which shortly presented the Americans with a list of 120 deserving veterans. Just by chance someone at the Mission checked out the list—Americans are learning to do that these days—and found that any relationship between those nominated and veterans was purely coincidental. All 120 were simply brothers, cousins, friends, creditors, debtors of people in the ministry.

Then the Americans went to veterans' groups themselves and advertised in the newspapers. Eventually the deserving recipients were found and chosen, and off they went to America. The Mission congratulated itself, both on the idea and on catching the fake list, and it was not until several weeks later that someone found out that each veteran had been forced to pay a bribe of 40,000 piastres (six months' pay at the very least) in order to get his passport so he could leave.

This corruption works from the top down, from the corps commander selling everything in his area, the corruption of venality, to the poor schoolteacher making only 1,400 piastres a month, selling questions and answers to exams to all of her students, making an additional 8,000 piastres a month—all to offset the terrible inflation, the corruption of survival. It is very bad and getting worse. Each day in the Vietnamese government and the Vietnamese Army it is a little more likely that if a position is any good it must be bought.

We have created a new class here, at a time when men are supposed to go out and die for their country. We are rewarding all the wrong values, the grafters, the black marketeers, the 20 per centers. There are some in the American Mission who believe that worrying about Asian corruption is naïve, that it is traditional, but I do not think this is true. One of the reasons for the success of the other side has been its relative lack of corruption. The corruption here has long since* passed the marginal phase and now dominates and indeed paralyzes the society. Unless it is checked and checked quickly and ruthlessly it is impossible to win this war.

The corps commanders are the worst, particularly in Two, Three, and Four Corps (there is too much fighting these days in the first corps area, near the Demilitarized Zone, for very much profiteering). They have become the new warlords of Vietnam, holding a certain balance of power which in the past has supported, or not supported, the government in Saigon. They buy and sell almost everything conceivable and a few things which are inconceivable.

They sell the province and district chiefs' jobs: up to three million piastres for a province chief's job; one million or more for a district chief's job, plus of course a monthly kickback, varying from 10,000 piastres a month to 10 per cent of the chief's budget. A division commander's job may cost as much as five million piastres.

The profits vary. Smaller fry make money off what are known here as ghost soldiers, the 30 per cent of a unit roll which does not exist—dead or never existed—but for which the commander still draws money. But the bigger men make the real money off the new construction wave. Every-

*Corruption has always been a problem here, as has American indifference to it. In 1963, when Marine Major General Victor Krulak was assigned by President Kennedy to find out whether or not the war was being won, he sent the American military command here a questionnaire with about sixty questions. One was: "Is there government corruption?" The answer: "To our knowledge there is not."

thing that is built has its take, an immense percentage. Nothing can be done without bribery, and the bribes go to the highest officials in the region.

Then there are the vast amounts of material brought in by the Americans. The docks become a gold mine, as do the bars which the Americans frequent. One corps commander is the opium king. In the Delta there is massive taxation on the rice harvest, which slips out illegally to Cambodia while Vietnam imports most of its rice. Along the Cambodian border there is a thriving two-way illicit traffic—rice and beer going out, food, fish, and clothes coming in.

A division commander like Nguyen Van Minh in the 21st Division (lower Delta) will make an agreement at rice harvest time to share the profits on collected taxes with absentee landlords and thereupon launch operations for that purpose. He will share also in the profits of outgoing charcoal and of trucking beer and supplies into the area. Minh is the prototype of the new Vietnamese officer. He is very popular with the Americans, speaks good English, knows American staff styles, and is on the surface quite cooperative. In Saigon among the Americans his division is considered a good one. But in the area, provincial advisers who are not directly in his chain of command feel that he is vastly overrated and that his division does not pursue the Vietcong all that actively.

The province chiefs make theirs in construction (faked sealed bids, with Americans there to watch the surface honesty—one province chief even created his own proxy building company) and local smuggling. In Kien Phong and Chau Doc provinces, district chiefs along the border are so wealthy that they have to kick back at least 50,000 piastres a month to their superiors. The price for certifying that Cambodian fish is indigenous Vietnamese fish is two piastres a kilo, and since as much as 20,000 kilos may enter a day, the profits are very handsome indeed.

In Bien Hoa, typical of those provinces where there are large numbers of Americans, bars are big business: at Tet alone the province chief has made an estimated 10 million piastres from the bars. He gets an estimated kickback of 10,000 piastres a month from each bar and he periodically extorts more by threatening to open new ones. The Americans have documented his corruption, but so far he has managed to stay in power.

And this works down. The assistants to these men, assistant province chiefs and district chiefs, buy their jobs and then make the payoffs back by selling positions under them. The assistant district chief for security sells police jobs and the police get their smaller payoffs at resource checkpoints or working the bars. Finally everyone is selling something: 5,000 piastre bribes to get a driver's license, 20,000 piastres to get a Honda out of the docks, 6,000 piastres to get a free place on a military aircraft, 50,000 piastres to get permission to have a job with the Americans.

Someone both honest and capable like General Nguyen Duc Thang, head of revolutionary development, is almost overwhelmed by this cynicism. He is trying to run an honest program, and corruption has become his favorite subject with visitors. An able Vietnamese friend of mine was offered a province in the Delta to run. He went there for a month and was told at the end of the month to kick in. He asked where he would find the money. That is your problem, the corps commander said. He immediately asked to be relieved. "It is very bad," he said. "If you are not one of them you become a threat to them and very dangerous." The handful of Americans who are fighting the massive corruption are numbed by the problem now. One of them told me, "You fight like hell to get someone removed and most times you fail and you just make it worse than ever. And then on the occasions when you win, why hell, they give you someone just as bad who's a little more careful about it. I mean he's been warned about you, that you're a little smarter than the other long noses, and the guy you had relieved, why they promote *him*."

There was for a time earlier this year an American Mission committee on corruption, but it met three times and has not met in six months. The problem is so delicate that it can only be handled by the very highest Americans, and indeed it is so delicate even there that it may not be discussed in the blunt and strong terms which it demands. A real attack on it, and real punishment, have yet to come, and there lingers among fair-minded Americans here a good deal of doubt that the government has either the desire or the capacity to take strong steps.

I have described this at length not just because the corruption is so serious and so corroding, but also because there is a new and growing Mission view of the war, a view which I think is the product of frustration in pacification and other nation-building programs. It says, in effect: military power will not win the war alone, and though the government is weak and indeed frequently venal, and Arvin is a myth, we Americans are doing so many things, so much gear is going into so many places, that relentlessly, almost in spite of ourselves, we are producing results.

"We are smothering them into victory," one very high official said. The failure of the past, this official added, was not just weak people and a weak policy, although that is now acknowledged. It was a lack of resources: 15,000 Americans and a half billion dollars a year simply weren't enough.

This is a philosophy that is at times quite well argued here, and it has the advantage of admitting the weakness of our Vietnamese. But I am not so sure: the failures of the past were deeply tied not so much to lack of resources—we always had more helicopters than the enemy—but to lack of leadership, motivation, unity. I am not sure but that the more resources we feed into this country, the more we weaken the fiber and the more we corrode our own Vietnamese.

We flew over the southern part of Long An province. My guide, an experienced American here, pointed down to the strange scene: deserted pathways leading nowhere, mud paths leading up to shacks which barely existed, a few deserted huts still left. "You know what that is?" he asked. I shook my head.

"Strategic hamlets," he said. "All that's left. You can see the outlines of where they used to be, where they built up the mud for paths. Part of the scenic beauty of Long An. Vacant since November 3, 1963, the first day the new government said they could all go; they left. I'm not even sure they waited that long. Those that we controlled, that is, and that was damn few enough. Mass desertion. Funny people, they preferred their ancestors' ashes to our barbed wire."

I looked down and he was right, there they were. One could still see the traces of the paths, neatly laid out, neatly eroding, and it all came back to me, the visits to Long An, and the other provinces, the hamlet program, the *key* to success, making the population turn on the enemy, all those fine charts showing that we were way ahead of schedule, only X hamlets programed and 3X completed.

In 1963 when Washington's confidence about the hamlets mounted and doubts mounted in the field, a young American civilian named Earl Young came down to take over Long An as province representative. Long An was allegedly almost completely government controlled; Young was appalled and quickly told Saigon that 80 per cent of Long An was VC controlled, and the war was virtually over in it. It was a report which jarred Saigon's sensitivities, and as a reward for this Paul Reveremanship a two-star American general tried to have Young fired.

Later in 1964 and 1965 Long An became a *hop tac* area, the spreading of oil slicks out from Saigon, the gradual driving back of the enemy. One American who was there said, "We knew what we wanted to do, but we couldn't get them to do it. There would be agreement, this was a priority operation and this or that program would be done, and they would nod and say yes, and then nothing would happen. You ask me why, I don't know why. If I had known why, I'd have been able to do something. So you'd send the word up to Saigon, and the top Americans there would say, 'Yes, look, we just talked to the Vietnamese about that problem and they're taking care of it—it's all okay.' And of course not a damn thing would happen."

In 1965, still almost completely Vietcong controlled, still squeezing Saigon, Long An was dubbed a National Priority Area. One American told me, "I don't know what happened to all the other national priority areas, but we couldn't cut it there. It was the same old goddamn story. You could tell the story of this country from Long An, like a dying man seeing his whole life flash before him. Their battalion commanders, peasants from the area who had everything to gain and nothing to lose if the VC won, had a rainbow waiting in this war. And up against them our little Arvin officers all from the upper or middle class, holding those damn baccalaureates, hating Long An a hell of a lot more than I ever did, with nothing to gain if there was a victory and a damn lot to lose down here, not wanting a bit to get wounded. So they tore us up when we went out. Most of the time the division advisers would be reporting how many operations they were on and all these things they were doing, and the troops wouldn't be doing anything at all, just sitting around and letting the VC have it free."

The National Priority Area never got off the ground there; Long An remained a particularly ugly sore. By late 1966 it remained as bad as ever (no American troops set foot there until September 1966) until by American estimates the VC controlled the entire rural province at night and all but 5 per cent during the daytime. Bridges were out, ferries were out, yet another try was made.

American troops were sent into the area and Colonel Sam Wilson, then Lodge's Mission coordinator, left his high Saigon post to try and oversee all operations there. He was somewhat appalled by what he found: "The province chief and the district chiefs do things for the people as if it were some form of largess. If a district chief wants to build a marketplace it doesn't really matter whether the village wants it or needs it—that's what it gets." But the Wilson experiment, started with the best of intentions, floundered too. There was always some doubt over just how much control he had over the American military; and the Vietnamese military was always divided between the province chief's wishes and the division commander's whims. Finally neither high nor low goals were reached.

Now, in late 1967, Long An is somewhat better. There is what one American who knows the past failures calls "marginal improvement or even better under difficult conditions." A brigade and a half of American troops, in addition to two Vietnamese regiments, are operating there. The Americans, working the difficult terrain, are paying a high price, but have hurt the tough Vietcong battalions in the area. Latest intelligence is that these battalions are at about 60 per cent strength, which means that they are still quite effective fighting forces. Security is somewhat better and some areas have been opened up.

But the local officials are no better, the Arvin forces are as bad as ever, and knowledgeable Americans speak of progress in muted tones, knowing it can vanish the next day. In addition, the Americans here—as elsewhere in the Delta—are wary of areas where they think local forces have reached an accommodation with the enemy. One Vietnamese described it to me in Long An: "They sit there and make their gentlemen's agreements. The VC let our people know when they want to move and not too much happens. If the boss comes down from Tan An, the local commander lets the VC know and the province chief arrives. So everyone walks around freely and the chief tells the local man what a fine commander he is."

Long An is at least without illusions.

One of the smaller wars in Vietnam these days is the one taking place between the American military command and the American reporters over that most time-honored subject, the quality of the Vietnamese Army. To the military they are constantly improving. To the reporters, nothing has changed. There is the same vast discrepancy between their statistics and their actual performances.

The other day an American officer was brought in to brief reporters on the Arvin units in his area. The briefing was standard: the officer patiently and politely went through his line about better leadership, better motivation, better morale. But the area is close to Saigon and most reporters have friends there; they listened in obvious disbelief. After the officer finished his briefing and was moving toward the door, one veteran reporter caught him, and asked what could really be done to shape Arvin up. "Fire all three goddamn division commanders and two-thirds of the regimental commanders," he said, and walked out the door.

Yet there are some here who claim that we have one last chance in Vietnam. The history of Vietnam in recent years has been littered with last chances. One follows another faithfully. But, say men whose judgment I have respected in the past, this is another: we have all the material and we have just had an election:* and perhaps now all the mistakes can be corrected. President Thieu will have the power he lacked before and we can get him to do these things which all his predecessors have failed to do. Thieu can use power; he can crush the little warlords.

Perhaps so, but one senses in Thieu a clever operator who will play it close to his vest. His ability to perform these late miracles is questionable. Give him six months, one very high American says. But what is it going to be at the end of it? Something dramatic—or just more statistics and briefings?

And the alternate solutions?

Putting American and Vietnamese troops together into joint units, thereby improving the morale of the Vietnamese—where tried so far in this country it has worked. . . . Giving the Americans complete command of Vietnamese forces, and giving them good American leadership. . . . Forgetting about the Vietnamese and bringing out one million more American troops and do the job right.

But instead I have a sense that we are once again coming to a dead end in Indochina. We have in the past narrowly staved off defeat several times in the South. In 1954 at Geneva, in 1956 with Diem, in 1961 with the Taylor report and the beginning of the American buildup, in 1965 with the commitment of American combat troops. Each time we have averted defeat and grabbed victory out of the hands of Hanoi, but in doing it, we have always been forced to up the price of the game. We have increased the stakes, so that now we stand with the present frustrating situation, neither victory nor defeat, a half-million troops, a heavy bombing program, with the military wanting more troops and more bombing. Yet

---

*The South Vietnamese election of September 1967 brought Gen. Nguyen Van Thieu to power, despite the fact that he had captured only thirty-five per cent of the vote. The election was also marked by considerable fraud and graft.

meanwhile we are more aware than ever of the frustrations of that particular war and of the strains that a commitment of half a million men places on our own society at home.

Or perhaps all the very best critics, such as the late Bernard Fall, will be proven wrong: you *can* gain a military victory without any decent political basis. You can simply grind out a terribly punishing war, year after year, using that immense American firepower, crushing the enemy and a good deal of the population, until finally there has been so much death and destruction that the enemy will stumble out of the forest, as stunned and numb as the rest of the Vietnamese people.

What would become of the country in this case I do not know. It could happen, but I doubt it. For though the highest Americans here have talked in terms of victory through a war of punishment and attrition, I have my doubts that we can win in a war of attrition. Attrition, after all, is not just a physical thing, it is a psychological state as well, and I wonder if they will fold first. Rather, the war is to them an immediate thing; it is their highest priority, their most important commitment, like the Israelis viewing the Arabs; they see it in terms of *survival,* while we are far away. We have our other fronts, other commitments, other priorities. We talk about this as a war of our national security, but we treat it as a war of luxury. Nothing shows this more than the casual way the war has been reported from Saigon to Washington, the willingness to pass on gentle fallacies instead of hard and cold truths. The general who tried to have Earl Young removed would, I am sure, give a very accurate report to Washington if the Vietcong were moving north from San Diego.

Perhaps. Perhaps. I do not think we are winning, and the reasons seem to me to be so basic that while I would like to believe my friends that there is a last chance opening up again in Vietnam, it seems to me a frail hope indeed. I do not think we are winning in any true sense, nor do I see any signs we are about to win. That is why this is such a sad story to write, for I share that special affection for the Vietnamese, and I would like to write that though the price is heavy, it is worth it. I do not think our Vietnamese can win their half of the war, nor do I think we can win it for them. I think finally we will end up lowering our sights, encouraging our Vietnamese to talk to their Vietnamese, hoping somehow they can settle what we cannot. That is what this country longs for right now, and it may well be that even if we stay here another five years, it is all we will end up with anyway.

About the Author

DAVID HALBERSTAM, born in New York City, graduated from Harvard in 1955, where he was managing editor of the *Crimson.* Thereafter he worked for the West Point, Mississippi *Daily Times Leader* and the Nashville *Tennessean* before joining the Washington bureau of the *New York Times* in 1960. In 1961 he was sent to the Congo by the *Times,* and after covering the fighting there for fifteen months, became the paper's correspondent in Vietnam in the fall of 1962 when he was twenty-eight years old.

This book, written when he was 29 and 30, reflects a reporter already pessimistic about the Vietnam War, and becoming more so. Twenty-odd years later it is fascinating as a reflection not only of the darkening clouds of Vietnam but also of America's changing attitudes about the war. Because of it the word "quagmire" quickly became part of the national vocabulary used to describe our involvement in Vietnam.

Halberstam's other books on Vietnam include *Ho,* a novel entitled *One Very Hot Day,* and the landmark political study, *The Best and the Brightest.* His most recent book is *The Reckoning,* an account of the Japanese challenge to American corporations.

About the Editor

DANIEL J. SINGAL is Associate Professor of History at Hobart and William Smith Colleges in Geneva, New York. He is a graduate of Harvard College and received his Ph.D. from Columbia University in 1976. His published works include *The War Within: From Victorian to Modernist Thought in the South, 1919–1945,* which won a number of prizes, among them the 1983 Ralph Waldo Emerson Award given by Phi Beta Kappa. A Guggenheim Fellow in 1984–1985, he lives with his wife and two children in Pittsford, New York.

A Note on the Type

The text of this book is set in CALEDONIA, originally a Linotype face designed by W. A. Dwiggins. It belongs to the family of printing types called "modern face" by printers—a term used to mark the change in style of type-letters that occurred about 1800. Caledonia borders on the general design of Scotch Modern, but is more freely drawn than that letter.

This version of Caledonia (called Gàel) was composed by ComCom, a division of Haddon Craftsmen, on a VideoComp 570 Pagesetter. It was printed and bound by R. R. Donnelley & Sons, Harrisonburg, Virginia.